JOURNAL FOR THE STUDY OF THE NEW TESTAMENT
SUPPLEMENT SERIES
96

Executive Editor
Stanley E. Porter

Editorial Board
Richard Bauckham, David Catchpole, R. Alan Culpepper,
Joanna Dewey, James D.G. Dunn, Craig A. Evans, Robert Fowler,
Robert Jewett, Elizabeth Struthers Malbon, Dan O. Via

JSOT Press
Sheffield

The Colossian Controversy

Wisdom in Dispute at Colossae

Richard E. DeMaris

Journal for the Study of the New Testament
Supplement Series 96

Copyright © 1994 Sheffield Academic Press

Published by JSOT Press
JSOT Press is an imprint of
Sheffield Academic Press Ltd
343 Fulwood Road
Sheffield S10 3BP
England

Typeset by Sheffield Academic Press
and
Printed on acid-free paper in Great Britain
by Bookcraft
Midsomer Norton, Somerset

British Library Cataloguing in Publication Data

A catalogue record for this book is available
from the British Library

ISBN 1-85075-473-X

CONTENTS

Acknowledgments	7
Abbreviations	9

Chapter 1
AN INTRODUCTION TO THE COLOSSIAN PHILOSOPHY PUZZLE — 11
   Rationale for Studying the Colossian Philosophy — 11
   The Interpretive Problems and a Proposed Solution — 14

Chapter 2
A HISTORY OF SCHOLARSHIP ON THE COLOSSIAN PHILOSOPHY — 18
   Gnosis, Gnosticism, Jewish Gnosticism, and Gnostic Judaism — 18
   Departure from the Jewish-Gnostic Model — 27
   Ascetic, Apocalyptic, and Mystical Judaism — 30
   Hellenistic Syncretism in First-Century Asia Minor — 33
   A Philosophical Background for the Colossian Philosophy — 36
   Conclusion — 38

Chapter 3
INTERPRETING THE POLEMICAL CORE IN COLOSSIANS — 41
   Isolating the Polemic: Considerations of Method — 41
   Translation of the Polemical Core in Colossians (2.8, 16-23) — 45
   Exegesis of the Polemical Core — 46
   Assessment of Other Interpretations of
      the Colossian Philosophy — 73

Chapter 4
THE HISTORICAL AND SOCIAL SETTING OF THE COLOSSIAN
PHILOSOPHY — 98
   The Philosophical Climate in the New Testament Era — 100
   Demonology in the Early Roman Empire — 104
   Philosophical Purification — 108

A Philosophy according to the World	114
The Social Location of the Colossian Philosophers	118
The Philosophers in the Colossian Congregation	126
Conclusion	131

Chapter 5
THE CONTROVERSY IN COLOSSIANS 134
   The Polemical Core in its Epistolary Context 135
   A Debate over Knowledge 140

Epilogue
THE COLOSSIAN PHILOSOPHY AND THE CONFLICT AT
COLOSSAE TODAY 146

Bibliography 150
Index of References 161
Index of Authors 168

ACKNOWLEDGMENTS

An earlier version of this study was a dissertation completed in 1990 at Columbia University and Union Theological Seminary. The idea for it originated in a graduate seminar at Union on the Christology of the Pauline hymns. Raymond E. Brown, J. Louis Martyn, and Thomas Robinson encouraged me to investigate the early Christian community at Colossae through the Colossian hymn (Col. 1.15-20) and the polemic in that letter against the so-called 'philosophy' (2.8). With their help I decided to make the Colossian philosophy the subject of my doctoral dissertation. Holland Hendrix and Robin Scroggs at Union saw the work through to completion. Their combined expertise—Hendrix in Hellenistic philosophy and Anatolian Judaism, Scroggs in the Pauline corpus—proved crucial. Both provided valuable comments on my work and much encouragement, before and after the defense.

The current version of the study benefited from a significant rewriting based on additional research, particularly in the area of archaeology. Preparation of entries for the *Anchor Bible Dictionary* on 'Philosophy' and 'Element, Elemental Spirit' forced me to refine my thinking on these two key terms.[1] Response to papers presented at the annual meeting of the Society of Biblical Literature in 1990 and 1991 proved useful in revising this study.[2] Most of all, introduction to, and research in, the field of archaeology provided me with more information about western Asia Minor in the early Roman Empire, which allowed me to say more about the likely social realities in and around Colossae in the first century CE. My thanks go to the National

---

1. R. DeMaris, 'Philosophy', *ABD*, V, p. 346; 'Element, Elemental Spirit', *ABD*, II, pp. 444-45.
2. R. DeMaris, 'Whence Comes Wisdom? The Crux of Conflict at Colossae', paper presented at Annual Meeting of the SBL, New Orleans, November 17 1990; '"According to the Elements of the World" (Colossians 2.8): The Colossian Opponents' Wisdom and the Sapiential Tradition in Hellenistic Judaism', paper presented at Annual Meeting of the SBL, Kansas City, November 25 1991.

Endowment for the Humanities and Valparaiso University's Committee on Creative Work and Research for making possible summer research trips to Greece. Thanks also go to the American School of Classical Studies at Athens, whose incomparable holdings in Mediterranean archaeology were an ideal resource for major portions of my revisions.

The staff of Sheffield Academic Press have been very supportive from start to finish. Encouragement to bring more archaeological evidence to bear on the Colossian philosophy came from Dr David Hill, who also gave me several important bibliographical leads. Directors David Clines and Philip Davies have been easy to work with, and desk editor Helen Tookey has saved this book from many errors. Those that remain, including any mistranslations from German, French, or Greek, are my responsibility.

These acknowledgments would be incomplete without mention of those here at Valparaiso University who have been instrumental to my work and even my well-being. My many fine colleagues in the Theology Department, especially Betty DeBerg, Jon Pahl, and Walt Rast, have created an atmosphere of collegial support and intellectual stimulation matched by few other places. My student assistant Joanne Oestreich spent hours on the tedious task of making minor editorial and punctuation changes, and Jamie Huston proved to be a capable proofreader. The interlibrary loan manager at Valparaiso University's Moellering Library, Dorothy Wodrich, met my frequent requests without complaint. I am also deeply grateful to the Ziegler family, whose generous contributions to Valparaiso University made the publication of this study possible.

Finally and of greatest importance, I thank my parents and most of all my colleague at Valparaiso and partner in life, Sarah Glenn DeMaris, whose undying patience and love have inspired me day after day.

R.E.D.
Feast of St Tarasius 1994

ABBREVIATIONS

ABD	D.N. Freedman (ed.), *Anchor Bible Dictionary*
AnBib	Analecta biblica
ANRW	*Aufstieg und Niedergang der römischen Welt*
ARW	*Archiv für Religionswissenschaft*
ATANT	Abhandlungen zur Theologie des Alten und Neuen Testaments
BAGD	W. Bauer, W.F. Arndt, F.W. Gingrich and F.W. Danker, *A Greek–English Lexicon of the New Testament and Other Early Christian Literature*
BARev	*Biblical Archaeology Review*
BDF	F. Blass, A. Debrunner and R.W. Funk, *A Greek Grammar of the New Testament and Other Early Christian Literature*
BEvT	Beiträge zur evangelischen Theologie
Bib	*Biblica*
BJS	Brown Judaic Studies
BSac	*Bibliotheca Sacra*
CahRB	Cahiers de la *Revue biblique*
CBQ	*Catholic Biblical Quarterly*
CII	*Corpus inscriptionum iudaicarum*
EKKNT	Evangelisch-katholischer Kommentar zum Neuen Testament
EPRO	Etudes préliminaires aux religions orientales dans l'empire romain
EvT	*Evangelische Theologie*
ExpTim	*Expository Times*
FB	Forschung zur Bibel
HNT	Handbuch zum Neuen Testament
HTKNT	Herders theologischer Kommentar zum Neuen Testament
HTR	*Harvard Theological Review*
JBL	*Journal of Biblical Literature*
JSNT	*Journal for the Study of the New Testament*
JSNTSup	*Journal for the Study of the New Testament*, Supplement Series
JTS	*Journal of Theological Studies*
LPGL	G.W.H. Lampe, *A Patristic Greek Lexicon*
LSJ	Liddel–Scott–Jones, *A Greek–English Lexicon*

MeyerK	H.A.W. Meyer (ed.), Kritisch-exegetischer Kommentar über das Neue Testament
NovTSup	*Novum Testamentum*, Supplements
NRSV	New Revised Standard Version
NTD	Das Neue Testament Deutsch
NTS	*New Testament Studies*
PGM	K. Preisendanz (ed.), *Papyri graecae magicae*
PTMS	Pittsburgh Theological Monograph Series
PVTG	Pseudepigrapha Veteris Testamenti graece
QD	Quaestiones disputatae
RevExp	*Review and Expositor*
RHR	*Revue de l'histoire des religions*
RSR	*Recherches de science religieuse*
SBLDS	SBL Dissertation Series
SBLSBS	SBL Sources for Biblical Study
SBLSCS	SBL Septuagint and Cognate Studies
SBLTT	SBL Texts and Translations
SBM	Stuttgarter biblische Monographien
SCHNT	Studia ad corpus hellenisticum novi testamenti
SD	Studies and Documents
SJT	*Scottish Journal of Theology*
SNT	Studien zum Neuen Testament
SNTSMS	Society for New Testament Studies Monograph Series
ST	*Studia theologica*
SUNT	Studien zur Umwelt des Neuen Testaments
TDNT	G. Kittel and G. Friedrich (eds.), *Theological Dictionary of the New Testament*
TLZ	*Theologische Literaturzeitung*
TU	Texte und Untersuchungen
UNT	Untersuchungen zum Neuen Testament
WUNT	Wissenschaftliche Untersuchungen zum Neuen Testament
ZKT	*Zeitschrift für katholische Theologie*
ZNW	*Zeitschrift für die neutestamentliche Wissenschaft*
ZTK	*Zeitschrift für Theologie und Kirche*

Chapter 1

AN INTRODUCTION TO THE COLOSSIAN PHILOSOPHY PUZZLE

Rationale for Studying the Colossian Philosophy

W. Schenk's article on postwar research on Colossians, appearing in a recent *ANRW* volume, reveals a striking aspect of current work on that letter.[1] He restricts himself to two topics and thereby indicates the dual preoccupation of Colossians scholars: (1) authorship of the letter and its relationship to other Pauline letters, and (2) the identity of the party combated by the letter's polemic. In short, apart from those two subjects and perhaps the Colossians hymn (1.15-20), Colossians receives little attention from NT scholars.

This highly focused scholarly activity has produced varied results. With regard to authorship, the consensus on the letter's authenticity has moved steadily in the past fifteen to twenty years. Until the early 1970s most scholars included Colossians among the genuine letters of Paul or considered the question of authorship open. In 1974, when N. Perrin presented his arguments for pseudonymity, he acknowledged being in a distinct minority in the matter.[2] Others who examined the issue observed that the scholarly consensus was divided.[3] By the late 1970s, however, scholars were more and more deciding for pseudonymity,[4] so that by 1984 R. Brown estimated the percentage of those arguing for pseudonymity at sixty.[5] Among several factors

---

1. W. Schenk, 'Der Kolosserbrief in der neueren Forschung (1945–1985)', *ANRW* II.25.4, pp. 3327-64.
2. N. Perrin, *The New Testament: An Introduction* (New York: Harcourt Brace Jovanovich, 1974), p. 121.
3. For example, W. Bujard, *Stilanalytische Untersuchungen zum Kolosserbrief* (SUNT, 11; Göttingen: Vandenhoeck & Ruprecht, 1973), p. 12.
4. J. Burgess, 'The Letter to the Colossians', in G. Krodel (ed.), *Ephesians, Colossians, 2 Thessalonians, the Pastoral Epistles* (Proclamation Commentaries; Philadelphia: Fortress Press, 1978), p. 41.
5. R. Brown, *The Churches the Apostles Left Behind* (New York: Paulist Press, 1984), p. 47.

prompting this shift in the consensus was the analysis of W. Bujard, which appeared in 1973.[1] His systematic study of the letter's style, syntax, and structure augmented earlier arguments based on theological content[2] and evidently tipped the scales in favor of pseudonymity.[3] In light of these developments, I will refer to the author of Colossians as 'the letter writer' in this study.[4]

No similar shift in the scholarly consensus has taken place in the identification of the group at Colossae whose practices and beliefs, which I will call the Colossian philosophy (Col. 2.8), are opposed by the letter writer. More accurately, any consensus that did exist at the beginning of the twentieth century has been steadily eroded, particularly since World War II. In recent decades certain reconstructions have had periods of relative ascendancy with respect to others, but none has caught and held the assent of anything approaching a majority. In short, no consensus currently exists.

This division in opinion, while it could engender pessimism about ever solving the Colossian philosophy puzzle, has in fact stimulated a rich variety in reconstructions of the philosophy. Surprisingly, however, book-length studies of the Colossian controversy have been few. F. Francis's dissertation of 1965 and L. Congdon's of 1968 offered substantial treatments of the issue, but a generation passed until T. Sappington's study of 1991.[5] The relative dearth of detailed studies and the still unresolved debate over the Colossian philosophy point to the value of additional investigations.

Lending necessity to undertaking such a work is the scholarship of E. Schweizer on Colossians. The early and mid-1970s saw the appear-

1. Bujard, *Kolosserbrief*.
2. For example, E. Lohse, *Colossians and Philemon* (Hermeneia; Philadelphia: Fortress Press, 1971), pp. 177-83.
3. M. Kiley, *Colossians as Pseudepigraphy* (The Biblical Seminar; Sheffield: JSOT Press, 1986), ch. 2; P. Pokorný, *Colossians: A Commentary* (Peabody, MA: Hendrickson, 1991), p. 10.
4. Feminist scholarship has questioned the assumption that the Bible was written exclusively by men, but in the case of Colossians female authorship seems highly unlikely, so I will refer to the letter writer as 'he'.
5. F. Francis, 'A Re-Examination of the Colossian Controversy' (PhD dissertation, Yale University, 1965); L. Congdon, 'The False Teachers at Colossae: Affinities with Essene and Philonic Thought' (PhD dissertation, Drew University, 1968); T. Sappington, *Revelation and Redemption at Colossae* (JSNTSup, 53; Sheffield: JSOT Press, 1991).

1. An Introduction to the Colossian Philosophy Puzzle 13

ance of several articles in German bearing directly or indirectly on the Colossian philosophy. In 1976 Schweizer's EKKNT commentary on Colossians was published.[1] His interpretation of the Colossian philosophy has also received steady exposure in English; several English-language articles gave interpreters a taste of his work before the translation of his commentary in 1982, and recently (1988) a very important article bearing on Col. 2.8 and 20 appeared in *JBL*.[2]

Making Schweizer's work particularly noteworthy is the new departure it represents in scholarship on the Colossian philosophy. Schweizer located the Colossian philosophy against the background of Greco-Roman philosophy, a tradition neglected by virtually all interpreters of Colossians, who regularly turned to Judaism or Gnosticism in their reconstructions. The depth and comprehensiveness of Schweizer's analysis combined with its innovativeness qualify it as a major development in Colossian studies, one deserving of consideration regardless of the popularity it gains among scholars. The very useful collection of milestone essays on the Colossian philosophy, *Conflict at Colossae*, appearing in 1973 and revised in 1975,[3] is now incomplete; an article representing Schweizer's reconstruction should be included among these important earlier essays. In the meantime, it is vital to assess the impact of Schweizer's work on the problem of identifying the Colossian philosophy, a task that no scholar has yet undertaken in any detail.

If progress could be made in identifying the Colossian philosophy, the letter's value as a mirror of early Christianity and its environment

---

1. E. Schweizer, 'Die "Elemente der Welt" Gal 4,3.9; Kol 2,8.20', in O. Böcher and K. Haacker (eds.), *Verborum Veritas: Festschrift für Gustav Stählin* (Wuppertal: Brockhaus, 1970), pp. 245-59; 'Versöhnung des Alls. Kol 1,20', in G. Strecker (ed.), *Jesus Christus in Historie und Theologie* (Tübingen: Mohr, 1975), pp. 487-501; *Der Brief an die Kolosser* (EKKNT; Zurich: Benziger Verlag; Neukirchen–Vluyn: Neukirchener Verlag, 1976).

2. E. Schweizer, 'Christ in the Letter to the Colossians', *RevExp* 70 (1973), pp. 451-67; 'Christianity of the Circumcised and Judaism of the Uncircumcised: The Background of Matthew and Colossians', in R. Hamerton-Kelly and R. Scroggs (eds.), *Jews, Greeks and Christians: Religious Cultures in Late Antiquity* (Leiden: Brill, 1976), pp. 245-60; *The Letter to the Colossians* (Minneapolis: Augsburg, 1982); 'Slaves of the Elements and Worshipers of Angels: Gal 4.3, 9; Col 2.8, 18, 20', *JBL* 107 (1988), pp. 455-68.

3. F. Francis and W. Meeks (eds.), *Conflict at Colossae* (SBLSBS, 4; Missoula, MT: Scholars Press, rev. edn, 1975).

would increase. Already the christological hymn at 1.15-20 has proven to be a gold mine of information about early Christian beliefs. Additional information mined from the letter would enable the interpreter to place those beliefs and that hymn in a concrete context. In other words, pinpointing the identity of the Colossian philosophy would provide the interpreter with some specifics about the Colossian situation and thus facilitate the re-creation of the community's situation and experience. The usefulness of reconstructing the Colossian philosophy did not escape Schweizer: along with his reconstruction he sketched a history of the Colossian community based on a comparison of the Colossian hymn, philosophy, and the letter writer's own perspective.[1]

An accurate portrait of the Colossian philosophy would also help make sense of the letter to the Colossians as a whole and the writer's objective(s) in composing it, since determining a document's purpose rests to a great degree on deducing the situation or problem it addresses. Such a portrait would illuminate the scope and contour of the letter writer's polemic against the philosophy and thus in all likelihood reveal the place of that polemic in the letter as a whole. Determining the letter's occasion and purpose and, for that matter, composing a history of the Colossian congregation belong to the latter stages of this study, but the first step toward that history is to offer the reader a convincing reconstruction of the Colossian philosophy, which is the primary objective of this study.

The Interpretive Problems and a Proposed Solution

To say that controversy was common and factionalism rife in the earliest churches has become a truism among NT scholars. What remains disputed and the subject of intense study is the exact nature of those controversies and the identity of the parties that often tore at the fabric of early Christian congregations. Detailing such matters is a difficult task because of the limited sources available for documenting life in the earliest churches. Typically, only a letter writer's polemic remains as evidence for reconstruction, so that even when a source exists it may have limited value. For a polemic can just as easily obscure as it can accurately capture the controversy troubling a

1. Schweizer, *Letter to the Colossians*, pp. 125-34; 'Christ in the Letter', pp. 451-66.

1. An Introduction to the Colossian Philosophy Puzzle

congregation and the parties to that controversy.

Some NT epistles do allow us to catch a good glimpse of an opposed position or party. At many turns in Paul's letter to the Galatians, the reader meets him coming to grips with a group he opposes in that community. The Corinthian correspondence, too, does not fail to convey some information about those at the receiving end of Paul's verbal salvos, even though Paul consistently and perhaps intentionally[1] avoids naming his enemies. While there is not always consensus about the precise contours of the position combated in Galatia or Corinth, data for interpretation are relatively plentiful and straightforward.

Markedly less revealing is the letter to the Colossians. On the one hand, the letter writer makes it clear that his readers are to avoid something he calls the philosophy (2.8), and later on in ch. 2 he cites and rejects specific practices of the philosophy (2.16, 18, 21). On the other hand, the lack of clear boundaries to the polemic, the brevity and occasional obscurity of the manifestly polemical portions, ambiguity in the designations of the position combated, and uncertainties about the origin(s), nature, and purpose of the practices enjoined by the philosophy mean that many obstacles stand in the way of determining exactly what in the Colossian congregation troubled the letter writer and prompted his response.

Epitomizing the difficulties confronting the interpreter is the phrase θρησκεία τῶν ἀγγέλων, whose genitive construction allows several readings (Col. 2.18). All interpreters connect this phrase with the Colossian philosophy, but their understandings of it take them down widely diverging paths. Does the phrase mean religion instituted by angels, angelic worship (of God, presumably), or worship directed toward angels? Unfortunately, the relative clause that follows θρησκεία τῶν ἀγγέλων does not help the interpreter eliminate any of these three readings. On the contrary, the phrase ἃ ἑόρακεν ἐμβατεύων (NRSV: 'dwelling on visions') adds to the interpreter's troubles because it, too, admits a range in interpretations.

The last word of the relative clause just mentioned, ἐμβατεύω, is but one of many words bearing on the Colossian philosophy that appear at only this point in the NT. The many other *hapax legomena* in the obviously polemical portions of the letter point to the relative

---

1. So argues P. Marshall (*Enmity in Corinth: Social Conventions in Paul's Relations with the Corinthians* [WUNT, 2.23; Tübingen: Mohr, 1987]) based on his analysis of social convention and rhetorical technique (pp. 341-48).

obscurity of the vocabulary: φιλοσοφία (2.8), νεομηνία (v. 16), καταβραβεύω (v. 18), δογματίζω (v. 20), ἀπόχρησις (v. 22), ἐθελοθρησκία (v. 23), ἀφειδία (v. 23), and πλησμονή (v. 23). Because of their rarity, the search for the meaning of these terms sometimes forces the interpreter far afield, to contexts that may or may not clarify the meaning of the term as it is used by the author of Colossians.

Other difficulties, such as the grammatical roughness of Col. 2.23, also beset the interpreter, but the few cited already give the reader a taste of the problem facing any attempt at reconstructing the Colossian philosophy. The troublesome character of the Colossian polemic has frustrated many scholars and has spawned many reconstructions of the Colossian philosophy, each with its own distinctive set of solutions to the exegetical difficulties presented by the polemic. The variety in these exegetical solutions has encouraged scholars to introduce a variety of history of religions backgrounds to support their exegeses. The diversity in these reconstructions will be evident in the second chapter.

Such diversity in reconstructions dictates that the reconstruction I make must be undertaken with great care. Chapters 3 and 4, the heart of my analysis, move carefully from determining those portions of Colossians relevant to my investigation to interpreting those passages in detail, and then placing the resulting picture of the Colossian philosophy against a historical and social background. Such a procedure, while relying heavily on work in the history of religions, social history, and archaeology, will keep the key features of the philosophy uncovered in Colossians center stage and thus lead to a reconstruction that rings true to the letter and the situation it reflects. As a confirmation of this fidelity, chapter 5 will test the compatibility of my reconstruction with the letter as a whole.

This analysis reaches the following conclusions and results. It criticizes the tendency among existing reconstructions of the philosophy to classify it as either Jewish or pagan, or to label it syncretistic without accounting for why that particular blend of elements arose. This study offers instead a portrait of philosophically-inclined Gentiles drawn to the Jewish community and then to the Christian congregation by ideas and practices congenial with their view of the world. Central to the Colossian philosophy's outlook was the pursuit of divine knowledge or wisdom through (1) the order of the cosmic elements (2.8, 20), (2) a bodily asceticism that sets free the investigative mind (2.18, 23), and (3) intermediaries between heaven and earth (angels or demons; 2.18). These features are typical of Middle Platonism in the NT period. At the same time, the philosophy's calendar (2.16) and stress on humility (2.18, 23) indicate Jewish and Christian influences. Hence, the Colossian philosophy appears to be a distinctive blend of popular Middle Platonic, Jewish, and Christian elements that cohere around the pursuit of wisdom.

Chapter 2

A HISTORY OF SCHOLARSHIP ON THE COLOSSIAN PHILOSOPHY

Surveying the existing reconstructions of the Colossian philosophy will do more than confirm the existence of a major interpretive problem in Colossians or highlight the diversity of proposed solutions to that problem. It will give the reader a firm notion of what do and do not constitute the central interpretive issues according to exegetes of the Colossian philosophy, and it will offer a description of the important exegetical positions and history of religions analyses introduced and developed by scholarship to solve the Colossian philosophy puzzle. By doing so this chapter will make a refined statement of where the problem stands.

This survey will strive for completeness, but not in the sense that all modern critical reconstructions are recorded here. J. Gunther's list of scholarly opinion concerning the philosophy amounts to 44 possibilities,[1] and in the twenty years since he wrote many new assessments have appeared. A description of all these would prove prohibitively long. Besides, a large number of these reconstructions overlap significantly or are minor variations of long-established positions, so that citing them would not contribute to the reader's understanding of the key issues. By comprehensive I mean a detailed sketch of the profile and history of the important schools of interpretation, which includes the variations that exist within them and the degree to which they are related.

Gnosis, Gnosticism, Jewish Gnosticism, and Gnostic Judaism

Age has not lessened the importance of J.B. Lightfoot's analysis of the Colossian philosophy. F. Francis and W. Meeks chose his century-old

---

1. J. Gunther, *St. Paul's Opponents and their Background* (NovTSup, 35; Leiden: Brill, 1973), pp. 3-4.

2. A History of Scholarship on the Colossian Philosophy   19

essay to begin their presentation of seminal studies on the conflict at Colossae.[1] The reasons for this selection are clear. First, Lightfoot epitomized much of nineteenth-century opinion on Colossians.[2] Secondly, he set the terms of the twentieth-century debate about the identity of the philosophy.[3] The majority of interpreters, in both this century and the last, have found in the Colossian philosophy an unorthodox brand of Judaism, a Judaism characterized variously as heterodox, theosophical, speculative, ascetic, esoteric, heretical, or syncretistic. So unparalleled was this Judaism that many invoked a second background to account for the elements that seemed incompatible with Judaism. The favorite candidate here was Gnosticism or Gnosis.[4]

Lightfoot made a clear and convincing presentation of this interpretation.[5] Several features, he noted, marked what he called the Colossian heresy as Jewish: Sabbath observance (Col. 2.16), dietary concerns (v. 16), and, possibly, circumcision (v. 11). At the same time, its mystical and theosophical speculation, particularly about intermediaries that were objects of worship, pointed beyond the bounds of Judaism to an elementary form of Gnostic thought. Thus, he described the Colossian heresy as an intertwining of Judaism and Gnosticism, as Judeo-Gnostic. What specifically in the letter reflected the Gnostic flavor of the heresy? Lightfoot mentioned four aspects: (1) the concern for wisdom, evidenced by wisdom language in the letter (1.26-28;

---

1. J. Lightfoot, 'The Colossian Heresy', in Francis and Meeks (eds.), *Conflict at Colossae*, pp. 13-59. The essay first appeared in Lightfoot's commentary on Colossians entitled *St. Paul's Epistles to the Colossians and to Philemon* (London: Macmillan, 3rd edn, 1879).

2. See, for example, H. Meyer, *Kritisch Exegetisches Handbuch über die Briefe Pauli and die Philipper, Kolosser und Philemon* (MeyerK, 9; Göttingen: Vandenhoeck & Ruprecht, 5th edn, 1886), pp. 257-63.

3. J. Moffatt, *An Introduction to the Literature of the New Testament* (International Theological Library; New York: Charles Scribner's Sons, 3rd edn, 1925), p. 152; R. Yates, 'Colossians and Gnosis', *JSNT* 27 (1986), p. 56.

4. As few of the studies I describe in the following pages distinguish between Gnosticism and Gnosis, I group the two terms together, even though some scholars have drawn distinctions. See U. Bianchi (ed.), *The Origins of Gnosticism* (Studies in the History of Religions, *Numen* Supplement, 12; Leiden: Brill, 1967), p. xxvii; R. Wilson, *Gnosis and the New Testament* (Philadelphia: Fortress Press, 1968), pp. 6-9.

5. Lightfoot, 'Colossian Heresy', pp. 27-32.

2.2-4, 23; 3.16); (2) the cosmological speculation suggested in the word πλήρωμα (1.19; 2.9-10); (3) the emphasis on intermediate beings—thrones, dominions, principalities, authorities (1.16; 2.15), and angels (2.18)—and the call to subservience to them (2.18); and (4) an extreme asceticism going beyond ritual or cultic motivations (2.23). As for the meeting of Jewish and Gnostic thought, Lightfoot described a history of their interaction into which he placed the Colossian heresy. Based on Josephus's account of them, Lightfoot detected the seeds of Gnosticism in the party of the Essenes, particularly in their asceticism and angelology. Outside Palestine, similar mixtures of Judaism and Gnosticism must have arisen, thereby providing the setting in which the Colossian heresy emerged. By the second century, of course, Gnosticism had departed radically from Jewish thought, but even then certain versions of Gnosticism—Lightfoot mentions the system of Cerinthus—betrayed Jewish roots. A clear line of development, therefore, stretched from Judaism to full-fledged Gnosticism along which the Colossian heresy fitted.

For the next three quarters of a century most reconstructions of the Colossian philosophy remained within the parameters set by Lightfoot's analysis, although few placed as balanced an emphasis as Lightfoot had on Judaism and Gnosticism with respect to the question of background. Scholars stressing the former mined the apocalyptic, ascetic, and mystical seams of the Jewish tradition for correspondences to the philosophy. Publication of the Dead Sea Scrolls encouraged the effort. On the other hand, growing reliance on Gnosis or Gnosticism as a key interpretive background for the NT, particularly in German scholarship in the first half of this century, meant that the philosophy's correspondences to it were fully articulated. Characteristic of both these trends in scholarship was the tendency to stress the Jewish or Gnostic background of the Colossian philosophy at the expense of the other. Some of the best reconstructions were one-sided in this regard.

Writing nearly four decades after Lightfoot, M. Dibelius emphasized the Gnostic rooting of the philosophy.[1] He classified it as a

---

1. I summarize here M. Dibelius, 'The Isis Initiation in Apuleius and Related Initiatory Rites', in Francis and Meeks (eds.), *Conflict at Colossae*, pp. 61-121, esp. pp. 82-90. This essay first appeared in German in 1917 and is most readily accessible in Dibelius's collected essays. See 'Die Isisweihe bei Apuleius und verwandte Initiations-Riten', in G. Bornkamm and H. Kraft (eds.), *Botschaft und Geschichte* (2 vols.; Tübingen: Mohr, 1953–56), II, pp. 30-79.

2. A History of Scholarship on the Colossian Philosophy

Gnostic mystery religion and paid scant attention to the features of the philosophy generally recognized as Jewish.

To Dibelius the primary features of the philosophy combated in Colossians mirrored a mystery cult, and initiatory practices in particular. First came the matter of angels (2.18), whom Dibelius equated with the elements of the world (στοιχεῖα τοῦ κόσμου; 2.8, 20) and the principalities and powers (1.16; 2.10, 15) and understood as enslaving deities.[1] He interpreted the philosophy's devotion to them on the basis of a text describing Isiac mystery initiation, namely, Apuleius's *Metamorphoses* (11.23). There the initiate is 'ravished through the elements' in a ceremony that brings him immortality. But while Lucius, the protagonist of that text, relied on Isis to make his way past the elements, according to Dibelius the initiate into the Colossian mystery pacified the cosmic powers by worshiping them, following the practices of Persian element worship.

The second feature proving the existence of a mystery at Colossae was the occurrence of the word ἐμβατεύω in the letter (2.18). Based on inscriptional evidence for the presence and use of the term at the Apollo sanctuary at Claros, Dibelius concluded that the term belonged to the technical vocabulary of the Colossian cult and denoted initiation into it. With these two pieces of the Colossian puzzle solved, the rest fell easily into place: (1) the term mystery (μυστήριον) in Colossians (1.26, 27; 2.2; 4.3) reflected the existence of a mystery cult at Colossae, (2) the term tradition (παράδοσις; 2.8) referred to initiation procedure, (3) asceticism (ἀφειδία; 2.23) was a prerequisite of the initiate, and (4) self-chosen religion (ἐθελοθρησκία; 2.23) denoted the voluntary nature of the mystery cult.

Besides the Persian influence on it, Dibelius noted several things about the cult that suggested its Gnostic orientation.[2] The lack of any reference to Hellenistic gods constituted a strong argument from silence. The mystical and speculative flavor of the philosophy pointed to Gnosticism. And the fact that the Naassenes, an established Gnostic group, underwent mystery initiation made it probable that earlier Gnostic mysteries had existed.

---

1. The full argument appears in his *Die Geisterwelt im Glauben des Paulus* (Göttingen: Vandenhoeck & Ruprecht, 1909), pp. 81, 137, 227-30.
2. Later versions of Dibelius's argument stressed the Gnostic element in the Colossian philosophy. Cf. M. Dibelius and H. Greeven, *An die Kolosser, Epheser, an Philemon* (HNT, 12; Tübingen: Mohr, 3rd edn, 1953) pp. 38-39.

Dibelius garnered wide support for his reconstruction in the decades that followed. His classification of ἐμβατεύω (2.18) as a technical term for mystery initiation had its supporters,[1] and his grouping of the elements and angels with the principalities and powers and his identification of them all as enslaving cosmic deities dominated scholarship on the topic.[2] In addition to enjoying support for the key elements of his argument, his full reconstruction was well received. Recently Lohse reiterated and affirmed the position in some detail. He concluded that the philosophy's pursuit of knowledge and world-negating character clearly marked it as Gnostic or at least pre-Gnostic, while the philosophy's cultic practices took the form of a mystery religion.[3]

In spite of the ostensibly Jewish origin of some of its practices, even Dibelius's minimizing of any Jewish background for the philosophy attracted adherents. The arguments for Dibelius's understatement ran as follows. What originally were Jewish practices—Sabbath observance (2.16) and so forth—had taken on a radically new meaning in a philosophy focused on the elements and not on the Law.[4] J. Gnilka summarized the position pithily: 'A Jewish structure has been filled with a foreign spirit'.[5]

Not all who emphasized the Gnostic orientation of the Colossian philosophy, however, gave the Jewish elements in it such an insignificant role. G. Bornkamm's version of the Gnostic hypothesis, appearing in 1948, differed from Dibelius's in important ways.[6] He followed

---

1. S. Eitrem, 'ΕΜΒΑΤΕΥΩ'. Note sur Col. 2, 18', *ST* 2 (1948), p. 93.
2. H. Schlier, *Principalities and Powers in the New Testament* (QD; New York: Herder & Herder, 1961), pp. 11-39; G. Macgregor, 'Principalities and Powers: The Cosmic Background of Paul's Thought', *NTS* 1 (1954–55), pp. 17-28.
3. Lohse, *Colossians and Philemon*, pp. 129-30.
4. H. Conzelmann, 'Der Brief an die Kolosser', in J. Becker, H. Conzelmann and G. Friedrich (eds.), *Die Briefe an die Galater, Epheser, Philipper, Kolosser, Thessalonicher and Philemon* (NTD, 8; Göttingen: Vandenhoeck & Ruprecht, 15th edn, 1981), p. 192; E. Lohmeyer, *Die Briefe an die Philipper, an die Kolosser und an Philemon* (MeyerK, 9; Göttingen: Vandenhoeck & Ruprecht, 11th edn, 1956), p. 122 n. 2.
5. J. Gnilka, *Der Kolosserbrief* (HTKNT, 10.1; Freiburg: Herder, 1980), p. 168.
6. I summarize here Bornkamm's essay 'The Heresy of Colossians', in Francis and Meeks (eds.), *Conflict at Colossae*, pp. 123-45. The German original, 'Die Häresie des Kolosserbriefes', first appeared in *TLZ* 73 (1948), pp. 11-20, and later in

Dibelius in classifying the elements (στοιχεῖα) as world-ruling deities, identical with the angels of 2.18 and the other intermediate powers mentioned in Colossians. But he parted company with Dibelius in arguing that the Colossian heretics regarded the στοιχεῖα not as tyrannical powers demanding veneration but as bearers of the divine fullness (πλήρωμα). He reached this conclusion based on his reconstruction of the heresy's position from the polemic in Col. 2.9-10. As in Dibelius's interpretation, redemption and deification came with initiation into the στοιχεῖα cult. But adherence to the cult, according to Bornkamm, also entailed obedience to the ritual and ascetic prescriptions, the δόγματα (2.14, 20), imposed by the στοιχεῖα.

Several features of this στοιχεῖα cult marked it as Gnostic. The very designation of the heresy, φιλοσοφία (2.8), and the reference to παράδοσις betokened the special doctrines and secret traditions typical of Gnosticism. In addition, the heresy's central feature, its στοιχεῖα theology, was akin to Gnostic speculation about the aeons. On the surface, of course, identifying the στοιχεῖα with the divine fullness seemed contradictory to Gnostic emanation theology, which regarded the intermediate cosmic powers as denizens of the world of darkness and hostile to the world of light. But, Bornkamm argued, the Gnosticism represented by the *Corpus Hermeticum* and the so-called *Mithras Liturgy* regarded the στοιχεῖα as divine, for in both texts the initiate's rebirth was achieved through those very powers.

Besides grounding it in Gnosticism, Bornkamm attributed several aspects of the Colossian heresy to a Jewish provenance. The festivals and holy days (2.16), the dietary restrictions (2.16, 21), and circumcision (2.11), which may have been required by the Colossian heretics, obviously came from Jewish law. And the characterization of these laws by the false teachers as a reflection (σκιά; 2.17) of a divine reality signaled a Jewish understanding of the Law. Moreover, the description of the στοιχεῖα cult as devotion to angels (θρησκεία τῶν ἀγγέλων; 2.18) and the role of the elements/angels as the transmitters and guardians of the cult's regulations marked the heresy as Jewish, since angels and speculation about their roles figured prominently in Judaism of that time.

Bornkamm's collected essays: *Das Ende des Gesetzes: Paulusstudien* (BEvT, 16; Munich: Chr. Kaiser Verlag, 1952), pp. 139-56.

Bornkamm's examination of Colossians resulted in a highly refined presentation of the Gnostic background of the Colossian philosophy. At the same time, he emphasized the Jewish character of many of its features, thus dissenting from Dibelius's earlier dismissal of Jewish influence. In so doing he came closer than Dibelius to Lightfoot's description of the Colossian philosophy as Judeo-Gnostic. What emerged from his analysis as the seedbed of the Colossian heresy was a Jewish Gnosticism similar to that which he found in the *Book of Elchasai* and the *Pseudo-Clementines*. That such a syncretistic Judaism thrived in Asia Minor and incorporated Persian elements was clear, Bornkamm argued, from the existence of the Hypsistos cult in the Roman imperial period which combined Jewish, Persian, and local pagan features.

Bornkamm's analysis, like Dibelius's, has proven persuasive to interpreters of Colossians. A case in point is the recent commentary of A. Lindemann which described the philosophy as a blend of Jewish and Gnostic elements showing influence from the mystery religions.[1] Analyses acknowledging Jewish features but focusing on the Gnostic orientation of the philosophy also abound in the English-speaking world. G. Beasley-Murray's examination of Colossians 2 concluded that at several points Jewish elements had been incorporated into a Gnostic teaching which at Colossae was decidedly legalistic.[2] R. Martin, who recognized a Jewish source for many of the philosophy's practices, pointed to the philosophy's angel/στοιχεῖα cult and pronounced dualism as evidence of the central role a Gnostic background played in it.[3]

The publication of the Nag Hammadi documents signaled a new phase in the articulation of a Gnostic background for the philosophy. Scholars turned to them in part to resolve an issue that had troubled and divided proponents of the Gnostic thesis:

> The relationship between the 'elements of the universe' [2.8, 20] and the 'fulness' [2.9-10] is not entirely clear; the powers could be understood as representatives of the divine fulness [following Bornkamm] or as

---

1. A. Lindemann, *Der Kolosserbrief* (Züricher Bibel Kommentare NT, 10; Zurich: Theologischer Verlag, 1983), pp. 82-84.
2. G. Beasley-Murray, 'The Second Chapter of Colossians', *RevExp* 70 (1973), pp. 473, 478.
3. R. Martin, *Colossians: The Church's Lord and the Christian's Liberty* (Grand Rapids: Zondervan, 1973), pp. 12-19, 92-95.

2. A History of Scholarship on the Colossian Philosophy

dangerous principalities who block the way to the 'fulness' and allow free passage only after they have received due reverence [following Dibelius].[1]

It troubled H.-M. Schenke that the angelic elements were held in such high esteem by the Colossian philosophers when full-fledged Gnosticism placed the intermediate cosmic powers in the camp of the demiurge. Siding with Dibelius, Schenke resolved this apparent contradiction by identifying the elements as archons and denying their connection with the divine realm. Accordingly, the worship given them by the philosophers was a ruse, a necessary deception undertaken by the beings of light living in this world of darkness. This interpretation, supported by Schenke's interpretation of a passage from the *Hypostasis of the Archons*, made sense of a key component in the philosophy's praxis: humility (ταπεινοφροσύνη). The Colossian Gnostics had to endure humiliating subservience to the archons/elements with indifference until they escaped this realm.[2]

Precisely the opposite understanding of the cosmic elements appeared in A. Moyo's argument for a Gnostic understanding of the Colossian philosophy. Moyo turned to *Eugnostos the Blessed* and *Sophia of Jesus Christ* to substantiate his claim that at least some Gnostic circles viewed the cosmic powers in a positive light. Siding with Bornkamm, he concluded that the Colossian philosophers located the divine fullness in the angels/elements/powers, which accounted for their worship of them.[3]

Not all those adhering to a Jewish-Gnostic reading of the Colossian philosophy joined the ranks of Dibelius and Bornkamm by placing primary interpretive emphasis on Gnostic thought in their reconstructions. With the publication of the Dead Sea Scrolls, another aspect of Lightfoot's analysis—the correspondence he found between the Essenes and the philosophy—became the focal point of research for some scholars. Now available were the primary texts of the Essene community on the Dead Sea, so that Lightfoot's work could be tested and enlarged. Naturally, attention to the Scrolls led to an emphasis on the Jewish background of the Colossian philosophy.

---

1. Lohse, *Colossians and Philemon*, p. 128.
2. H.-M. Schenke, 'Der Widerstreit gnostischer und kirchlicher Christologie im Spiegel des Kolosserbriefes', *ZTK* 61 (1964), pp. 395-99. For a recent version of this interpretation, see Pokorný, *Colossians*, pp. 117-20.
3. A. Moyo, 'The Colossian Heresy in Light of Some Gnostic Documents from Nag Hammadi', *Journal of Theology for Southern Africa* 48 (1984), pp. 34-35.

E. Saunders saw his study of Qumran theology as verification of the affinity Lightfoot had posited between Essene and heretical Colossian thought. The features of the heresy he isolated—pursuit of esoteric wisdom, ritual perfection, and asceticism—varied little from the elements Lightfoot had found in common between the Essenes and the Colossian heretics: (1) concern for wisdom, (2) angelology, and (3) ritual and ascetic practices.[1] Saunders located ample documentation for all these features in the Dead Sea Scrolls.

Like Lightfoot, Saunders refrained from concluding that the similarities between the thought and praxis at Qumran and Colossae indicated a historical connection. Rather, both represented a dualism impregnated by a style of thought known as Gnostic, and they testified to its pervasiveness. He ended his study in this way:

> Bishop Lightfoot's nineteenth century hypothesis of a discernible affinity between the Colossian heresy and the Gnostic Judaism exhibited in the Essene sect is further corroborated as we move from the descriptive accounts of Philo and Josephus to the primary literature of the sect at Qumran. No identity of origin can be documented between the Colossian heresy and Qumran heterodoxy, but the literature from the Dead Sea sect amplifies the sparse references in the Colossian polemic, permitting us to obtain a clearer understanding of the forms of syncretistic Judaism which proved a disturbing influence in many of the Christian congregations in Asia Minor.[2]

Like Saunders, E. Yamauchi began with the Dead Sea Scrolls in his search for the roots of the Colossian philosophy. Much of what he found there was congenial with the thought and praxis of the philosophy. In matters of practice Colossae and Qumran shared scrupulous eating habits and intense concern for calendrical matters, especially Sabbath observance. Conceptually, the philosophy's interest in secret knowledge or mysteries and in angels revealed an Essene background.[3] On the other hand, some significant features of the philosophy showed little affinity to Qumran, anticipating instead later Gnosticism. Yamauchi detected at Colossae a soteriology that approximated

---

1. E. Saunders, 'The Colossian Heresy and Qumran Theology', in B. Daniels and J. Suggs (eds.), *Studies in the History and Text of the New Testament* (SD, 29; Salt Lake City: University of Utah Press, 1967), pp. 134-35.
2. Saunders, 'Colossian Heresy', pp. 141-42.
3. E. Yamauchi, 'Qumran and Colossae', *BSac* 121 (1964), pp. 142-47.

2. A History of Scholarship on the Colossian Philosophy

Gnostic rather than Essene thought.[1] As a consequence, he judged that the philosophy represented a stage of transition between Essene heterodoxy and Gnosticism. Yamauchi would have concurred with the designation that L. Johnson attached to the philosophy: Gnostic Judaism.[2]

Departure from the Jewish-Gnostic Model

Jewish-Gnostic understandings of the Colossian philosophy, especially those emphasizing the Gnostic side, dominated scholarly reconstructions through the first half of this century and remain popular today. Even before World War II, however, this line of scholarship had its critics. H. Rongy, writing in the late 1930s, acknowledged the Jewish features of the philosophy and even accepted Dibelius's interpretation of ἐμβατεύω as evidence of a mystery initiation in the philosophy, but he found arguments for the Gnostic orientation of the philosophy to be unconvincing.[3] While admitting that the philosophy went beyond the circle of Judaism, he refused to introduce a Gnostic background, concluding that the philosophy represented a type of syncretism with little coherence.

The publication of the Dead Sea Scrolls triggered even greater criticism. Much as they had encouraged an increased emphasis on the Jewish side of the philosophy by scholars adhering to a Jewish-Gnostic reading, the writings at Qumran also allowed articulation of a position that departed substantially from that model. S. Lyonnet's articles of the 1950s and 1960s were a prime example of the assault on the ruling Jewish-Gnostic thesis and the replacement of it with a purely Jewish reading.[4]

---

1. Yamauchi, 'Qumran and Colossae', p. 151.
2. L. Johnson, 'Beware of Philosophy', *BSac* 119 (1962), p. 302.
3. H. Rongy, 'Les erreurs combattues dans l'épître aux Colossiens. II,16-19', *Revue ecclésiastique de Liège* 30 (1938–39), pp. 245, 247-48; 'La réfutation des erreurs de Colosses. Col. II, 8-15', *Revue ecclésiastique de Liège* 31 (1939–40), p. 220.
4. S. Lyonnet, 'L'épître aux Colossiens (Col. 2,18) et les mystères d'Apollo Clarien', *Bib* 43 (1962), pp. 417-35; 'Saint Paul et le gnosticisme: L'épître aux Colossiens', in Bianchi (ed.), *The Origins of Gnosticism*, pp. 538-51; 'Paul's Adversaries in Colossae', in Francis and Meeks (eds.), *Conflict at Colossae*, pp. 147-61. The French original of this last article appeared as part of an essay entitled 'L'étude du milieu littéraire et l'exégèse du Nouveau Testament', *Bib* 37 (1956), pp. 27-38.

First, Lyonnet attacked those defending a predominantly Gnostic reading of the Colossian philosophy on several fronts. He argued that the vocabulary attributed to the false teachers was not exclusively Gnostic, and, in some instances, not from them but the letter writer himself: (1) the terms πλήρωμα and σῶμα could come just as readily from Stoic vocabulary, (2) ἀρχαί and ἐξουσίαι had a Jewish provenance, and (3) στοιχεῖα was Pauline (cf. Gal. 4.3, 9). Moreover, the philosophers' involvement with intermediaries and mediatorial powers had a Jewish, not Gnostic, ring. The letter writer's polemic, according to Lyonnet, concentrated on angels, the Law, and wisdom, all subjects of Jewish thought. Lyonnet also took Dibelius to task over the term ἐμβατεύω, finding no correspondences between its use in Colossians and in the sanctuary inscriptions at Claros. Instead, he cited the word's occurrence in 2 Macc. 2.30 as the closest analogy, and argued that the letter writer introduced it into the conflict.

Second, Lyonnet presented Judaism as the background that best illuminated the Colossian conflict. Specifically, he saw much in common between the philosophy and the Dead Sea Scrolls, although he declined to posit a historical connection between the two: (1) an emphasis on the calendar; (2) an ascetic perspective, especially in matters of food and drink; (3) a drive for wisdom; and (4) a lively angelology. Central to both as well was the Law, evidenced at Colossae in the letter writer's strong anti-Law polemic. So central was it to the philosophers, according to Lyonnet, that the Law had displaced Christ from his mediatorial role. Because of the Law's prominence, those who assisted in its promulgation, the angels, occupied center stage in the philosophy. Their importance was nicely captured in the phrase θρησκεία τῶν ἀγγέλων, which referred not to a cult devoted to angels but to the religious and moral practices delivered and guarded by angels.

While not as aggressive in his attack on the Jewish-Gnostic interpretation of the Colossian philosophy, W.D. Davies was as certain as Lyonnet of the philosophy's affinity to Essene thought.[1] To support his claim that Col. 2.11-23 had a predominantly Jewish character, Davies located specific points of contact between the Scrolls and the

1. Davies's skepticism about the value of introducing Gnosticism or Jewish Gnosticism into analyses of the Dead Sea Scrolls extended to his treatment of the Colossian philosophy. See his *Christian Origins and Judaism* (London: Darton, Longman & Todd, 1962), pp. 107, 134-38, 158-60.

2. A History of Scholarship on the Colossian Philosophy

philosophy. Both emphasized calendrical matters, particularly Sabbath observance; distinctions in dietary matters; asceticism; access to special wisdom or knowledge; angelology; and a dualistic viewpoint that saw this world populated by evil forces. Making the connection between the Dead Sea Scrolls and Colossians tighter was an exact verbal parallel: the uncommon expression 'body of flesh' appeared in 1QpHab 9.2 and in Col. 1.22 and 2.11, and the nuance of the phrase in 1QpHab 9.2 and Col. 1.22 was the same.[1]

Lyonnet's criticism of the Jewish-Gnostic model did not go unchallenged, nor did his heavy dependence on the Dead Sea Scrolls in interpreting the Colossian philosophy. M. Braun's extensive study of the Qumran documents in relation to the NT suggested only partial overlap between the Scrolls and Colossians. Whereas the former's purity was cultic in orientation, Braun detected an ascetic purity at Colossae that went beyond cultic concerns. A more glaring difference lay in the lack of any reference to the elements of the world, a key phrase at Colossae, in the Scrolls.[2] Despite these objections, scholars came more and more to regard the Scrolls as the key documents for understanding the philosophy.[3]

At the same time, Lyonnet's criticisms encouraged a full-scale reappraisal of the major exegetical positions taken by the Jewish-Gnostic thesis. The 1960s saw the appearance of major studies that went further than Lyonnet in challenging the three exegetical pillars of the Jewish-Gnostic thesis: the 'elements of the world' (Col. 2.8, 20) equated with the angels (2.18), principalities, and powers (2.10, 15) and regarded as powerful cosmic deities; the 'religion of angels' read as an objective genitive meaning devotion to the angels; and ἐμβατεύω understood as a term for mystery initiation. In their respective monographs on the 'elements of the world', both A.J. Bandstra and A.W. Cramer rejected the identification of the

---

1. W.D. Davies, 'Paul and the Dead Sea Scrolls: Flesh and Spirit', in K. Stendahl (ed.), *The Scrolls and the New Testament* (New York: Harper, 1957), pp. 166-68.
2. H. Braun, *Qumran und das Neue Testament* (2 vols.; Tübingen: Mohr, 1966), I, pp. 229-32; II, pp. 178, 290, 292-98.
3. Gunther, *St. Paul's Opponents*, p. 314-15; W. Foerster, 'Die Irrlehrer der Kolosserbriefes', in W. van Unnik and A. van der Woude (eds.), *Studia Biblica et Semitica* (Wageningen: Veenman, 1966), p. 79; N. Kehl, 'Erniedrigung und Erhöhung in Qumran und Kolossä', *ZKT* 91 (1969), pp. 364-94.

elements as world-ruling angelic spirits.[1] Bandstra concluded that the elements referred to the fundamental forces inherent in the world, Cramer that they were the natures of the present evil world; both noted that Paul saw them as equivalent to the Law.[2] As for the phrase 'religion of the angels', Lyonnet's rejection of the Jewish-Gnostic reading received support from Francis's arguments for a subjective genitival reading of the phrase: the philosophers pursued a vision of angelic worship (2.18), that is, of the angels worshiping God in heaven.[3] Francis also undertook a thorough analysis of ἐμβατεύω. The action of entering conveyed in that word, he concluded, referred not to initiatory entry into a mystery cult but visionary entry into heaven.[4]

Ascetic, Apocalyptic, and Mystical Judaism

The massive reassessment of how the definitive features of the Colossian philosophy were to be understood opened the door to a line of scholarship markedly different from the Jewish-Gnostic school. The new departure limited the search for analogies to the Colossian philosophy to the Judaism of the time. But emphasis did not fall as it had in Lyonnet's work so heavily on the Dead Sea Scrolls. Evidently in response to critics of the Scrolls–Colossae connection, both those hostile and those sympathetic to the new approach,[5] the pursuit of a

---

1. A. Bandstra, *The Law and the Elements of the World* (Kampen: Kok, 1964), p. 44; A. Cramer, *Stoicheia tou kosmou: Interpretatie van een nieuwtestamentische term* (Nieuwkoop: de Graaf, 1961), p. 174. See also J. Blinzler, 'Lexikalisches zu dem Terminus τὰ στοιχεῖα τοῦ κόσμου bei Paulus', in *Studiorum Paulinorum Congressus Internationalis Catholicus 1961* (AnBib, 17–18; 2 vols.; Rome: Pontifico Instituto Biblico, 1963), II, pp. 429-43; and N. Kehl, *Der Christushymnus im Kolosserbrief* (SBM, 1; Stuttgart: Katholisches Bibelwerk, 1967), pp. 138-61.
2. Bandstra, *Law and the Elements*, p. 68; Cramer, *Stoicheia*, pp. 175-76.
3. F. Francis, 'Humility and Angelic Worship in Col. 2.18', in Francis and Meeks (eds.), *Conflict at Colossae*, pp. 176-80. This essay appeared originally in *ST* 16 (1962), pp. 109-34.
4. F. Francis, 'The Background of EMBATEUEIN (Col. 2.18) in Legal Papyri and Oracle Inscriptions', in Francis and Meeks (eds.), *Conflict at Colossae*, pp. 197-99.
5. Congdon's stress on the Jewish background of the Colossian philosophy does not keep her from noting significant differences between the Scrolls and the philosophy ('False Teachers', pp. 251-53, 268).

2. A History of Scholarship on the Colossian Philosophy

comprehensive background for the Colossian philosophy embraced the full range of contemporary Jewish literature and the OT pseudepigrapha in particular.

Francis's dissertation, and the series of articles that sprang from it, represented the most elaborate exposition of the new proposal.[1] Francis focused his efforts on the practices prescribed by the philosophy, paying scant attention to the issues of intermediate powers or Christology because he regarded these as irrelevant matters to the Colossian controversy. At the center of its praxis, according to him, lay the philosophy's enjoyment of θρησκεία τῶν ἀγγέλων. Taken as a subjective genitive in construction, this phrase denoted the philosophers' access to the worship of God undertaken by the angelic host, an activity in which some in the Qumran community also joined (1QSb 4.25-26; 1QH 3.20-22; 11.13-14). This foretaste of the heavenly state came through a mystical vision and journey, the achievement of which was the goal of the philosophy's praxis. The careful observance of dietary regulations, engagement in humiliation, and the practice of rigorous bodily asceticism effected a purification that prepared one for the receipt of revelation, as it did in contemporary Jewish apocalyptic literature (*2 Bar.* 5.7ff.; 9.2–10.1; 12.5–13.1; 21.1ff.; 43.3; 47.2ff.; *4 Ezra* 5.13-20; 6.31, 35; 9.23-25; 12.51–13.1) and OT tradition (Exod. 19–20). Thereupon one could gain entry (Col. 2.18; ἐμβατεύω) into the heavenly realm. This mystical ascent, the fruit of a rigorism based on the Law, gave some at Colossae a taste of what they had seen (ἑόρακεν)—the angelic host adoring God—and was, therefore, their assurance of salvation.

Francis's placement of the Colossian philosophy in the ascetic, mystical strand of contemporary Judaism attracted the interest of many scholars. Bandstra, for instance, explored the OT pseudepigraphical literature further and found another correspondence between it and the philosophy.[2] Noting a polemic stressing God's unmediated activity in the world in Jewish apocalypses of the NT period, he located the

---

1. F. Francis, 'A Re-Examination of the Colossian Controversy' (PhD dissertation, Yale University, 1965); 'Visionary Discipline and Scriptural Tradition at Colossae', *Lexington Theological Quarterly* 2 (1967), pp. 71-81. See also his 'Background of EMBATEUEIN' and 'Angelic Worship'.

2. A. Bandstra, 'Did the Colossian Errorists Need a Mediator?', in R. Longenecker and M. Tenney (eds.), *New Dimensions in New Testament Study* (Grand Rapids: Zondervan, 1974), pp. 329-43.

same theme in the Colossian philosophy, arguing that its adherents saw no need for Christ's mediation and could achieve their salvific vision independently. Bandstra based his interpretation, in part, on Col. 2.2-4, reading in the letter writer's polemic he found there a claim by the philosophy to have direct access to the treasures of wisdom and knowledge. This phrase, 'treasures of wisdom', Bandstra located in 2 Bar. (44.14; 54.13) where it is associated with the throne of God, which he labeled the epicenter of Jewish mystical speculation. In other words, this was additional proof that the Colossian philosophy showed signs of contact with early Jewish mysticism.

C. Evans joined Francis and Bandstra in locating the Colossian philosophy 'against the background of Jewish mysticism, the sort of mysticism found at Qumran, in apocalyptic and pseudepigraphical writings, and in later Rabbinic traditions'.[1] He largely confirmed the findings of both scholars and augmented their reconstructions with his own analysis of the phrase 'elements of the world'. He refrained from endorsing Bandstra's position entirely, for he found no polemic against a divine mediator in either Jewish literature of the time or in Colossians. But he supported Bandstra's argument that the philosophy claimed to have direct access to the treasures of wisdom and knowledge (Col. 2.3). Along with their pursuit of this divine wisdom, Evans argued, the Colossian mystics sought the secret knowledge embodied in the 'elements of the world'. The letter writer, he concluded, challenged this claim of wisdom and the means of acquiring it in his polemic of ch. 2.[2]

Others added their voices to the thesis that the Colossian philosophy could best be understood in the milieu of Jewish apocalyptic mysticism. R. Yates's confidence in being able to place the philosophy against such a background was clearly evident in his critique of the Jewish-Gnostic proposal, one of the most recent.[3] He conceded no more than that some of the philosophy's features could have served as the soil from which an interest in gnosis and full-fledged Gnosticism emerged. F.F. Bruce concluded that *merkabah* mysticism was the tradition most comparable with the Colossian philosophy, and C. Rowland turned to Jewish apocalyptic literature to explain the vision of angels he found

1. C. Evans, 'The Colossian Mystics', *Bib* 63 (1982), p. 204.
2. Evans, 'Colossian Mystics', pp. 199-202.
3. R. Yates, '"The Worship of Angels" (Col. 2.18)', *ExpTim* 97 (1985), p. 14; 'Colossians and Gnosis', pp. 58-59.

mentioned in Col. 2.18.[1] Most recently, Sappington undertook an extensive survey of apocalyptic literature, resulting in further refinement of Francis's reconstruction.[2]

Hellenistic Syncretism in First-Century Asia Minor

The attack launched by Rongy, Lyonnet, and others on the Jewish-Gnostic reconstruction prompted not only radical departures from it but also modifications in it. Reflected in this attack and the responses to it was the growing reluctance in the period after World War II to invoke a Gnostic background. The scholarly consensus about the origin(s) and pervasiveness of Gnosticism shifted as the century progressed, with skepticism replacing the earlier enthusiastic employment of Gnosticism in NT interpretation.

In addition to this trend in NT scholarship and the criticism of the Jewish-Gnostic proposal it encouraged, proponents of the latter had themselves recognized interpretive problems with it and sought to improve it. Schenke's analysis of the Colossian philosophy offers a good example of the attempt to overcome difficulties in the Jewish-Gnostic thesis. As noted before, he saw real difficulty in reconciling the Colossian philosophy's στοιχεῖα/angel cult with the Gnostic denigration of intermediate powers.[3] Accordingly, he modified Bornkamm's position on the στοιχεῖα/angels in order to achieve a reconciliation.

Not all were confident, however, that a reconciliation could be so easily achieved. Noting the same problem as Schenke—that the worship of elements appeared antithetical to Gnostic thought—H. Hegermann saw no solution and reached this conclusion: 'The worship of elements is not Gnostic'.[4] Taking this position placed Hegermann in opposition to the Jewish-Gnostic proposal, particularly as it was articulated by Dibelius and Bornkamm. Yet he otherwise adhered closely to the exegetical and history of religions positions reached by those two. Hegermann determined the Colossian philosophy to be a typical

---

1. F. Bruce, 'Colossian Problems. Part 3: The Colossian Heresy', *BSac* 141 (1984), pp. 201-204; C. Rowland, 'Apocalyptic Visions and the Exaltation of Christ in the Letter to the Colossians', *JSNT* 19 (1983), pp. 75-77.
2. Sappington, *Revelation and Redemption*, p. 21, esp. n. 5.
3. Schenke, 'Widerstreit', p. 395.
4. H. Hegermann, *Die Vorstellung vom Schöpfungsmittler im hellenistischen Judentum und Urchristentum* (TU, 82; Berlin: Akademie Verlag, 1961), p. 163.

example of Hellenistic syncretism. He relied on Dibelius's analysis of ἐμβατεύω as evidence that the philosophy was a mystery religion. Bornkamm's work had also influenced him, for he stressed the Jewish features of the philosophy and favored the *Mithras Liturgy* as the document providing the best analogies to the philosophy.[1] In other words, apart from abandoning all talk of Gnostic influence, Hegermann remained entirely within the parameters of the Jewish-Gnostic reconstruction delineated by German scholarship. For him, the Colossian philosophy was a Jewish mystery cult to the angels.

The analysis of J. Lähnemann went into much greater depth than that of Hegermann, but it yielded similar results. He regarded talk of Jewish Gnosticism at Colossae as chimerical, but relied heavily on the insights of Dibelius and Bornkamm about the nature and origins of the philosophy.[2] Key to understanding the philosophy, according to Lähnemann, was Colossae's location near the major east–west trade route of Asia Minor. From Greece came the philosophy's stress on wisdom and its structure as a mystery religion; from the east came Persian element worship and Jewish practices. Mixed with these features were two local religious influences: calendrical interests reflected a concern about nature, a preoccupation of the regionally popular Men cult, and a rigorous asceticism typified Phrygian-born religious traditions like the Cybele cult and Montanism.[3] In short, the Colossian philosophy epitomized Anatolian syncretism.

Hegermann and Lähnemann are but two examples of what in recent decades has become a distinctive line of scholarship on the Colossian philosophy. Owing much to the Jewish-Gnostic thesis, this school nonetheless modified that position, dropping any argument for a Gnostic presence. The search for the roots of the philosophy focused instead on the pagan tradition that combined with Jewish elements to form the Colossian philosophy amalgam. The new reconstruction's indebtedness to the Jewish-Gnostic proposal showed in its interpretation of three key features of the Colossian philosophy: (1) the θρησκεία τῶν ἀγγέλων designated an angel cult; (2) the term ἐμβατεύω indicated that the philosophy took the form of a mystery religion; and (3) the στοιχεῖα τοῦ κόσμου referred not to Jewish

---

1. Hegermann, *Vorstellung vom Schöpfungsmittler*, pp. 161-62.
2. J. Lähnemann, *Der Kolosserbrief: Komposition, Situation und Argumentation* (SNT, 3; Gütersloh: Gerd Mohn, 1971), pp. 81, 86, 99-101.
3. Lähnemann, *Kolosserbrief*, pp. 82-100.

2. A History of Scholarship on the Colossian Philosophy

law, religious regulations, or elementary principles but to powerful cosmic divinities. As was the case with proponents of the Jewish-Gnostic reading, emphasis on the Jewish or pagan features of the philosophy varied with the interpreter. But all characterized the Colossian philosophy as markedly syncretistic.

T. Kraabel called the Colossian philosophy a brand of Anatolian Judaism which had absorbed much from its Lydian–Phrygian environment. He documented the importance of religious festivals and dietary matters in Anatolian Judaism and noted the same emphases in the Colossian philosophy (Col. 2.16, 21).[1] Added to the Jewish foundation of the philosophy were features characteristic of Anatolian piety, whether Jewish, Christian, or pagan: an extreme asceticism, and attention to mediating deities, sometimes referred to as ἄγγελοι. The latter element in particular played a central role in the philosophy, to judge from its concern with the cosmic στοιχεῖα and devotion to angels. Engendering such a development was Jewish interest in, and speculation about, angels.[2]

Unlike Kraabel, Gnilka found pagan elements to be more definitive of the Colossian philosophy than Jewish features. The philosophy most closely resembled a Hellenistic mystery religion, Gnilka argued, for it spoke the language of initiation (ἐμβατεύω) and promised escape from the cosmic powers, much as Isis freed Lucius from world-ruling fate in Apuleius's *Metamorphoses*. The debt Gnilka owed to Dibelius for this interpretation was great, and it extended even to the treatment of the philosophy's Jewish features, which Dibelius had dismissed as insignificant. While there were ostensibly Jewish features in the philosophy, they had been entirely incorporated into a Hellenistic pagan outlook, according to Gnilka. He surmised that proselytes to the philosophy had brought them in, but that the motivation behind these Jewish practices was now entirely different.[3] Here, then, was an interpretation at some distance from Kraabel's, yet the differences were not programmatic but matters of nuance. For both relied primarily on Dibelius and Bornkamm for their understanding of the

---

1. T. Kraabel, 'Judaism in Western Asia Minor under the Roman Empire with a Preliminary Study of the Jewish Community at Sardis, Lydia' (PhD dissertation, Harvard Divinity School, 1968), pp. 141-42.
2. Kraabel, 'Judaism in Western Asia Minor', pp. 142-46.
3. Gnilka, *Kolosserbrief*, pp. 167-69.

philosophy; they differed only in the weight they placed on the various elements that formed the Colossian philosophy hybrid.

A Philosophical Background for the Colossian Philosophy

Compared to the many other proposals for the background of the Colossian philosophy, suggestions that it was a brand of Hellenistic philosophy or at least heavily influenced by it have commanded little support. Literature of the late nineteenth and early twentieth centuries did little more than mention this approach and then defend one of the more popular views already treated above.[1] Only after World War II did Hellenistic philosophy receive greater attention, and even then not to the degree that other backgrounds enjoyed.

E. Percy's analysis of the epistle to the Colossians appeared immediately after the war. In it he noted that the severity of the asceticism called for by the Colossian philosophy went beyond the pursuit of ritual purity and reflected instead the motivation and outlook of a philosophically oriented piety. Percy cited examples from Apollonius of Tyana's life in arguing that a neo-Pythagorean or neo-Platonic perspective came closest to accounting for the Colossian philosophy's insistence on a strict asceticism of the body (Col. 2.23).[2] He concluded that the Christian philosophers at Colossae exhibited strong influence from 'late Greek speculation and ascetic piety'.[3]

A more recent study by G. Caird observed the same stress on the ascetic and the avoidance of the sensual at Colossae. This emphasis assumed a mind–body dualism, Caird argued, which was clear evidence for a non-Jewish component in a philosophy otherwise showing strong Jewish influence. The practical orientation of the philosophy, what Caird called its concern with morality, marked it as a typical Hellenistic philosophy, so he speculated that Stoic elements had joined Jewish elements to form the Colossian philosophy.[4]

Going much further than either Percy or Caird, Schweizer argued

---

1. Meyer, *Handbuch*, pp. 258-59; Moffat, *Introduction*, pp. 152-53.
2. E. Percy, *Die Probleme der Kolosser- und Epheserbriefe* (Acta Regiae Societatis Humaniorum Litterarum Lundensis, 39; Lund: Gleerup, 1946), pp. 141-42.
3. Percy, *Probleme*, p. 143.
4. G. Caird, *Paul's Letters from Prison* (New Clarendon Bible; Oxford: Oxford University Press, 1976), pp. 162-64.

2. A History of Scholarship on the Colossian Philosophy 37

that Hellenistic philosophy provided the key to unraveling the entire Colossian philosophy puzzle. Schweizer's analysis of the Colossian controversy, which began with a study of the στοιχεῖα τοῦ κόσμου in 1970, took a direction that was critical of both the Jewish-Gnostic and exclusively Jewish interpretations of the philosophy. Rejecting the former's identification of the elements as world-ruling deities and the latter's identification of them as legal regulations or the Mosaic law, Schweizer stressed the philosophical background of the στοιχεῖα as the four constituents of the cosmos.[1]

Schweizer turned again and again to the Greek philosophical tradition for insights into the Colossian philosophy.[2] His analysis of Colossians isolated three features he considered central to the philosophy: (1) the prescriptions concerning food, drink, and festivals based on human, not divine, authority; (2) exercises in self-abasement, including the devotion to angels and ascetic practices that may have entailed fasting and sexual abstinence; and (3) concern with the cosmic στοιχεῖα which bind humanity to the world (Col. 2.20). He saw little that was distinctly Jewish in all this, that is, in secular legalism, radical asceticism, and concern with the στοιχεῖα. Rather, Schweizer proposed that these features made sense from a perspective dominant in contemporary philosophical circles: a pessimistic outlook assuming the instability and transitoriness of the world and encouraging the flight of the higher element in the human makeup to the immortal, celestial realm. In support of this interpretation he cited a summary of neo-Pythagorean teachings from the first century BCE recorded by Diogenes Laertius (*Lives of Eminent Philosophers* 8.25-33). That text describes the constitution of the world from the στοιχεῖα. The interplay between these elements produces an inherently unstable world and, as a consequence, a human existence that is mortal. Naturally, the immortal part of human beings strives to escape this lower realm, an undertaking that requires a purity achieved by a regimen of abstinence from certain foods, the proper worship of gods and heroes, and various cleansings and lustrations. This outlook and program, Schweizer argued, corresponded closely to the Colossian philosophy with its sense of enslavement in the world by the στοιχεῖα, expectation of an ascent

1. Schweizer, '"Elemente der Welt"', pp. 245-59.
2. Schweizer, *Letter to the Colossians*, pp. 127-33; 'Zur neueren Forschung an Kolosserbrief (seit 1970)', in J. Pfammatter and F. Furger (eds.), *Theologische Berichte 5* (Zurich: Benziger Verlag, 1976), pp. 173-80.

to a heavenly realm, possibly anticipated by mysteries (Col. 2.17-18), abstinence from certain foods and angel worship (vv. 16, 18)—Schweizer noted that Philo equated the angels with heroes (*Plant.* 4 §14)—and, possibly, advocacy of baptism (v. 12). Even in the mention of Sabbath observance (v. 16), Schweizer found little more than Jewish trimmings on what was an essentially Pythagorean philosophy. And the legalism alive in Colossae was of a pagan sort, which Ignatius later combated as a Judaism of the uncircumcised (*Phld.* 6.1).[1]

Conclusion

This survey of the important reconstructions of the Colossian philosophy has been structured so that each study presented has been classified according to the major exegetical positions it takes and the history of religions background(s) it champions. There appear to be five distinct schools of interpretation, each with its own history and relationship with the other schools, and each well represented in contemporary scholarship.

Jewish Gnosticism. This proposal regards Gnostic thought as essential for understanding the Colossian philosophy, to the extent that in some versions of this proposal the Jewish elements are considered vestigial.

Gnostic Judaism. This thesis, while adhering to the exegetical findings of the Jewish-Gnostic proposal, emphasizes the Jewish side of the Colossian philosophy. Nevertheless, where the philosophy goes beyond the circle of Judaism, this thesis calls upon Gnostic thought for explanation.

Ascetic, Apocalyptic, Mystical Judaism. This reading departs from every version of the Jewish-Gnostic thesis, both in matters of exegesis and background, and relies exclusively on Jewish sources for the reconstruction of the Colossian philosophy.

Hellenistic Syncretism. This hypothesis, representing a modification of the Jewish-Gnostic proposal, focuses on the religious milieu of Asia Minor—its indigenous religious impulses, the distinctive features of Anatolian Judaism, and Asia Minor as the place where Greek and Eastern thought met—as the key for interpreting the Colossian philosophy.

---

1. Schweizer, *Letter to the Colossians*, pp. 127-28; 'Christianity of the Circumcised', pp. 245-55.

2. A History of Scholarship on the Colossian Philosophy

Hellenistic Philosophy. This interpretation, also an heir of the Jewish-Gnostic proposal, explores Hellenistic philosophy for a key or the key to the Colossian philosophy puzzle.

The reason for structuring the survey in this way lies in the light it casts on the contours of the Colossian philosophy puzzle. By now the reader should have some grasp of the philosophy's salient elements and the interpretive difficulties they pose to any attempt at reconstruction. These problematic features have received further definition in the presentation of the proposed interpretations of them.

None of the reconstructions of the Colossian philosophy commands a consensus of scholarly opinion at the present, but this survey of them allows some observations and provisional conclusions about the current method of approaching Colossians and the value of certain reconstructions and history of religions backgrounds. At the very least it is worth noting that an overwhelming number of scholars recognize a distinct threat to the Colossian community reflected in the letter. Hence, M. Hooker belongs to a rather insignificant minority of Colossians scholars when she concludes that Colossians contains no clear reference to the supposed error and that the letter writer's warnings in ch. 2 arose from a general pressure to conform to the pagan environment.[1] The vast majority of scholars are convinced that the author is combating opponents or a well-defined faction in the Colossian community, or that at the very least he has in mind an established set of beliefs and practices that he finds objectionable and that warrant his opposition. Interestingly, even Hooker concedes that the letter reflects the advocacy of certain specific practices at Colossae.[2]

With respect to the history of religions analyses of the philosophy, the developments within each school of interpretation just narrated may indicate the viability of one or another background in the interpretation of the philosophy. Those reconstructions that root the philosophy solely in Judaism, for instance, took inspiration from Lyonnet yet took exception to his heavy reliance on the Dead Sea Scrolls in the search for correspondences to the Colossian philosophy.

---

1. M. Hooker, 'Were there False Teachers in Colossae?', in B. Lindars and S. Smalley (eds.), *Christ and Spirit in the New Testament* (Cambridge: Cambridge University Press, 1973), pp. 318, 329. This article reappears as ch. 10 in M. Hooker, *From Adam to Christ: Essays on Paul* (Cambridge: Cambridge University Press, 1990).

2. Hooker, 'False Teachers in Colossae?', p. 327.

While they made Lyonnet's criticism of the Jewish-Gnostic proposal their own, Francis, Bandstra, and others broadened the scope of their search to include the full range of contemporary Jewish literature, especially the OT pseudepigrapha. This development suggests that an interpretation of the Colossian philosophy against the background of the Scrolls alone may run into difficulties.

Those scholars finding some form of Gnosticism at Colossae reside in a house divided. Indicative of this is the tension that exists between the two major proponents of this school, Dibelius and Bornkamm. How the στοιχεῖα/angels are understood, either positively or negatively, largely dictates one's interpretation of the philosophy, and the opposing views expressed in Dibelius's and Bornkamm's analyses have not been resolved. On the contrary, the debate among advocates of the Jewish-Gnostic position continues, as the articles of Schenke and Moyo attest. This unresolved controversy naturally detracts from the appeal of the Jewish-Gnostic reconstruction.

Beyond these observations about developments in particular schools of interpretation, one important general impression comes from this survey of existing reconstructions. The most comprehensive, coherent, and (in my opinion) convincing reconstructions of the Colossian philosophy appear to disregard or dismiss a fundamental aspect of the philosophy, which is its essentially syncretistic nature. Dibelius, Francis, and Schweizer alike place the features of the philosophy against a single background, either pagan or Jewish. On the other hand, the many who recognize and stress the philosophy's syncretism have produced fragmented pictures of it. For the most part they fail to account for the particular blending of Jewish and pagan features in the philosophy, nor do they describe the historical and social contexts that would have fostered such a syncretism.[1] Such is the state of research on the Colossian philosophy, and such are the hazards of reconstructions grounded in history of religions. All too easily the interpreter either introduces several backgrounds without accounting for how they cohere or allows a single background to direct the reconstruction.

---

1. For example, J. Stewart, 'A First-Century Heresy and its Modern Counterpart', *SJT* 23 (1970), pp. 428-30; W. House, 'Doctrinal Issues in Colossians. Part 1: Heresies in the Colossian Church', *BSac* 149 (1992), p. 59.

Chapter 3

INTERPRETING THE POLEMICAL CORE IN COLOSSIANS

Isolating the Polemic: Considerations of Method

An additional observation arises from the survey of Colossian philosophy reconstructions just completed: the locus of data about the philosophy lies in Colossians 2. Because of the scarcity of that data scholars have examined every line of the letter in the search for information about the philosophy. Some detect traces of it in ch. 1, others in ch. 3.[1] But every reconstruction undertaken to date has rested primarily on evidence gleaned from ch. 2, where the letter writer warns his readers about specific beliefs and practices.

The language of Colossians 2 draws the attention of the interpreter, for it conveys a mood of open combat absent from the rest of the letter. Indicative of this polemic is the author's borrowing of a phrase, apparently from a position he opposes, in order to challenge it (Col. 2.21): '"Do not handle, do not taste, do not touch"'. Moreover, unlike the paraenesis of ch. 3, the exhortations of ch. 2 are directed against disrupters of the community: would-be abductors (v. 8) or judges (vv. 16, 18) who seek to seduce or coerce the author's readers into practices he considers valueless. Nowhere is the chapter's combative edge sharper than in the contrast the author makes between life according to Christ (vv. 6-7) and philosophy, that is, life according to human tradition, according to the στοιχεῖα τοῦ κόσμου, and *not* according to Christ (v. 8). It may well be that other passages in Colossians embody the author's polemic and therefore might prove useful in reconstructing the combated position, but, because the author's attack is so focused and relatively direct in ch. 2, the contours of the position he opposes appear there in greatest relief.

Within ch. 2 itself certain sections counter a specific threat more

---

1. Ch. 1: Gunther, *St. Paul's Opponents*, p. 15; ch. 3: Bornkamm, 'Heresy of Colossians', pp. 133-34.

directly than others. The first imperative of the letter occurs in 2.6, and from then on the chapter bristles with commands that warn the readers of the letter about the threats facing them (vv. 8, 16, 18). Prior to 2.6, the chapter contains no obvious polemic and appears to offer the interpreter little information about the philosophy. Rather, vv. 1-5 conclude what Lähnemann calls the presentation of the author's apostolic commission, which begins at 1.24.[1] Once he establishes his apostolic authority, the letter writer can act on that authority by instructing, directing, and warning the community, which is precisely what he begins to do at 2.6.

The letter's change in content in v. 6 and following signals a major transition in the letter as a whole. All of ch. 2 lies in the body of the letter—as opposed to the introduction (1.1-23) or conclusion (4.7-18)—where the author articulates the main points of the letter.[2] Within the body of the typical Greek letter, according to J. White's analysis, there are three parts: body-opening, body-middle, and body-closing. In Colossians, 2.5 ends the body-opening and 2.6 introduces the body-middle, where the letter writer presents his full argument and the implications of that argument for his readers (2.6–4.1).[3] Confirmation of this structure comes from the vocabulary the author employs in this portion of the letter: he signals the transition to the body-middle and each step in it with the consecutive coordinating conjunction οὖν (2.6, 16; 3.1, 5, 12).

The function of οὖν in Colossians merits close examination not only because it marks the beginning of the body-middle of the letter. Besides providing the transition to the section of the letter where the author wages his attack on the philosophy (2.6), another occurrence of οὖν at 3.1 announces the transition away from talk about the philosophy to paraenetical material the author wishes to impart to his readers. Moreover, οὖν subdivides the polemical portion of ch. 2 (2.6-23) at v. 16, just as two occurrences of οὖν do in the author's exhortations of ch. 3 (3.5, 12).

---

1. Lähnemann, *Kolosserbrief*, p. 32. See also Lohse, *Colossians and Philemon*, p. 3; Pokorný, *Colossians*, p. 25.
2. J. White, *The Form and Function of the Body of the Greek Letter* (SBLDS, 2; Missoula, MT: Scholars Press, 2nd edn, 1972), p. 168; G. Cannon, *The Use of Traditional Materials in Colossians* (Macon: Mercer University Press, 1983), p. 172.
3. White, *Greek Letter*, passim; Cannon, *Traditional Materials*, p. 156. See also Pokorný, *Colossians*, pp. 25-26.

3. Interpreting the Polemical Core in Colossians

How exactly does the οὖν of 2.16 function in the polemic of 2.6-23? To answer this question, the interpreter must determine whether the οὖν operates transitionally, as it does at 2.6 and 3.1, or more in its inferential or resumptive capacity.[1] Apparently, readers are to infer that with the erasure of the bond against them (2.14), food and calendar regulations are no longer in force (2.16). Yet the οὖν also coincides with the resumption of the author's warnings to his readers, marked by the reappearance of a syntactical pattern: negative + indefinite pronoun + imperative (2.8, 16, 18). Vocabulary that occurred earlier in the author's polemic (at 2.8) also returns in 2.16: στοιχεῖα τοῦ κόσμου (2.8, 20) and παράδοσις τῶν ἀνθρώπων/ἐντάλματα καὶ διδασκαλίας τῶν ἀνθρώπων (2.8, 22). These syntactical and lexical repetitions suggest that the conjunction οὖν functions resumptively in v. 16; the letter writer *resumes* the explicit warnings he began in 2.8.

If the letter writer begins his attack on the philosophy in 2.6-8 and continues it in vv. 16-23, are vv. 9-15 an interlude in the polemic of ch. 2? This subsection appears to possess none of the explicit polemic of vv. 8, 16-23; at the very least the letter writer has relaxed his direct offensive against the philosophy. Instead of the straightforward directions and warnings to the community typical of vv. 6-8 and 16-23, vv. 9-15 have a noticeably different style and content. The author evidently relied heavily on traditional material—perhaps baptismal liturgy—to compose this section of Colossians.[2] Moreover, this portion of Colossians more than any other shows signs of dependence on earlier Pauline letters; Sanders notes striking agreements between Col. 2.12-13 and Rom 6.4 (and 4.24) and between Col. 2.10 and 1 Cor. 15.24.[3] This reliance produces a passage altogether different from the surrounding material, variously described as hymnic or liturgical in flavor.[4] Consequently, scholars have increasingly come to the conclusion that vv. 9-15 contain little or no polemic against the philosophy and therefore have minimal value in reconstructing the

---

1. BDF, §451; H. Smyth, *Greek Grammar* (Cambridge, MA: Harvard University Press, 1920), §2964.
2. Cannon, *Traditional Materials*, p. 37; Bujard, *Kolosserbrief*, p. 227; Lähnemann, *Kolosserbrief*, p. 20.
3. E. Sanders, 'Literary Dependence in Colossians', *JBL* 85 (1966), pp. 40-44.
4. Lähnemann, *Kolosserbrief*, p. 20; Cannon, *Traditional Materials*, p. 11; Percy, *Probleme*, p. 40.

philosophy.[1] If vv. 9-15 do embody a polemic aimed at the philosophy, it is so indirect an attack that the features of the philosophy appear only faintly and inexactly.

Removing vv. 9-15 from 2.6-23 does not, however, bring the interpreter to the undisputed polemical core of Colossians. With regard to 2.6-8, scholars invariably pay less attention to vv. 6-7 than v. 8,[2] for in that verse the letter writer first mentions the philosophy. Moreover, it is the vocabulary and syntax of v. 8, not 6 and 7, that reappear in vv. 16-23. Whether or not Lähnemann is correct in asserting that vv. 6-7 introduce vv. 9-15 and v. 8 introduces vv. 16-23,[3] postwar scholarship consistently limits the polemical core to, and bases its reconstruction of the philosophy on, Col. 2.8, 16-23.[4] While they embody the most explicit attack on the philosophy in the letter, these mere nine verses of ch. 2 probably do not constitute the whole polemic in Colossians. To focus on these verses is, therefore, a conservative approach in that it likely underestimates what Colossians reveals about the philosophy. Particularly if the philosophy's potential or actual disruption of the community is the cause or one of the causes of the letter, more than nine verses are directed to that situation.

Nevertheless, good reasons exist for limiting—at least initially— what one examines as evidence for reconstruction: first, inclusion of additional material may direct the interpreter away from the passage that, according to the consensus of scholarship, contains the most direct, concrete characterization of the philosophy; and second, the significant differences in previous reconstructions and their respective characterizations of the philosophy mandate the tightest control over what constitutes the data for reconstruction.

This conservative approach should guide each step of the reconstruction. Just as the interpreter must be wary of augmenting the

---

1. Lähnemann, *Kolosserbrief*, p. 115; Percy, *Probleme*, p. 137; Gunther, *St. Paul's Opponents*, p. 15; White, *Greek Letter*, p. 177; Schweizer, *Letter to the Colossians*, pp. 126-27.
2. Beasley-Murray, 'Second Chapter of Colossians', p. 470.
3. Lähnemann, *Kolosserbrief*, p. 49.
4. Percy, *Probleme*, p. 137; Congdon, 'False Teachers', p. 6; Schweizer, *Letter to the Colossians*, pp. 126-27; Sappington, *Revelation and Redemption*, p. 144; F. Francis, 'The Christological Argument of Colossians', in J. Jervell and W. Meeks (eds.), *God's Christ and His People: Studies in Honour of Nils Alstrup Dahl* (Oslo: Universitetsforlaget, 1977), p. 194.

3. *Interpreting the Polemical Core in Colossians* 45

evidence from 2.8, 16-23 with information from the remainder of Colossians, interpretation of the philosophy's features and placement of them against a history of religions background must be undertaken with extreme care. The observation about previous reconstructions made at the close of the last chapter bears repetition here: all too easily the interpreter either introduces several backgrounds without accounting for how they would have come together or allows a single background to direct the reconstruction. Filling out the meager evidence we have about the Colossian philosophy with information from an invitingly clarifying history of religions background or backgrounds poses the same hazards as supplementing the evidence from within Colossians itself.

Historical reconstruction necessarily entails speculation,[1] a necessity made all too evident by the paucity and ambiguity of the evidence for the Colossian philosophy. Still, by hypothesizing as little as possible, the interpreter allows the evidence at hand to have the loudest possible voice. This methodological simplicity and cautiousness Francis calls the 'minimalist' approach.[2] While this method seeks to account for all the features of the Colossian philosophy, it favors the comprehensive hypothesis that is also the simplest.

Translation of the Polemical Core in Colossians (2.8, 16-23)

With the relatively undisputed kernel of the Colossian polemic isolated, the stage is set for a systematic analysis of it. I begin with a translation of the polemical core, Col. 2.8, 16-23, which will serve as a useful reference point for the exegesis that follows and thus lend clarity to the coming pages.

> 2.8 See to it that no one becomes your abductor through philosophy and empty deception, according to human tradition, according to the elements of the world, but *not* according to Christ.
> 16 Therefore, let no one judge you in eating and drinking or with regard to a festival or new moon or Sabbath,
> 17 which are a shadow of the things to come, but the substance is Christ.
> 18a Let no one decide against you, commanding humility and devotion to angels,

---

1. Francis and Meeks (eds.), *Conflict at Colossae*, pp. 4-6.
2. Francis, 'Christological Argument', p. 194. See also his 'Colossian Controversy', pp. 20-21.

18b which he has seen upon close scrutiny,
18c puffed up without basis by his fleshly mind,
19 and *not* holding to the head, from whom the whole body, nourished and knit together through its joints and ligaments, grows with a growth that is from God.
20 If you died with Christ, parted from the elements of the world, why do you submit to rules as if living in the world?
21 'Do not handle, do not taste, do not touch',
22a referring to things all of which are destined for destruction by being consumed,
22b according to human commandments and teachings,
23 which, though they pass for wisdom in achieving would-be devotion, humility, and severe treatment of the body, are of no worth with respect to fleshy indulgence.[1]

Exegesis of the Polemical Core

The translation above should prove especially useful to the reader given the structure of the exegesis that follows, for the order of analysis suggested by the polemical core does not lead the interpreter in a phrase-by-phrase fashion. The interpreter cannot expect the polemic to be uniformly valuable with regard to what it reveals about the philosophy, so some phrases deserve more attention than others. Where the letter writer is the most derogatory and disparaging may be the least revealing, especially where his criticisms are sweeping and general. On the other hand, the letter writer had to identify what he rejected, and it is in this descriptive language that the interpreter probably finds the most information about the philosophy, although sometimes even that language may be slanted. Given the nature of the polemic and the goals of this study, a verse-by-verse analysis would serve little purpose.

Rather, recurring vocabulary and syntactical patterns in the core dictate another course. Because the language the letter writer uses to qualify what he calls philosophy in Col. 2.8—elements of the world, human tradition—reappears in 2.20 and 2.22b, treating these verses or portions of verses together seems reasonable. Likewise, language

---

1. A well-supported ($\mathfrak{P}^{46}$, B) textual variant that eliminates the 'and' after 'humility' in v. 23 would support the following translation: 'which, though they pass for wisdom in achieving would-be devotion and humility through severe treatment of the body, are of no worth with respect to fleshy indulgence'.

3. Interpreting the Polemical Core in Colossians

employed to describe the philosophy's practices first appears in 2.16 and 2.18a, then returns in vv. 21 and 23, which makes it logical to group together these parts of the polemical core in the exegesis. Not only does certain vocabulary recur in the polemical core, but also certain syntactical patterns: the negative + indefinite pronoun + imperative construction in 2.8, 16, and 18a, and the relative clauses beginning 2.17, 18b, 22a, and 23. These latter clauses deserve undivided treatment because in them the letter writer comments on the practices of the philosophy, expressing his many reasons for rejecting them. At points in these clauses, as he articulates his complaint against the philosophy, he also appears to reproduce the rationale offered by the philosophers for their practices. Accordingly, these relative clauses and the various rationales expressed in them belong together in the following exegesis, where they can receive undivided and especially close attention.

The coming pages will revolve around these three aspects of the philosophy: the designations of the philosophy, its practices, and the intellectual underpinning of its practices.

Designations of the Position Combated by the Letter Writer
φιλοσοφία. While the verses of central importance to the reconstruction of the Colossian philosophy, 2.8, 16-23, express an unequivocal condemnation of it, that which is attacked remains rather elusive. The terms used by the letter writer to identify what he opposes are equivocal. A distinct possibility exists that the initial identification of the threat combated, φιλοσοφία, may not come from the author's polemical vocabulary but from those practicing this philosophy at Colossae. For the appellation has no pejorative sense per se,[1] and the letter writer takes pains to add a clearly derogatory label, 'empty deception' (κενῆς ἀπάτης), then disparagingly qualifies the philosophy as something in accord with human tradition.

Yet even if φιλοσοφία is a self-designation of a group at Colossae, the term's semantic breadth prevents the interpreter from viewing that group clearly. The term φιλοσοφία was applied to a good deal more than the thinking of Stoics, Academicians, and Peripatetics. By the Hellenistic period it could refer to the study and scientific treatment of, or speculation about, any subject. Besides intellectual disciplines,

---

1. LSJ, p. 1940; O. Michel, 'φιλοσοφία, φιλόσοφος', *TDNT*, IX, p. 187.

φιλοσοφία could also denote prescribed training or, more broadly, a way of life. It comes as no surprise, then, that the first-century BCE writer Diodorus of Sicily uses the verb φιλοσοφέω to describe the discipline undertaken by the Chaldeans of Babylon, a group he compares to Egypt's priestly class. Their lifelong devotion to the study of astrology and divination he calls φιλοσοφία (2.29.1-4).

Determining the nuance of the term in Colossians is especially difficult because the occurrence at 2.8 is a *hapax legomenon* in the NT. Nor does the term appear frequently in Jewish literature of that time. In the entire LXX φιλοσοφία occurs only in *4 Maccabees*, which is rather fitting since that book claims to treat a most philosophical topic (φιλοσοφώτατον λόγον): whether devout (εὐσεβής) reason rules the emotions (1.1). While proving that it does, the author concomitantly demonstrates that the Jewish religion (θρησκεία), rather than being foolish philosophy (5.11), meets the highest goals of Greek philosophy, for it instills in its practitioners the cardinal virtues of rational judgment, self-control, courage, and justice (5.22-24). In addition, it fosters piety (εὐσέβεια), a virtue that Socrates included in the philosophical life, according to Xenophon (*Mem.* 1.4.1-19). Worth noting here is the apologetic line *4 Maccabees* takes. Although his case is made more plausible by the semantic breadth of φιλοσοφία and Greek writers' recognition of philosophical elements in barbarian cultures, the author of *4 Maccabees* bases his depiction of Judaism as a legitimate philosophy on the former's promotion of the latter's traditional ideals.

Philo takes a similar position, stressing the correspondence between Jewish piety and Greek philosophy. His treatment of the Sabbath is a case in point (*Vit. Mos.* 2.39 §§211-16). The day of rest prescribed by Jewish law allows for the pursuit of wisdom (φιλοσοφέω) and the study of the ancestral φιλοσοφία (211, 216). He concludes the discussion by describing Jewish places of prayer as schools of prudence, courage, temperance, justice, and piety (216). In other words, the synagogue appears to be a house of philosophy.

Josephus, too, stresses the correspondences between Judaism and the Greek philosophical tradition. According to him, the various parties of pre-70 CE Jewish society, the Pharisees, Sadducees, and Essenes, represent the three long-lived φιλοσοφίαι of the Jews (*Ant.* 18.1.2. §11; cf. *War* 2.8.2 §119). After introducing them, he gives an outline of the tenets and practices of each, much like an epitome of a philo-

3. Interpreting the Polemical Core in Colossians

sophical school or thinker (*Ant.* 18.1.3-5 §§12-22). Of importance here is Josephus's identification of groups *within* Judaism as philosophies, for it suggests that the term φιλοσοφία can have a narrower referent, at least in Josephus's mind, than Judaism as a whole.

What does the Hellenistic Jewish use of the term suggest about its meaning in Col. 2.8? φιλοσοφία's breadth may obscure what the term refers to in Colossians, but its evident apologetic value increases the likelihood that the word came not from the letter writer but from his opponents. Were they, like *4 Maccabees*, Philo, and Josephus, presenting a religious tradition as a form of Greek philosophy, or was their way of life a full-fledged Hellenistic philosophy? Even if it was the former, claiming the designation φιλοσοφία entailed pointing out correspondences between Greek philosophy and the apologist's tradition. In the case of the Colossian philosophers, the case they made for claiming the designation φιλοσοφία must have had merit, for the letter writer adopted this neutral, even positive, appellation to refer to something he otherwise describes in religious terms (2.16, θρησκεία; 2.23, ἐθελοθρησκία) or derogates altogether. At the very least, then, the designation φιλοσοφία indicates some correspondence between the Colossian philosophy and Greek philosophy, and it may mean that the Colossian philosophy was a type of Hellenistic philosophy.

Human Tradition, Commandments and Teachings. Subsequent designations of the threat are potentially ambiguous, too, even though they specify the type of philosophy the letter writer combats. The phrase κενῆς ἀπάτης does not help in identifying the object of derogation, because that aspersion could be applied to anything objectionable to the polemicist, but the elaboration of the initial designation in 2.8 as a philosophy according to human tradition (κατὰ τὴν παράδοσιν τῶν ἀνθρώπων) could prove to be a revealing qualification. While the phrase is obviously not a self-designation of the opposed group— few groups in antiquity would have claimed human rather than divine sanction—it constitutes a key element in the letter writer's criticism of the position he opposes, judging by the occurrence of a similar phrase, κατὰ τὰ εντάλματα καὶ διδασκαλίας τῶν ἀνθρώπων, in 2.22. By qualifying the φιλοσοφία as one according to human tradition, the author is able to distinguish and draw a contrast between types of philosophy: a human-based philosophy versus a φιλοσοφία κατὰ Χριστόν. He may also have had in mind another dichotomy: ἡ παράδοσις τοῦ Χριστοῦ versus ἡ παράδοσις τῶν ἀωθρώπων. For Col. 2.6 speaks of receiving (παραλαμβάνω) and walking (περιπατέω), language associated with the receipt of, and adherence to, Jewish legal traditions or halakah. In 2.6 the author makes Χριστόν the object of the two actions, for he is the content of the Christian tradition.

The contrasts the letter writer draws in 2.8 effectively fuel the polemic he begins there, but the interpretive question is whether the phrase κατὰ τὴν παράδοσιν τῶν ἀνθρώπων illuminates the position under attack. The use of this phrase and a similar polemic elsewhere in early Christian literature should help determine an answer. Both Mark and Matthew record a confrontation between the Pharisees and Jesus over the failure of the latter's disciples to follow Jewish purity law (Mk 7.1-23; Mt. 15.1-20). To justify their laxity, Jesus contrasts the Pharisaic tradition (παράδοσις) of the elders with the commandment of God, citing Isa. 29.13, a passage in which Yahweh condemns Israel's superficial and misdirected allegiance (Mk 7.6-7). Much as Israel mistakenly taught as doctrine the commandments of human beings (διδάσκοντες διδασκαλίας ἐντάλματα ἀνθρώπων; Mk 7.7), the Pharisees have displaced the commandments of God with their own tradition, namely, τὴν παράδοσιν τῶν ἀνθρώπων (Mk 7.8; cf. Mt. 15.6-9). In Mark, therefore, the ἐντάλματα ἀνθρώπων (cf. Col. 2.22) and the παράδοσις τῶν ἀνθρώπων (cf. Col. 2.8) both constitute derogatory references to the Jewish, specifically Pharisaic, oral law.

Elsewhere in the NT this type of expression and polemic does not have so specific a reference. In his attack on those of the circumcision group (1.10), the author of Titus condemns them as proponents of Jewish myths and ἐντολαῖς ἀνθρώπων (1.14). Are these commandments halakah? It is difficult to say.[1] Tit. 3.9 mentions quarrels over the law, which may or may not point to a dispute over halakah. In short, the interpreter cannot be sure what ἐντολαῖς ἀνθρώπων refers to in Titus.

Another NT letter, Galatians, opens with a polemical contrast akin to that in Col. 2.8. Paul lays claim to an apostleship through Christ and God, not ἀπ' ἀνθρώπων nor δι' ἀνθρώπου (1.1), and to a divinely revealed gospel, as opposed to an εὐαγγέλιον κατὰ

---

1. M. Dibelius and H. Conzelmann, *The Pastoral Epistles* (Hermeneia; Philadelphia: Fortress Press, 1972), p. 137.

3. Interpreting the Polemical Core in Colossians

ἄνθρωπον (1.11). Taken to its logical end, this polemic would stigmatize the Torah-obedient missionaries Paul opposes as humanly-chosen apostles and their message as coming from a human source. But Paul does not apply the negative side of the contrast to his enemies, as critical as he is of them (5.12) and as much distance as he later puts between the Law and God (3.19-20). Rather, Paul denies human authorization for his apostleship and message in order to bolster his own authority and the authority of his message.

What do these various parallel cases suggest about the significance of the aspersion ἡ παράδοσις τῶν ἀνθρώπων in Colossians? Evidence from the Synoptic tradition, which contains the closest verbal correspondences, indicates that the philosophy adhered to halakah. But a halakah-affirming philosophy would presumably have upheld the Torah as well, and there is no obvious polemic concerning the Law in Colossians. The word νόμος does not even occur. Furthermore, that which the letter writer classifies as human tradition hardly resembles Jewish halakah. He apparently regards the commands of Col. 2.21, 'Do not handle, do not taste, do not touch', and the initial phrase of v. 22, 'referring to things all of which are destined for destruction by being consumed', as human commandments and teachings (v. 22b). And while one could reasonably argue that one verb appearing in the commands, ἅπτω, belongs to Jewish legal traditions, since it occurs regularly in Leviticus, no case can easily be made for the other two verbs. Furthermore, the explanatory note opening v. 22 bears no resemblance to Jewish halakah.

Although exact verbal agreements between the two are fewer, the Galatian polemic corresponds most closely to that of Colossians. Both employ a contrast between human and divine authorization. In Colossians, the phrase ἡ παράδοσις τῶν ἀνθρώπων plays a key role in the distinction the letter writer makes between the tradition he imparted to the community (Col. 2.6-7) and that of the philosophy. The phrase appears, therefore, to reveal little about what is being spurned, a conclusion confirmed by Galatians, where Paul uses this polemical element to distinguish and legitimate his own authority rather than to give the reader accurate information about his opponents. In other words, this qualification of the φιλοσοφία tells us nothing about the Colossian philosophy.

The Elements of the World: τὰ στοιχεῖα τοῦ κόσμου. The letter writer does not end his criticism of the Colossian philosophy in 2.8 with his ascribing it to human tradition; he also labels it a philosophy according to the elements of the world (φιλοσοφία κατὰ τὰ στοιχεῖα τοῦ κόσμου). Since these two qualifications of philosophy are parallel in construction (κατά + phrase) and stand side by side, the interpreter may be tempted to posit a relationship between them. Perhaps the στοιχεῖα, qualified as τοῦ κόσμου, constituted the principles or rudiments of the tradition. They may have been the essential principles of knowledge behind the tradition, thus forming the epistemological basis of the philosophy, or they may only have been simple elements of teaching in it (cf. Heb. 5.12).

Other possible translations for στοιχεῖα abound because the term admits a range of meanings.[1] στοιχεῖον denoted not just an elementary principle but any simple unit, such as a pitch or tone in music, a syllable or letter in grammar, a line or point in mathematics, or a basic constituent of the physical world. It also came to stand for components of the celestial realm, that is, a star or planet, and at some point, the spirit, divinity, or δαίμων connected or identified with celestial bodies.[2] These latter associations emerged after the composition of Colossians, so their relevance to Colossians is highly disputed.[3]

What is not uncertain is the regular use of στοιχεῖα as a reference to the four basic components of the cosmos according to Greek philosophy: earth, water, air, and fire.[4] This is most often what Hellenistic Jewish writers had in mind when they used the term. Every occurrence in the LXX appears to reflect this usage (Wis. 7.17; 19.18; *4 Macc.* 12.13). And of the dozens of times the term appears in Philo, the vast majority refer to the four components of the world. Early Christian literature also shows ready familiarity with this usage. When

---

1. W. Wink offers a thorough presentation of the term's breadth in *Naming the Powers: The Language of Power in the New Testament* (Philadelphia: Fortress Press, 1984), pp. 67-82. Such breadth does not, however, justify Wink's contention that the στοιχεῖα of Col. 2.8 and 2.20 refer to two different things (pp. 74-77).

2. LSJ, p. 1647; BAGD, pp. 768-69.

3. G. Delling, 'στοιχέω, συστοιχέω, στοιχεῖον', *TDNT*, VII, p. 682; Bandstra, *Law and the Elements*, p. 44; Cramer, *Stoicheia*, p. 174.

4. Lohse, *Colossians and Philemon*, p. 97, esp. n. 30; Blinzler, 'τὰ στοιχεῖα τοῦ κόσμου', p. 440; D. Winston, *The Wisdom of Solomon* (AB, 43; Garden City, NY: Doubleday, 1979), p. 173.

3. Interpreting the Polemical Core in Colossians

the author of 2 Peter writes of the overthrow of the cosmos, he appears to be in touch with Stoic eschatology by including the dissolution of the four elements in his description (3.10, 12). Hermas compares a couch with four feet to the world and the four στοιχεῖα (*Herm. Vis.* 3.13.3). Such evidence gives considerable support to the position that the στοιχεῖα in Colossians refer to the four physical elements.

This interpretation is made more certain by the letter writer's qualification of στοιχεῖα. He adds the genitive τοῦ κόσμου, a phrase that seems not to have had the same connotation as the genitive τῶν ἀνθρώπων or to have been added solely as a derogation. In Philo's case, whenever he writes about τὰ στοιχεῖα τοῦ παντός (*Flacc.* 15 §125; *Virt.* 11 §73), or the στοιχεῖα φύσεως (*Vit. Mos.* 2.46 §251), or τὰ στοιχεῖα τοῦ κόσμου (*Aet. Mund.* 21 §109), his subject is *always* the four elemental constituents of the cosmos. D. Rusam reached the same conclusion in his study of pagan Greek literature from the second century CE.[1] In light of this consistent usage, it will not suffice to regard the στοιχεῖα at Col. 2.8 as nothing more than the principles or elements of the tradition mentioned in that verse. The addition of τοῦ κόσμου appears to be the author's confirmation, as it is in Philo and elsewhere, that he refers to the four elemental components *of the cosmos*.

A second reference to the στοιχεῖα at 2.20 may shed further light on the significance of τὰ στοιχεῖα τοῦ κόσμου in Colossians. The verse reads, 'If you died with Christ, parted from (ἀπό) the elements of the world, why do you submit to rules (δογματίζω) as if living in (ἐν) the world?' Once again, the στοιχεῖα seem to have a connection with a tradition of some sort, for if one has not parted from the στοιχεῖα, one still adheres to δόγματα (cf. 2.14), which may be components of a tradition. Yet such a reading would ignore the letter writer's qualification of the στοιχεῖα in v. 20 as τοῦ κόσμου. If anything, v. 20 reveals that the importance of the τοῦ κόσμου should not be underestimated, because the logic of the verse connects the στοιχεῖα τοῦ κόσμου with κόσμος. While they are not interchangeable, in this verse both terms seem to denote a sphere of existence or arena of activity that one can part *from* or live *in*. At least the prepositions ἀπό and ἐν suggest it. If this is correct, then the emphasis in the phrase στοιχεῖα τοῦ κόσμου would naturally fall on the τοῦ

---

1. D. Rusam, 'Neue Belege zu den στοιχεῖα τοῦ κόσμου (Gal 4,3.9; Kol 2,8.20)', *ZNW* 83 (1992), pp. 124-25.

κόσμου, pointing to the cosmic aspect of στοιχεῖα, which is precisely the nuance the word has when understood as the four elemental components of the cosmos.

How the phrase τὰ στοιχεῖα τοῦ κόσμου could denote a plane of existence or realm of activity becomes clear from the literature I have already cited. For Philo also refers to the στοιχεῖα as the four powers (δυνάμεις; *Aet. Mund.* 21 §§107-108) and Hermas notes that the world is ruled (κρατεῖται) by them (*Herm. Vis.* 3.13.3). In other words, the four elements are not simply types of passive matter but also the cosmological principles that define and underpin the universe. Since they are the roots and branches of the cosmos, the phrase στοιχεῖα τοῦ κόσμου could serve as a fitting and precise reference to the cosmic sphere.

Paul's use of στοιχεῖα τοῦ κόσμου in Galatians further clarifies the significance of the phrase in Colossians, even though one cannot assume that the author of Colossians knew that letter. There, in heated debate with teachers commending Torah obedience to the community, Paul compares life under the Law to enslavement to the στοιχεῖα τοῦ κόσμου (3.23–4.7, esp. 4.1, 3, 5). The latter condition is that of the pagan Gentile who does not know God and is therefore subject to those things that are not by nature gods (4.8), that is, it would seem, to the στοιχεῖα. In other words, for Gentile Christians to endorse and obey the Law is virtually a return to their former enslavement as pagans.

What are the στοιχεῖα τοῦ κόσμου in this context? The logic of Paul's argument suggests overlap between the Law and the στοιχεῖα. While they are not to be equated, Paul's second mention of στοιχεῖα in Gal. 4.9, where he calls them weak and impotent (ἀσθενῆ καὶ πτωχά), ostensibly strengthens that correspondence, because elsewhere Paul also calls the Law weak, it having been made so (ἠσθένει) by the flesh (Rom. 8.3). The common trait between them, however, is not that they both denote religious ordinances and rules, a reading of στοιχεῖα (cf. Gal. 4.9-10) made impossible when Paul acknowledges that some mistake them for gods (4.8). Nor does Paul here picture world-ruling deities (cf. 4.8), since the Law clearly is not a divinity. Rather, the στοιχεῖα and the Law have a common *function*; they both engender human bondage. Moreover, they both operate in the same sphere, for the κόσμος is the location of the weakened Law's operation, along with the other enslaving forces: the στοιχεῖα,

3. Interpreting the Polemical Core in Colossians 55

σάρξ, sin, and death.[1] Paul's use of the στοιχεῖα in Galatians confirms, therefore, what I have concluded about them: they were regarded as the four powers that constituted and defined existence in the cosmos.

As powers that constitute and define the universe, the στοιχεῖα could be thought of as guiding principles in the world. Some at Colossae, according to the letter writer, articulated a philosophy *according to* the elements of the world. Some at Colossae—the question in v. 20 implies—have produced regulations from lives lived according to the στοιχεῖα. Thus the elements may have served the philosophers as principles of knowledge, as the epistemological basis of their way of life. But, anterior to that function, the στοιχεῖα τοῦ κόσμου were most likely thought of as cosmological principles, the four elements that constituted the world. Evidence from Christian, Jewish, and pagan literature contemporary with Colossians makes this conclusion fairly certain.[2]

Conclusion. The designations of the threat at Colossae consist of terms and phrases that vary considerably in what they reveal about that threat. On the one hand, ascribing the philosophy to human tradition (Col. 2.8) and labeling its demands and precepts human commandments and teachings (2.21-22) give the interpreter little positive evidence for reconstructing the philosophy. On the other hand, the terms φιλοσοφία and στοιχεῖα, particularly since the latter is qualified with τοῦ κόσμου, suggest a great deal more about what the letter writer opposes at Colossae. The use of the two terms outside Colossians allows the interpreter to narrow the possible interpretations of the terms. Both point—φιλοσοφία probably, στοιχεῖα uneqivocally—to a philosophical background.

Can the interpreter conclude that the Colossian opponents followed a philosophy according to the elements of the world? Probably so. στοιχεῖα is paired with the negative 'human tradition' in 2.8 and appears again in v. 20 in a pointedly polemical question phrased by the letter writer, so it is not clear from the polemic that στοιχεῖα came from those practicing the philosophy at Colossae. On the other

---

1. Bandstra, *Law and the Elements*, pp. 68-71; cf. Cramer, *Stoicheia*, pp. 174-76.
2. Delling, 'στοιχέω, κτλ', p. 684; Schweizer, 'Slaves of the Elements', p. 466.

hand, στοιχεῖα τοῦ κόσμου has no negative connotation per se, and some facet of the philosophy made the phrase appropriate for identifying the philosophy, if in fact the letter writer introduced the phrase rather than borrowing it from his opponents. Hence, if the philosophers did not use exactly this language to describe themselves, the letter writer has at least accurately approximated the position of the philosophy by saying that it conforms to the στοιχεῖα τοῦ κόσμου.

The Practices of the Philosophy: Their Nature and Aim
Food and Calendar. If the designations of the threat at Colossae vary greatly as to the light they shed on the Colossian philosophy, what it required of its adherents is more plainly described and thus may reveal more of the philosophy's character. Col. 2.16 introduces in blunt fashion its practices. The letter writer warns his readers about those passing judgment with regard to food, drink, and the calendar (2.16). Accordingly, the interpreter may assume that those who practiced the philosophy at Colossae were concerned with precisely such matters. With regard to the calendar, the author refers to the annual, monthly, and weekly observances that the philosophers keep, namely festivals (ἑορτή), the new moon or first of the month (νεομηνία), and Sabbath (σάββατα). What does the listing of these observances tell the interpreter about the philosophy? The series corresponds to enumerations of Jewish holy days in the LXX (Hos. 2.13; 1 Chron. 23.31; 2 Chron. 2.3; 31.3). Evidently, then, the philosophy contained a Jewish element, a conclusion that finds obvious confirmation in the very mention of Sabbath. ἑορτή and νεομηνία might also refer to pagan observances, but not σάββατα.[1]

Concern about food and drink may also point to a Jewish background, but this is less certain. Jewish law had long distinguished between clean and unclean foods (Lev. 11.1-47; cf. Deut. 14.3-20). While this was not the case with drinks, the undertaking of a vow or fast could mean abstinence from certain drinks, such as wine, or strong drink of any kind (cf. the Nazirite vow: Judg. 13.14; Num. 6.2-4; cf. Amos 2.12; cf. fasting: Exod. 34.28; Deut. 9.9, 18; cf. Philo, *Vit. Mos.* 2.4 §24).[2] Illustrative of these dietary concerns is Daniel's resolution to avoid defilement by consuming the king's rich

1. See for example Plutarch, *Def. Orac.* 14 (417C); *Is. et Os.* 42 (368A).
2. L. Goppelt, 'πίνω, πόμα, πόσις, πότος, ποτήριον, καταπίνω, ποτίζω', *TDNT*, VI, p. 136.

3. *Interpreting the Polemical Core in Colossians* 57

food and wine (Dan. 1.8). He limits his diet to vegetables and water (1.12). Although Daniel's refusal of the king's wine appears not to be linked to a fast or Nazirite vow, it may rest on an apprehension about the possible pollution of the wine which could have resulted from its contact with something unclean. Or perhaps the king's wine had been consecrated to a foreign deity and had thereby become unfit for Daniel's consumption.

The eating of food previously consecrated to pagan gods created controversy among early Christians. The letter of 1 Corinthians deals at two points with this problem. Paul addresses the knowledgeable Christian who understands that idols have no real existence and who consequently eats food offered to those idols without compunction (1 Cor. 8.1-13). Weaker Christians, however, could consider themselves defiled by such a practice. Thus Paul admonishes those with understanding to use their knowledge and liberty wisely and discreetly. Paul reiterates this position two chapters later: nothing of God's creation is unfit for eating, but one should not offend those who would be troubled by the eating of food offered to idols (10.23–11.1).

The letter to the Romans contains a similar discussion (ch. 14). Although it is the weak in faith who have reservations about certain foods (14.2; meat? cf. v. 21) and wine (v. 21) and who observe certain days (vv. 5-6; Sabbath?), their scruples in these matters deserve respect. This is the case even though Jesus, as Paul notes (14.14), declared all foods clean (cf. Mk 7.19). As in the Corinthian community, the strong in faith must not cause the weak to stumble. And as a sign of mutual respect, the one abstaining from certain food must not pass judgment (κρίνω) on the one who does not share that scruple (Rom. 14.3).

The Colossian controversy bears some resemblance to the Roman situation in particular. A conflict has arisen in Colossae over food, drink, and the observance of certain days (Col. 2.16). One group—the interpreter assumes the practitioners of the philosophy—passes judgment (κρίνω) on those who fail to follow its food, drink, and calendar prescriptions.

The motivation for these regulations may also be similar to what Paul encounters at Rome and Corinth: a concern for purity manifest in a sacral calendar and a clean/unclean distinction. Despite Paul's reminders that such considerations no longer apply to the Christian (1 Cor. 10.23, 26; Rom. 14.14, 20), Jewish tradition regarding cultic and ritual purity obviously continued to exercise considerable influence in the earliest Christian communities.

Pagan religious and philosophical traditions could also have fostered this concern about purity. Chapter 14 of Romans not only describes practices rooted in Jewish tradition, such as the keeping of a certain day in honor of the Lord (14.5-6), but also those without strong Jewish antecedents, such as a strictly vegetarian diet (14.2; λάχανα, not the term in Dan. 1.12; cf. 4 Ezra 9.23-25; 12.51).

At Colossae, too, the drive for purity goes beyond the cultic and ritual practices typical of Judaism, even though the sacral calendar reflected in 2.16 clearly has Jewish roots. At Col. 2.21 the letter writer records several commands issued by his opponents: '"Do not handle, do not taste, do not touch"'. These commands could be read as a call to distinguish between clean and unclean food, and thus reflect distinctively Jewish concerns, but the context of the letter suggests otherwise. The explanatory remark that immediately follows in v. 22—'referring to things all of which are destined for destruction by being consumed'—could apply not just to certain foods but to *all* food and drink. In light of v. 22a, therefore, the commands of v. 21 may advocate complete rather than selective abstinence.

The advocacy of fasting could have arisen from within Judaism, but again information from the polemical core pushes the interpreter beyond what is clearly Jewish. Whatever the source of the philosophers' praxis, v. 23 suggests that one of the aims of the praxis is to achieve the severe treatment of the body (ἀφειδία σώματος). Whether control of the body also had cultic or ritual implications is unclear, but it is clear that purity concerns typical of Judaism are no longer primary motivations.

What can be concluded about the calendar and food concerns of the philosophers? Their praxis obviously draws from Judaism in matters of the calendar, and this is probably the case in matters of food and drink as well. For all this Jewish rootage, however, the goal of the philosophy's praxis lies to some extent beyond typically Jewish ends, for the philosophers' food and drink regulations had as one of their aims the severe treatment of the body.

Humility and Worship of the Angels. Verse 23 lists two other matters that may have been central to the activities of the philosophers: proper religious service (θρησκεία), to which the letter writer apparently

3. Interpreting the Polemical Core in Colossians

added the disparaging ἐθελο- (self-made, self-chosen, or would-be), and humility (ταπεινοφροσύνη). Such language echoes an earlier portion of the polemical core that mirrors a demand of the philosophy: 'Let no one decide against you, commanding humility and devotion to angels' (2.18a). There, religious service is specified as a θρησκεία τῶν ἀγγέλων; the term for humility in v. 18 is the same as in v. 23. The mention of ταπεινοφροσύνη and some form of θρησκεία twice in the small polemical core of Colossians means that these were the primary points of contention between the letter writer and the philosophy. Yet the polemic does not reveal whether the *philosophers* themselves would have given them such prominence. They would probably have denied that their devotion or religious service was self-chosen or would-be (ἐθελο-; 2.18); that prefix has the markings of polemic. Otherwise, the language does not appear openly polemical. Humility and devotion may have been the focal points of the philosophers' praxis.

From all indications, humility (ταπεινοφροσύνη) belonged to the prized virtues of the earliest church (Phil. 2.3; 1 Pet. 5.5; cf. 1 Pet. 3.8; Mt. 18.4; 23.12; Lk. 14.11; 18.14). Even the author of Colossians, though he condemns the philosophers' insistence on it, includes humility in his list of desirable traits later in the letter (Col. 3.12). Perhaps he saw in their ταπεινοφροσύνη a humility that was misguided, much like the humility that Paul's Corinthian opponents found in him (2 Cor. 11.7; cf. 10.1). What the letter writer found objectionable may be indicated by the association of humility with bodily asceticism in 2.23, which suggests that humbling oneself according to the philosophy included or was accomplished by a self-abasement that included bodily mortification. On the other hand, he may have taken issue with a humility linked to the θρησκεία τῶν ἀγγέλων (v. 18). For, while humility and lowliness before God was deemed appropriate by early Christian writers (Jas 4.10; 1 Pet. 5.6), a self-abasement that included devotion to angels would probably have been viewed as humility before an altogether inappropriate party.

This explanation of the letter writer's objection to the philosophy's humility rests on rendering θρησκεία as worship and reading τῶν ἀγγέλων as an objective genitive indicating the object of worship, namely, the angels. There are, of course, other possible readings of this phrase. The τῶν ἀγγέλων could be a subjective genitive and consequently denote the worship of God along with or in the manner of angels, that is, angelic worship. The term θρησκεία could refer broadly to religious service, ritual, custom, or simply religion, so the phrase might signify a religion instituted by angels. Sorting out the likeliest of these possibilities is no simple task, because all three find support in literature contemporary with Colossians. As to the breadth of the term θρησκεία, that is readily established. In James the term lacks any ritual or cultic sense, referring primarily to pious and ethical conduct (1.26-27). In contrast to this, Philo uses the term to denote the ritual or formal aspect of religion as distinct from piety (*Det. Pot. Ins.* 7 §21). Elsewhere θρησκεία refers to religious observance (*Fug.* 7 §41) or to temple service or tradition (*Leg. Gai.* 37 §298). Josephus applies the term to the religious ceremonies of the temple as well (*War* 4.5.2 §324). In short, θρησκεία serves as a reference to the many sides of religion. In addition, it may refer to a religious tradition in general. It is used in this way at Acts 26.5 and *4 Macc.* 5.13. Josephus employs θρησκεία in like fashion (*Ant.* 19.5.2 §283).

θρησκεία also stands for the act of worship. Its use in Wis. 14.18 conveys the meaning of worship or devotion. When the genitive case connects θρησκεία to another noun, the latter usually becomes the object of the action or verbal idea present in the former. Accordingly, the phrase θρησκεία τοῦ θεοῦ reads 'worship of God' (Josephus, *Ant.* 4.8.44 §306; 8.8.4 §225; 17.9.3 §214; cf. *1 Clem.* 45.7). The same rendering holds true for plural objects and even objects an author does not regard as worthy of worship. Thus the phrase θρησκεία θεῶν is properly translated 'worship of gods' even in Hellenistic Jewish literature (Philo, *Spec. Leg.* 1.58 §315; cf. Wis. 14.27). Instances of the subjective genitive do appear in the literature, however. The phrase τῇ Ἰουδαίων θρησκείᾳ means 'to the Jews' religion' or 'to the Jewish religion' (Josephus, *Ant.* 12.5.4 §253; cf. *4 Macc.* 5.7). Two other examples of the subjective genitive occur in the works of Josephus (*War* 2.10.4 §198; *Ant.* 16.4.3 §115), but these occurrences do not mean that the genitive construction is common. On the contrary, Josephus' corpus contains some fifteen examples of θρησκεία followed by an objective genitive, which makes the subjective genitive comparatively rare. In summary, while this lexical and syntactical evidence precludes any decisive argument regarding the translation of the phrase θρησκεία τῶν ἀγγέλων, it does suggest a probable reading: 'worship directed to angels'.

3. Interpreting the Polemical Core in Colossians

Even with this probable reading, however, uncertainty about the meaning of θρησκεία τῶν ἀγγέλων remains because the term ἄγγελος presents the interpreter with a range of meanings and associations. Speculation about angels blossomed in post-exilic Jewish thought, resulting in a proliferation of their functions. *1 Enoch* portrays the variety of their roles nicely. Their range of activity stretches from the intercessory (47.2; 99.3) to the punitive (53.3). They are seen as the controlling spirits of natural phenomena (60.16-22) and are linked with cosmic powers and forces (61.10; cf. 40.9). Moreover, opposed to the hierarchy of good angels is a group of fallen angels that is the root of various evils (6.2-7; 19.1; 69.2ff.).

This developed angelology appears in the NT as well. Revelation in particular is aware of the various functions assumed by angels. It links them to stars (1.20), portrays them as governors of the four winds (7.1), casts them as agents of punishment and destruction (9.15), and distinguishes a hierarchy of good angels from bad ones (12.7; cf. 2 Cor. 11.14; 2 Pet. 2.4). The question arises, then, whether or not the author of Colossians had a specific kind of ἄγγελοι in mind. Is it the φιλοσοφία's involvement with what he considers *fallen* angels that so perturbs him, or angels per se?

Other NT documents connect the angels with cosmic powers and authorities. 1 Peter, for instance, lists ἀγγέλων, ἐξουσιῶν, and δυνάμεων together (3.22; cf. *1 En.* 61.10), which raises the question of the relationship between the ἄγγελοι of Col. 2.18 and the ἀρχαί and ἐξουσίαι of 2.15.[1] The interpreter must bear in mind, however, that the author of Colossians does not specify the kind of angels he speaks of in 2.18. As for the ἀρχαί and ἐξουσίαι of 2.15, that is language that the letter writer introduces, as 2.15 lies outside the polemical core.

Philo's understanding of angels complicates matters even more. In a discussion about the inhabitants of the air, he mentions bodiless souls (ψυχαί; *Plant.* 4 §14). The purest of these, he says, are what Moses called angels and the Greeks called heroes (ἥρωας). Elsewhere he identifies the angels as δαίμονες (*Gig.* 4 §16). In other words, Philo joins Jewish angelology to Hellenistic demonology. The implications of this merger for Colossians are clear. If the author equates the angels with heroes or δαίμονες, as Philo does, then the phrase

1. W. Grundmann, G. von Rad and G. Kittel, 'ἄγγελος, ἀρχάγγελος, ἰσάγγελος', *TDNT*, I, p. 86.

'worship of angels' in Col. 2.8 may be a reference to a common feature of Greco-Roman religiosity: devotion to demons or heroes (cf. Rev. 9.20).[1]

The Anatolian setting of the Colossian philosophy underscores the importance of Philo's equation and the ambiguity it introduces. Numerous inscriptions from western Asia Minor dedicated to Michael, Gabriel, or simply to the archangel, many found in Christian churches, all dating well after the first century CE, point to Jewish influence.[2] Yet the same region produced epigraphical dedications to angels—again, these are late relative to Colossians—betraying no obvious Jewish or Christian influence.[3] In these cases one would understand ἄγγελοι as messengers or mediators between god(s) and humankind along the lines of Hermes.[4] Because the Colossian philosophy might reflect an earlier stage of Anatolian pagan speculation about messenger or mediatorial figures, the interpreter cannot regard the reference in Col. 2.18 to angels as certain evidence of Jewish influence.

Conclusion. The examination of θρησκεία τῶν ἀγγέλων just completed confirms an aspect of the Colossian philosophy that emerged earlier, in the discussion of its calendrical and food concerns: a Jewish background alone will not readily account for all the features of the philosophy. While speculation about angels flourished within first-century Judaism, worship directed to angels pushes the interpreter to the edge of and even beyond this tradition. If Philo's equating of angels with heroes or demons reflects speculation outside Judaism about messenger figures, as Anatolian evidence suggests, the inter-

---

1. A recent study by F. Brenk provides an overview of this phenomenon ('In the Light of the Moon: Demonology in the Early Imperial Period', *ANRW* II.16.3, pp. 2068-145).

2. W. Ramsay, *The Cities and Bishoprics of Phrygia* (2 vols.; Oxford: Clarendon Press, 1895–97), II, pp. 541, 558, 675, 741-42 (inscriptions #404, 442, 678); C. Roueché, *Aphrodisias in Late Antiquity: The Late Roman and Byzantine Inscriptions* (*Journal for Roman Studies* Monograph, 5; London: Society for the Promotion of Roman Studies, 1989), pp. 154-57, 178, 180-82 (inscriptions #92, 94, 124, 132, 133).

3. F. Sokolowski, 'Sur le culte d'angelos dans le paganisme grec et romain', *HTR* 53 (1960), pp. 226-29.

4. M. Nilsson, 'The High God and the Mediator', *HTR* 56 (1963), p. 116. See also F. Cumont, 'Les anges du paganisme', *RHR* 72 (1915), pp. 160, 165.

preter may find pagan influence even in the reference to angels. Yet the philosophy had roots in Judaism to the extent that it adopted a Jewish calendar, and it belonged in the Christian circle because of the stress it placed on humility. Hence, while this look at the philosophy's praxis brings the interpreter a clearer view of its individual features, the identity of the philosophy remains elusive, for the philosophy as a whole has a complex character defying simple classification.

Warrant and Wisdom in the Philosophy
Besides designating what he opposed at Colossae and condemning certain practices advocated there, the letter writer details his objections to the philosophy in lengthy relative clauses (Col. 2.17, 18b-19, 22a-23). These portions of the polemic are a source of information about the philosophy, a source I have already tapped, particularly when vocabulary from elsewhere in the polemic appears there. My use of these clauses up to this point, however, belies the difficulty of gauging how illuminating material from this part of the polemic is, for only pieces of those clauses accurately mirror the philosophy. In the case of Col. 2.17, for example, where the letter writer explains why he rejects the food and calendar regulations of the philosophers, he evidently allows the interpreter no view of his opponents. It might be tempting to find in the phrase 'shadow of things to come' (σκιὰ τῶν μελλόντων) the philosophy's rationale for the practices of v. 16: they reflect or anticipate a coming reality (Heb. 10.1; 8.5). Yet paired with σῶμα, σκιά has a decidedly negative meaning, because it is an *undesirable* second—a mere shadow or appearance—to the real or substantial (Philo, *Dec.* 17 §82; *Migr. Abr.* 2 §12).[1] Consequently, σκιά appears to come from the letter writer's vocabulary and not the philosophy's. Verse 17 simply registers his biting criticism of the praxis: the practices of v. 16 are a *mere* shadow; they obscure reality. Hence, the verse offers no clue as to what motivated the practices of v. 16. Fortunately, other relative clauses in the polemical core provide the interpreter with more information about the philosophy.

ἃ ἑόρακεν ἐμβατεύων *and the Fleshly Mind.* Verse 18b begins with the relative pronoun ἅ, which signals a transition from the point-blank rejection of specific practices to the letter writer's comments

---

1. S. Schulz, 'σκιά, ἀποσκίασμα, ἐπισκιάζω', *TDNT*, VII, pp. 395-96. This reading contradicts Francis, 'Christological Argument', pp. 205-206.

about them and reasons for rejecting them, although the second component of the signal (ἐστιν) is lacking. In this instance, unlike v. 17, the letter writer appears to begin his argument for dismissing the practices condemned in v. 18a by articulating the position of the φιλοσοφία, for the language of v. 18b is descriptive, not critical. Evidently, he describes in order to make his criticism, which follows immediately, the more pointed. As a consequence, he reveals information about the philosophy in the act of launching his negative assessment.

In Col. 2.18b the letter writer recounts the philosophy's warrant for the exercise of humility and the devotion to angels. In doing so he continues the attack begun at the start of v. 18 against any who would decide against those in the Christian community. The person who would condemn is the logical subject of ὁράω; his insistence on certain practices is based on what he has seen. The Greek verb here, ὁράω, refers to perception at various levels, from visual perception to mental recognition, insight, or spiritual vision.[1] The precise meaning of ὁράω in Col. 2.18b depends to a great extent on the significance of the participle ἐμβατεύω which stands immediately after it in the verse. ἐμβατεύω is a *hapax legomenon* in the NT, but instances of it elsewhere offer the interpreter some indication of the nuance of the term in Colossians. In classical literature the word denotes the act of entering or setting foot on or in. Because it was used to describe entry into a holy place or precinct, the word also came to refer to religious initiation. In addition, ἐμβατεύω could mean entering or coming into possession of something.[2]

In Hellenistic Jewish literature the term appears infrequently. The only occurrence of ἐμβατεύω in Josephus is in the *Antiquities*, where he recounts the story of Moses and the burning bush (2.12.1 §265). Because the deity dwells on Sinai, he writes, shepherds do not venture to set foot on it. In the LXX ἐμβατεύω appears in the narrative in Joshua about tribal Israel's entering into possession of the promised land (Josh. 19.49, 51). Other occurrences of ἐμβατεύω in the LXX also reflect its classical usages, but there is one exception to this. The verb appears four times in 1 Maccabees, all in a military context. Accordingly, the term denotes forceful entry or invasion (12.25; 13.20; 14.31; 15.40). The exceptional use occurs in 2 Macc. 2.30, in

1. BAGD, pp. 577-78; LSJ, pp. 1244-45.
2. LSJ, p. 539.

3. Interpreting the Polemical Core in Colossians

the preface to the historical narrative portion of the book. In that verse the author describes the duties of the historian as investigation or scrutiny, that is, *entering deeply* into something (ἐμβατεύω), the discussion of accounts, and attention to details. Here ἐμβατεύω takes a figurative sense that is not among its classical usages but is a logical extension of its literal meaning. The participle of ἐμβατεύω also appears as an alternative reading to ἐμβαθύνοντες in Philo's *On Noah's Work as a Planter* (19 §80), where it has the same figurative sense.[1]

Depending on the precise meaning of ἐμβατεύω in Colossians 2.18b, there are several defensible translations of the phrase ἃ ἑόρακεν ἐμβατεύων. These may be multiplied by the possible syntactical relationships between the words of the phrase. The participle could be adverbially related to ἑόρακεν, or ἃ ἑόρακεν could be the object of the participle. If ἐμβατεύω has the figurative sense of 2 Macc. 2.30, possible renderings are 'which he has seen upon close scrutiny' or 'investigating closely what he has seen'. If ἐμβατεύω has a literal sense, the phrase could be rendered 'which things he has seen by coming into possession [of them]' or 'coming into possession of what he has seen'. The verb could refer to entry of some sort, possibly entry into a holy place, but in this case the phrase becomes intelligible only by speculating about what the phrase describes: 'which he has seen upon entering [it]' (what did he enter?); 'entering into what he has seen' (a vision and subsequent visit to what he envisioned? A revelation from or of heaven and a journey there?); 'which he has seen during initiation' or 'entering [in the initiation] that which he has seen'.

These last two translations with their mention of initiation become more inviting options in light of the fact that ἐμβατεύω occurs in inscriptions found at the Apollo oracle at Claros, a site none too far from Colossae. Although the Clarian inscriptions postdate the letter to the Colossians, they do confirm ἐμβατεύω's place in the vocabulary of mystery initiation in Asia Minor.[2] Could one of the philosophers at Colossae have received instructions about his praxis when he was

---

1. H. Preisker, 'ἐμβατεύω', *TDNT*, II, p. 535; L. Cohn and P. Wendland (eds.), *Philonis Alexandrini opera quae supersunt* (7 vols.; Berlin: Reimer, 1962–63), II, p. 149.
2. Dibelius, 'Isis Initiation', pp. 85-87; Lyonnet, 'L'épître aux Colossiens', pp. 417-20.

initiated into a mystery, or was he granted a glimpse of what he later entered during initiation? Possibly, though such a reconstruction probably places undue interpretive weight on one word and on one of many contexts in which the word appears.

The trouble confronting any literal reading of ἐμβατεύω lies in the speculation required to make sense of the word. In the case of those who read ἐμβατεύω as a reference to coming into possession of something or entering some place, conjecture about what one enters or gains possession of arises. Thus, Francis speculates that the unexpressed object of ἐμβατεύω is the heavenly realm, the place one enters and enjoys a heavenly vision (ὁράω).[1] But there is no sign of this heavenly journey elsewhere in the text. Likewise, contrary to those who posit that ἐμβατεύω denotes entry into a mystery cult, Colossians lacks any unequivocal reference to initiation.

By contrast, ἐμβατεύω taken in its figurative sense produces a reading needing no extensive explanation or elaborate hypothesis about the setting it assumes. The translation of ἃ ἑόρακεν ἐμβατεύων would be one of the first two I mentioned: 'which he has seen upon close scrutiny' or 'investigating what he has seen'.[2] What these translations imply is this: careful inquiry conducted by one of the philosophers has produced an insight regarded as authoritative for the philosophy. That insight justifies certain practices, namely, humility and angel worship.

The additional attraction of this interpretation lies in its echoing of a theme that has emerged already in this exegesis. In the opening salvo of his polemic (Col. 2.8), the letter writer blasts the basis of the philosophy by citing its alignment with human tradition and the στοιχεῖα τοῦ κόσμου rather than Christ. Now he launches anew this line of attack by reporting the basis for the philosophy's practice of humility and worship of angels: he who insists on such things perceived them by careful examination rather than by relying on the head (2.19), Christ, who is the true source of all knowledge and wisdom (2.3). Whatever this insight enjoyed by the philosopher is, the letter writer attributes it to his own close investigation. At this point, then, the stage is set for a resumption of the letter writer's blast against the epistemological underpinnings of the philosophy.

1. Francis, 'Background of EMBATEUEIN', p. 197.
2. Supporting this reading are A. Nock ('The Vocabulary of the New Testament', *JBL* 52 [1937], p. 133) and Preisker ('ἐμβατεύω', pp. 535-36).

3. Interpreting the Polemical Core in Colossians 67

What follows ἐμβατεύων in vv. 18 and 19 is decidedly derogatory. The assertion of authority by the philosophy, evidenced by an insistence on a certain praxis, and the rationale for that assertion clearly infuriate the letter writer, who regards these as pure arrogation. Accordingly, he attacks with full force. He heaps ridicule on the philosopher of v. 18b who bases on private insights his insistence on certain practices. There are no grounds (εἰκῇ), the letter writer counters in v. 18c, for the philosophy's demands. The fellow who asserts his authority was made arrogant (φυσιούμενος) by his mind, a mind the letter writer characterizes as fleshly (τῆς σαρκός). The unfortunate consequence of this groundless appropriation of authority is, according to the letter writer, the philosophy's detachment from the exclusive source of knowledge and warrant for practice, Christ. This arrogant fellow, by relying on the fruits of his own investigations, is failing to hold to the head.

Little in the polemical assault immediately following ἐμβατεύων appears to be of use in reconstructing the philosophy. The words immediately after ἐμβατεύω are quite derogatory and have a Pauline provenance, φυσιόω appearing elsewhere in the NT only in 1 Corinthians (4.6, 18, 19; 5.2; 8.1; 13.4) and εἰκῇ occurring predominantly in Paul's corpus (Rom. 13.4; 1 Cor. 15.2; Gal. 3.4; 4.11).[1] Accordingly, such vocabulary comes in all probability from the letter writer, whose indebtedness to Paul is obvious. The criticism at the beginning of v. 19, of not holding to the head (Christ), was obviously not coined by the philosophers either, nor does it give the interpreter much to go on in ferreting out the actual features of the philosophy. For the charge of disloyalty to Christ was widely applied by early Christian polemicists and, as a consequence, may obscure as much as illuminate the object of that criticism. Does the charge indicate that the Colossian philosophy was not even Christian? Perhaps, although its adherents may well have belonged to the Christian community at Colossae since they prized humility and exercised enough influence on Colossian Christians to be perceived as a threat. Was the philosophy's Christology deficient? Possibly, though the charge of 'not holding to the head' does not enable the interpreter to specify that deficiency.

The only part of the polemic following ἐμβατεύων in vv. 18c and 19 that is likely to reveal anything of the philosophy is the puzzling

---

1. Marshall, *Enmity in Corinth*, pp. 204-205.

phrase ὑπὸ τοῦ νοὸς τῆς σαρκὸς αὐτοῦ. There is strong indication that the term σάρξ was a favorite of the letter writer and may well have originated with him, since it occurs frequently in the letter, particularly outside the polemical core (1.22, 24; 2.1, 5, 11, 13, 18, 23; 3.22). But one can only guess at the inspiration behind the phrase as a whole, an expression unique in the NT. It may have been formulated by the author of the letter, even though Pauline thought tends to contrast mind and flesh rather than linking them (Rom. 7.25). Two analogous constructions occur at Col. 1.22 and 2.11 (both outside the polemical core), where the author speaks of the σῶμα τῆς σαρκός (+ αὐτοῦ in 1.22). The antecedent to these phrases appears to be an expression in the Dead Sea Scrolls, גוית בשרו (1QpHab 9.2), meaning simply physical body, as the Greek phrase denotes at Col. 1.22. The body of flesh in 2.11 may not refer strictly to the body but to the lower nature in human beings as well. Apparently, the letter writer, taking his lead from these expressions in 1.22 and 2.11, added τῆς σαρκὸς αὐτοῦ to ὑπὸ τοῦ νοός to produce the curious retort 'by his fleshly mind'. These considerations would indicate, therefore, the letter writer's, if not the philosophy's, affinity to the Dead Sea Scrolls.[1]

Why would the letter writer coin such an unusual phrase? This expression depicts a νοῦς caught up in the physical, lower realm; it portrays the mind as corrupted and depraved, however awkward the expression. If this expression is the work of the letter writer, as seems likely, its awkwardness suggests his manipulation of an antecedent phrase, perhaps the vocabulary or an actual claim of the philosophy. Behind this characterization may have stood the philosophy's assertion that the νοῦς was the agent of the close investigation and the recipient of the insight described earlier in the verse, a role for νοῦς common in philosophical thought.[2] The letter writer's addition of τῆς σαρκὸς αὐτοῦ to ὑπὸ τοῦ νοός would, therefore, represent a continuation of his effort to defuse any claim to authority the philosophy made.

The Wisdom of the Philosophy. The two relative clauses ending the polemical core (vv. 22-23) have already shed some light on, and in some cases confirmed, what other portions of the polemic say about

1. *Contra* Davies, *Christian Origins*, pp. 156-60.
2. Cf. Plutarch, *Gen. Socr.* 20 (588D) and *Def. Orac.* 40 (432C); J. Behm, 'νοέω, νοῦς, κτλ', *TDNT*, IV, pp. 954-58. Behm does not, however, think that the NT occurrences reflect Hellenistic philosophical or religious uses.

3. Interpreting the Polemical Core in Colossians 69

the praxis of the philosophy and the letter writer's description of it. I need not repeat here my analysis of ταπεινοφροσύνη, θρησκεία, or 'human commandments and teachings'. But these probes hardly exhaust Col. 2.22-23; the letter writer reveals a good deal more about the philosophy as he articulates his objections to it.

The explanatory remark opening v. 22—'referring to things all of which are destined for destruction by being consumed'—helped determine the significance of the commands in v. 21. The commands appear to call for fasting, not just selective abstinence, because *all* foods are destined for dissolution. That this is the philosophy's rationale for its praxis receives confirmation from the remainder of v. 22, which identifies the commands of v. 21 and the accompanying justification of v. 22a as *human* commandments and teachings, a characterization the letter writer applies to the philosophy earlier (v. 8).

What else does the explanatory note of v. 22a reveal about the philosophy? Initially the language of the explanation gives the interpreter few leads. ἀπόχρησις is a *hapax legomenon* in the NT, does not occur in the LXX, and is rare in classical literature. The word φθορά does appear elsewhere in the NT but its use in Col. 2.22 is distinctive, as all other occurrences pertain to *human* corruption or destruction, not the physical dissolution of foodstuffs (Rom. 8.21; 1 Cor. 15.42, 50; Gal. 6.8; 2 Pet. 1.4; 2.12, 19). A common thread, on the other hand, may link Col. 2.22 to many of these. In a philosophical setting φθορά denoted the physical dissolution inevitably faced by everything that comes into being.[1] This notion is common in Philo and aptly expressed in the phrases γένεσις δὲ φθορᾶς ἀρχή (*Dec.* 12 §58) and ἐν γενέσει καὶ φθορᾷ (*Spec. Leg.* 3.32 §178; cf. Plutarch, *Is. et Os.* 63 [376D]). This perspective seems to underlie the phrase πάντα εἰς φθοράν in Col. 2.22 and εἰς...φθοράν in 2 Pet. 2.12, the εἰς expressing purpose or end. If, as seems likely, the Colossian philosophy had relied at this point on vocabulary and thought with a philosophical provenance to articulate the reasons for its praxis, that would strengthen earlier conclusions I drew about the background of φιλοσοφία and στοιχεῖα τοῦ κόσμου.

Verse 23 tells the interpreter more about the significance of v. 22a because the relative clause there evidently refers both to the commands of v. 21 and the explanation of v. 22a. But the difficult

---

1. G. Harder, 'φθείρω, φθορά, φθαρτός, κτλ', *TDNT*, IX, pp. 94-96.

grammar of the verse leaves some doubt about what the letter writer is saying in it. I repeat my translation of v. 23 here: 'which, though they pass for wisdom in achieving would-be devotion, humility, and severe treatment of the body, are of no worth with respect to fleshy indulgence'. Other readings are possible, however. Since the author gives the reader no clear sign of where the subordinate concessive clause begins and ends and the preposition πρός has semantic breadth, B. Hollenbach maintains that the main clause runs, 'which things (actually) lead to the fulfillment of the flesh'.[1] B. Hanssler champions another reading based on a less common use of πρός: a comparative sense.[2] The resulting main clause reads, 'such things are not of any worth in comparison with the gratification of the flesh', which suggests to Hanssler that the letter writer attacks the philosophy by asserting that its asceticism is *no better than* libertinism.[3] To reach this interpretation, however, Hanssler pushes πρός beyond its likeliest meaning and must posit an asceticism versus libertinism debate behind v. 23. Therefore, while Hollenbach's reading is possible, Hanssler's is improbable.

Yet even Hanssler would agree that the letter writer included a subordinate concessive clause within the relative clause of v. 23, so that the differing interpretations of that verse do not obscure the begrudging concession the letter writer makes to his opponents. He concedes that the commands of v. 21 and the explanatory comment of v. 22a pass for wisdom—the interpreter presumes—*in the eyes of the philosophers*. In making this admission he gives his polemic a sharper edge, for even as he records the philosophy's claim of wisdom, he undercuts it by calling it illusory.

Besides implying that vv. 21 and 22a belong to the wisdom of the philosophy, v. 23 may say even more about the philosophy. For the concessive clause also reveals what the philosophers hoped to achieve with their wisdom: proper devotion, humility, and bodily asceticism. How exactly did the philosophers' wisdom achieve such objectives? A textual variant in v. 23 mentioned earlier would suggest that devotion

---

1. B. Hollenbach, 'Col. II.23: Which Things Lead to the Fulfilment of the Flesh', *NTS* 25 (1978–79), p. 254.
2. B. Hanssler, 'Zu Satzkonstruktion und Aussage in Kol. 2,23', in H. Feld and J. Nolte (eds.), *Wort Gottes in der Zeit: K.H. Schelkle Festschrift* (Düsseldorf: Patmos-Verlag, 1973), p. 143; Smyth, *Greek Grammar*, §1695.3.c.
3. Hanssler, 'Aussage in Kol 2,23', p.147.

and humility are achieved *through* severe treatment of the body. But even if the more widely-accepted reading is followed, the answer may appear in veiled form: it may be reflected in the letter writer's claim that the philosophers' practices are inadequate in the face of, or may even lead to, fleshy indulgence. Here the letter writer may be reversing the actual claim of the philosophers. Perhaps they saw in the abstinence embodied in the commands of v. 21 an antidote to the flesh and thus an adequate means of controlling the body. Whether the letter writer is rejecting this claim or turning it on its head—the broken grammar of the verse allows both possibilities—here as elsewhere he seems to rehearse enough of the philosophy's position in order effectively to contradict it.

Results of the Exegesis

This exegesis of the Colossian polemical core has not resolved every interpretive puzzle that exists there. The brevity and ambiguity of the core precludes certainty about some features of the philosophy. Nevertheless, in many cases I was able to rule out certain readings, in many I could establish probability, and in others I came to a readily defensible interpretation.

In the course of this exegesis there has emerged a fairly well-defined profile of the philosophy, evidenced by the recurrence of particular themes and elements. The twofold appearance of ταπεινοφροσύνη and θρησκεία (θρῆσκία) in a few short verses indicates the high probability of their importance to the philosophy. To what these two terms refer is mostly but not entirely clear: (1) the letter writer condemns the philosopher's humility but commends it in others (3.12); (2) θρησκεία probably refers to worship, and in the philosophers' case this likely means worshiping angels, but the term 'angels' admits a number of meanings and associations. Whatever their precise significance, v. 23 confirms the centrality of humility and devotion in the philosophy, because that verse suggests that they, along with (or by means of) the asceticism of the body, are objectives toward which the commands of v. 21 and the rationale of v. 22 are directed.

Also made clear by the exegesis is the diverse character of the Colossian philosophy, such that it can simultaneously recommend the prized Christian virtue of humility, worship of angels, and food and calendar regulations that include Sabbath observance. Several elements come not from any religious tradition but from the Greek philosophical tradition: the elements of the world (vv. 8, 20), the mind's investigative function (v. 18b, c), the inevitability of physical dissolution (v. 22a), and perhaps even the term φιλοσοφία (v. 8). Philosophically-rooted asceticism could probably even account for the Colossian dietary concerns, but these, along with the calendar regulations, probably have a Jewish source. Whatever their source, the polemic suggests what ends they serve in the philosophy. If I have grasped the logic of the explanatory note in v. 22a correctly, then the commands of v. 21 dictate abstinence not just from certain foods and drinks but from sustenance altogether. This call to fasting along with the calendrical observances enjoined by the philosophy may have included a cultic purpose: to prepare one for proper θρησκεία. But those practices evidently met other goals as well; they allowed the philosophers to keep tight rein over their bodies. Successful achievement of this bodily asceticism assured the philosophers that they could check the promptings of the flesh (v. 23). Here again we see the complexity of the philosophy: Jewish practices utilized to achieve a goal that is not exclusively or even distinctively Jewish. Nevertheless, while the philosophy does appear to be diverse and syncretistic, its various features cohere around certain goals.

While the letter writer directs much of his criticism against the practices enjoined by the philosophy, he also appears preoccupied with the rationale and warrant for that way of life. His polemic regularly moves beyond a condemnation of the philosophy's practices to a rejection of its authority and a disparagement of the bases of its practices and authority. If the characterization of the philosophy as rooted in human tradition (2.8, 22) says very little about the philosophy, at least it reveals that the letter writer judges the philosophy to rest on inadequate foundations. This line of attack reappears at several points: first, the philosophy rests on principles (στοιχεῖα) that no longer bear on the believer (2.8, 20); second, the investigation that facilitated or deciphered the vision of practices enjoined in v. 18a was conducted by a *fleshly* mind (v. 18c); and third, what constitutes wisdom among the philosophers is in fact inadequate and illusory (v. 23). As the letter writer rejects specific practices of those he opposes at Colossae, therefore, he also attacks the underpinnings of the philosophy's discipline.

Does the polemical core give the interpreter any further insight into the character of the letter writer's attack on the philosophy's wisdom?

3. Interpreting the Polemical Core in Colossians

Possibly so. The conflict over knowledge at Colossae appears to revolve around this question: how is wisdom achieved? This exegesis could not with complete certainty locate the phrase στοιχεῖα τοῦ κόσμου in the vocabulary of the philosophers, but the letter writer's use of the phrase in Col. 2.8 and 20 suggests that he understood them to be the epistemological principles of the philosophy, hence the qualification of the philosophy as κατὰ τὰ στοιχεῖα τοῦ κόσμου. How these στοιχεῖα (or whatever the philosophers themselves called their guiding principles) are used by the philosophy is not described, but the letter writer hints that the human mind is vital in the acquisition of knowledge in the philosophers' program. For it is the mind in v. 18—derogated by the author as fleshly—that both undertakes a careful investigation (of the στοιχεῖα?) and enjoys revelatory insight.

Assessment of Other Interpretations of the Colossian Philosophy

The exegesis of the Colossian polemic just completed represents one among many interpretations of the philosophy. I have already described the most important of these, and now, in support of my own reading, I shall make an evaluation of them. Such an undertaking will allow me to test and refine the results of my exegesis.

Meriting the closest attention are the analyses of Francis, Dibelius, and Schweizer. Besides their comprehensiveness and coherence, these reconstructions embody all the important exegetical options in interpreting Colossians and are the most prominent representatives of their respective schools of interpretation: the exclusively (apocalyptic, ascetic, mystical) Jewish reading, the Jewish-Gnostic reading, and the Hellenistic philosophical reading. Not to be slighted are Lyonnet and Bornkamm, authors of important reconstructions who offer noteworthy variations on Francis and Dibelius respectively. Because of its growing popularity among contemporary scholars, the Hellenistic syncretism model also deserves comment, although exegetically it varies little from the Dibelius–Bornkamm line.

The Ascetic, Apocalyptic, Mystical Jewish Reconstructions

The exegetical study that began this chapter placed ταπεινοφροσύνη and θρησκεία at the center of the philosophy as the primary objectives of its praxis and as its dominant features. How adequately do the existing interpretations treat these two aspects? In fact, both the Jewish-Gnostic and purely Jewish theses paid very close attention to the phrase θρησκεία τῶν ἀγγέλων and certain versions of both proposals offered interpretations of ταπεινοφροσύνη. Proponents of a purely Jewish background for the philosophy invariably read θρησκεία τῶν ἀγγέλων as a subjective genitive, a grammatical possibility that Judaism's monotheistic tradition made attractive. Taken as such, the phrase meant either the religion outlined in the Law that the angels delivered and oversee (Lyonnet) or the worship of God undertaken by the angels themselves (Francis). Francis, as we have seen, made these adoring angels in heaven the content of the philosophers' vision and he assigned ταπεινοφροσύνη, which he argued denoted fasting, ἀφειδία, and the regulations prescribed by the philosophy a preparatory role for that visionary (ἑόρακεν) exaltation and entry (ἐμβατεύων) into heaven.[1]

The Francis Reconstruction. For all the attention that Francis gives to θρησκεία and ταπεινοφροσύνη, however, his interpretation of these terms and the philosophy as a whole faces these problems: (1) significant evidence tells against his equating ταπεινοφροσύνη with fasting, (2) it is difficult to document a Jewish pattern of ascetic preparation and heavenly journey, and (3) he has an interpretation of θρησκεία τῶν ἀγγέλων that leads to an untenable reading of the polemical core.

In his interpretation of ταπεινοφροσύνη, Francis's efforts to equate it with a specific practice, fasting, may reflect to some degree his response to a feature common to many analyses of the Colossian philosophy. By emphasizing the philosophy's practices, Francis sought to correct the widespread assumption that the conflicts among early Christians are basically and determinatively ideational and confessional.[2] While credit goes to Francis for arguing that the philosophy's praxis and not its Christology lay at the heart of the conflict at Colossae, he tends either to reduce most features of the philosophy to specific practices or to ignore those, such as the στοιχεῖα, that do not point readily to practices.[3]

Francis can cite Jewish and Christian tradition that links humility to

1. The substance of Francis's interpretation is presented in 'Angelic Worship', pp. 167-81.
2. Francis and Meeks (eds.), *Conflict at Colossae*, p. 5.
3. Francis, 'Christological Argument', pp..192-208, esp. 203, 206.

3. Interpreting the Polemical Core in Colossians

fasting. He points to two OT passages where humiliation is understood to be achieved by fasting and mourning (Ps. 34[35].13-14; Isa. 58.3, 5). So closely is the former related to the latter two, Francis argues, that by the time *Hermas* was composed, humility was synonymous with fasting (*Herm. Sim.* 5.3.7; *Herm. Vis.* 3.10.6).[1] And Francis could appeal to my exegesis which concluded that on the basis of v. 22a, the commands of v. 21 are a call to fasting. But occurrences of the term in the NT demand a broader reading of it, for in all its appearances outside Colossians ταπεινοφροσύνη denotes an attitude or bearing rather than specific practices (Acts 20.19; Eph. 4.2; Phil. 2.3; 1 Pet. 5.5; cf. Mt. 18.4; 23.12; Lk. 14.11; 18.14; Jas 4.10). Within Colossians, at 3.12, ταπεινοφροσύνη hardly admits to being a reference to specific practices, so it is unlikely to have so specific or technical a sense in ch. 2. ταπεινοφροσύνη is not, therefore, equivalent to fasting.[2] Nor is it, as Francis claims,[3] a technical term at Colossae for a specific set of ascetic practices, as it *may* have been by the time of Tertullian.[4]

Also unconvincing is Francis's contention that a strand of Jewish thought understood that an ascetic regimen was preparatory not just for the receipt of revelation but for ascent and entry (ἐμβατεύω) into heaven as well. He must turn to relatively late writings to establish this connection, and many of the texts fail to support the claim he makes for them. While the *Greek Apocalypse of Ezra* does narrate Ezra's fasting and consequent visionary departure (1.3-7), it is considered such a distant Christian imitation of *4 Ezra* that most scholars place it several hundred years after *4 Ezra*, some as late as the ninth century CE.[5] Francis also cites *3 Enoch* which has Moses fasting 121 times until the habitations of *chashmal* (highest heaven) are opened to him (15B.2). But most scholars place *3 Enoch* in the fifth or sixth century

1. Francis, 'Angelic Worship', pp. 168-69.
2. Kehl, 'Erniedrigung', pp. 370-74.
3. Francis, 'Angelic Worship', p. 168.
4. Even as late as Tertullian, the connection between ταπεινοφροσύνη and specific ascetic practices is weak, according to R. Darling, 'TAPEINOSIS and Typology in the Study of Early Christian Asceticism' (paper presented at Annual Meeting of the SBL, Boston, December 5 1987). See also *LPGL*, p. 1374.
5. Charlesworth, *The Pseudepigrapha and Modern Research with a Supplement* (SBLSCS, 7S: Chico, CA: Scholars Press, 1981), p. 116; O. Wahl (ed.), *Apocalypsis Esdrae, Apocalypsis Sedrach, Visio Beati Esdrae* (PVTG, 4; Leiden: Brill, 1977), p. 7.

CE, and even Odeberg, who finds sections of it going back to the first century, considers ch. 15B to be very late.[1]

Documents closer in time to Colossians lack the exact pattern Francis seeks. The *Testament of Isaac*, whose date eludes scholars but may be 400 CE or earlier,[2] describes Isaac's ascetic practices (4.1-6) but fails to connect these in any way with his ascent into heaven (5.4; 6.1).[3] Somewhat earlier in date are the *Ascension of Isaiah* (late second century CE) and the *Apocalypse of Abraham* (end of the first century CE),[4] but again a clear pattern linking asceticism and ascent is lacking. In the former, mention of Isaiah's program of asceticism (2.7-11) comes well before, and has no clear connection with, his journey to heaven (ch. 7). The history of the document confirms this perceived gap, since the stories of Isaiah's martyrdom (1.1–3.12; 5.1-14) and vision (6.1–11.4) circulated separately until a Christian redactor joined them.[5] In the *Apocalypse of Abraham*, Francis's claim that revelation and heavenly journey are made contingent on abstinence from meat and wine ignores the point of the story: it is Abraham's sacrifice that brings about his vision and journey (chs. 9, 12, 15).

Jewish apocalypses contemporary with Colossians may regard ascetic practices as preparatory for the receipt of revelation, but one looks in vain for early examples of a connection between ascetic discipline and heavenly ascent or journey.[6] Enoch, in *1 Enoch*, makes his

---

1. J. Charlesworth (ed.), *The Old Testament Pseudepigrapha* (2 vols.; Garden City, NY: Doubleday, 1983–85), I, p. 229; H. Odeberg (ed.), *3 Enoch or the Hebrew Book of Enoch* (repr.; New York: Ktav, 1973 [1928]), part 1, pp. 41-42.
2. Charlesworth, *Pseudepigrapha and Modern Research*, p. 124.
3. Kehl, 'Erniedrigung', p. 371.
4. Charlesworth (ed.), *Pseudepigrapha and Modern Research*, pp. 68, 126; R. Charles (ed.), *The Ascension of Isaiah* (Translations of Early Documents, Series 1: Palestinian Jewish Texts; London: SPCK, 1917), pp. ix, x; G. Box (ed.), *Apocalypse of Abraham* (Translations of Early Documents, Series 1: Palestinian Jewish Texts; London: SPCK, 1918), p. xvi.
5. Charlesworth (ed.), *Old Testament Pseudepigrapha*, II, pp. 147-50.
6. Kehl, 'Erniedrigung', pp. 372-74. Two recent studies on the subject make no such connection. See M. Dean-Otting, *Heavenly Journeys: A Study of the Motif in Hellenistic Jewish Literature* (Judentum und Umwelt, 8; New York: Peter Lang, 1984), pp. 264-74; J. Tabor, *Things Unutterable: Paul's Ascent to Paradise in its Greco-Roman, Judaic, and Early Christian Contexts* (Studies in Judaism; Lanham, MD: University Press of America, 1986).

3. Interpreting the Polemical Core in Colossians

visionary ascent to heaven without ascetic preparation (ch. 14), as does the seer John in Revelation (4.1-2).

The third major difficulty with Francis's reconstruction arises from his treatment of θρησκεία. According to his reading, the θρησκεία τῶν ἀγγέλων of v. 18 refers to worship carried out by angels, but the θρησκεία of v. 23 denotes the worship performed by the philosophers, which the letter writer disparages as ἐθελοθρησκία, 'would-be worship'. This polemical addition to θρησκεία in v. 23 indicates, Francis argues, the focus of the author's attack: not the angelic worship of God per se but the philosophers' visionary experience and consequent adoption of angelic worship.[1]

But an obvious question arises: is the change in context from v. 18 to v. 23 so great that the two occurrences of θρησκεία do not refer to the same thing? It appears to me to be questionable whether the ancient reader or listener would have distinguished between the two occurrences of θρησκεία without the benefit of Francis's argument. It is more likely that they have a common referent, indication of which comes from a consideration of the letter writer's polemic: the letter writer is just as unhappy with the θρησκεία τῶν ἀγγέλων he attacks in v. 18 as he is with the ἐθελοθρησκία of v. 23. The polemic does not distinguish between the two. In all probability, then, neither should we.

The reading of θρησκεία τῶν ἀγγέλων my exegesis found more likely, worship directed to angels, avoids the pitfall faced by Francis's reconstruction. Evidently, because Francis sought to locate the Colossian philosophy solely against a Jewish background, he chose a less probable reading and thus avoided attributing to the philosophy a practice anathema to Jewish tradition. By doing so, however, he is forced into a disjointed and untenable reading of the polemical core.

The Lyonnet Reconstruction. There are other versions of the exclusively Jewish thesis that do not fall into the exegetical difficulties that trouble Francis's reading, but they have their own serious flaws. Second only to Francis's in comprehensiveness, Lyonnet's treatment of the philosophy nonetheless fails to be attentive to a key element of it. He pays scant attention to ταπεινοφροσύνη, which my exegesis placed at the center of the philosophy.

---

1. Francis, 'Angelic Worship', pp. 181-82.

More problematic is Lyonnet's reading of θρησκεία τῶν ἀγγέλων as a subjective genitive, although he does not join Francis in arguing that the two uses of θρησκεία in the polemical core refer to two separate things. Lyonnet sees in the phrase a reference to a group of practices regulating the moral life that the angels assisted in promulgating and now administer. In other words, θρησκεία τῶν ἀγγέλων is an oblique reference to the Law.[1] This circumlocution hardly seems to fit a Pauline context, however. Would Paul or a Paulinist—whoever wrote Colossians—have allowed θρησκεία—the philosophy's reference to the Law—to stand, if the matter under debate was Torah obedience? If the letter writer was really attacking the philosophy's requirement of the Law, one would expect an unequivocal reference to the Law in the polemical core, namely, mention of νόμος. His polemic would certainly have been strengthened by it. Instead, readers meet the verb δογματίζομαι in 2.20 and the related δόγματα outside the polemical core in 2.14, neither of which points unambiguously to the Law, and they find the letter writer criticizing a number of practices, not all of which have clear antecedents in Jewish observances. These are scarcely sufficient grounds for arguing, as Lyonnet does, that ch. 2 is dominated by an anti-Law polemic to which the anti-angel polemic is ancillary.[2]

Another difficulty in Lyonnet's reading emerges in the interpretation of ἐθελοθρησκία. Could the author really be derogating the philosophy's advocacy of the Law as a 'would-be religion', if he has already acknowledged that the θρησκεία promulgated by the angels is the religion of the Jews? Or could he describe the θρησκεία as 'self-willed' or 'self-chosen', suggesting that human beings had a hand in formulating or choosing it, when he has already noted the angelic role in instituting and administering it? None of these possible readings of ἐθελοθρησκία seems compatible with Lyonnet's reading of θρησκεία τῶν ἀγγέλων as a reference to religion based on the Law, promulgated and upheld by the angels.

Such are the problems that attend Lyonnet's version of the Jewish proposal. As was the case with Francis's interpretation, Lyonnet's insistence on reading θρησκεία τῶν ἀγγέλων as a subjective genitive construction leads to grave difficulties. Read as an objective genitive,

1. Lyonnet, 'Paul's Adversaries', pp. 149-50.
2. H. Weiss, 'The Law in the Epistle to the Colossians', *CBQ* 34 (1972), pp. 294-314, esp. 311.

3. Interpreting the Polemical Core in Colossians 79

on the other hand, as the exegesis that began this chapter favored, the problems that surround the interpretation of ἐθελο- vanish. It is no surprise that the author would blast the human worship of angels as a grossly inadequate θρησκεία, a would-be religion, or as a self-chosen undertaking, one inspired by a self-conceited visionary (2.18).

The Jewish-Gnostic and Related Reconstructions

Proponents of a Jewish-Gnostic background for the Colossian philosophy took as close a look as Francis and Lyonnet at the phrase θρησκεία τῶν ἀγγέλων. And they avoided a major stumbling block to the exclusively Jewish thesis by reading that phrase as an objective genitive, thus concurring with the conclusion of my exegesis. One version of the Jewish-Gnostic thesis, that of Schenke, also gave close attention to the term ταπεινοφροσύνη, a word the opening exegesis placed at the center of the philosophy. Initially, then, there is promise in the Jewish-Gnostic thesis, for it places its interpretive emphases correctly and follows the likeliest reading of θρησκεία τῶν ἀγγέλων.

The Dibelius–Bornkamm Reconstruction. The Jewish-Gnostic reconstruction also corresponds to my exegesis by paying close attention to the στοιχεῖα τοῦ κόσμου, but in doing so it misreads the significance of the στοιχεῖα for the philosophy, making them objects of worship. Several problems face the thesis that a Gnostic mystery religion devoted to the στοιχεῖα/angels existed at Colossae: (1) evidence for the divination and worship of the στοιχεῖα is late or suspect or both; (2) no text, including Colossians, supports the identification of the στοιχεῖα with the angels; (3) language in Colossians pointing unequivocally to mystery initiation is lacking; and (4) devotion to the στοιχεῖα cannot be successfully placed in any Gnostic tradition.

The two texts crucial to Dibelius's reconstruction, Apuleius' *Metamorphoses*[1] and the *Testament of Solomon*, fail as adequate evidence of a στοιχεῖα cult in the first century CE. In the former, the protagonist of the text, Lucius, faces the elements (Latin *elementa*) during his initiation into the Isis rites, as he makes his spiritual journey from death to rebirth as an immortal being (11.23). In that same passage, Lucius worships the infernal and celestial gods, which leads Dibelius to conclude that the elements, too, receive Lucius's

---

1. Dibelius, 'Isis Initiation', pp. 61-65, 74-78.

devotion. To support this conclusion, Dibelius cites the parallelism in a prayer to Isis (11.25)—'the gods rejoice, the elements serve'—as confirmation that the elements were conceived of as deities.[1] Yet neither the prayer nor the initiation identify the elements as gods. Lucius's movement or migration through the elements may be nothing more than the assault of the initiate by trials of water, fire, earth, or air, for such practices were common in mystery initiations.[2] As for the prayer, Apuleius does not seem to be deifying the elements as much as he is listing the various denizens and components of the cosmos that respond to Isis's commands: 'the stars move to your order, the seasons return, the gods rejoice, the elements serve. At your nod the breezes blow, clouds collect, seeds sprout, blossoms increase'. Isis is mistress of the universe, including the elements (2.28; 11.4), and Apuleius employs literary personification in Lucius's prayer to Isis to depict the obedience of every aspect of the world to her. It is unlikely, therefore, that Apuleius or the Isis devotees he portrays regarded the elements as divine entities.

Dibelius, conscious of the century-long gap between Apuleius and Colossians, introduced other texts to support his position.[3] By far the most important is a citation from the *Testament of Solomon*. At one point in that document, Solomon summons seven spirits or δαίμονες before him and commands them to identify themselves (8.1-2). They respond in this way: 'we are (the) elements, world rulers of the darkness' (ἡμεῖς ἐσμεν στοιχεῖα κοσμοκράτορες τοῦ σκότους) Here, then, is solid evidence for Dibelius's contention that the στοιχεῖα were thought of as animate cosmic rulers. Quite naturally the text connects these cosmic tyrants with fate and the coercive influence of the celestial bodies: one has the name Clotho and all have stars representing them (8.3-4). It is not far-fetched to think that some in the Greco-Roman world felt compelled to propitiate these entities, though the *Testament of Solomon* portrays Solomon as a manipulator, not worshiper, of them.

As indicative as this passage is of what the στοιχεῖα could denote, the uncertainty surrounding its date of composition limits its

1. Dibelius, 'Isis Initiation', p. 78.
2. G. Griffiths, *Apuleius of Madauros: The Isis-Book ('Metamorphoses', Book XI)* (EPRO, 39; Leiden: Brill, 1975), p. 302.
3. Dibelius and Greeven, *An die Kolosser*, pp. 27-29. See also Dibelius, *Geisterwelt*, p. 230.

3. Interpreting the Polemical Core in Colossians

pertinence to the interpretation of στοιχεῖα in Colossians. It is crucial to Dibelius's reading of Colossians to know not just *that* but also *when* the στοιχεῖα became divinized, but the *Testament of Solomon* cannot provide a firm answer. C. McCown, who compiled the standard edition of the *Testament of Solomon*, favored a third-century CE date, although he offered a range of dates in which it could have fallen, from 100 to 400 CE.[1] Even if it falls early in that range, the *Testament of Solomon* obviously came some time after Colossians, a fact confirmed by its dependence on NT expressions. Both the references to the κοσμοκράτορες τοῦ σκότους in 8.2 and to the κοσμοκράτορες τοῦ σκότους τοῦ αἰῶνος τούτου in 18.2 appear to rely on the phrase κοσμοκράτορας τοῦ σκότους τούτου in Eph. 6.12, and the series ἀρχαὶ καὶ ἐξουσίαι καὶ δυνάμεις of *T. Sol.* 20.15 seems to mirror the phrase πάσης ἀρχῆς καὶ ἐξουσίας καὶ δυνάμεως of Eph. 1.21.[2] These signs of dependence date the *Testament of Solomon* to a period subsequent to the NT, which indicates the document's limited value for interpreting what the στοιχεῖα mean in Colossians.

Bornkamm is no more successful than Dibelius in documenting the divination and worship of the στοιχεῖα in the first century CE because the two sources he cites are as late or inconclusive as Dibelius's.[3] In the so-called *Mithras Liturgy*, a supplicant seeks immortality for his only son with a prayer invoking, among many other things, fire, water, air, and earthly substance (*PGM* 4.475ff.). Bornkamm asserts that these elements had a divine aspect, for in or by means of them—noteworthy is the reference to immortal water (τῷ ἀθανάτῳ ὕδατι [4.507])—the initiate is transformed into a divine and incorruptible being. In the *Corpus Hermeticum* (13.11; cf. 13.20), the initiate and now-divinized protagonist Tat enjoys a vision of the cosmos in which he realizes that he is in all things, including ἐν γῇ, ἐν ὕδατι, and ἐν ἀέρι. Following the interpretive lead of R. Reitzenstein,[4] Bornkamm

---

1. C. McCown (ed.), *The Testament of Solomon* (UNT, 9; Leipzig: Hinrichs, 1922), pp. 106-108. See also Charlesworth (ed.), *Old Testament Pseudepigrapha*, I, pp. 940-43. McCown detects a core of first-century CE Palestinian material in the *Testament of Solomon*, but he does not include ch. 8 in this early stratum (pp. 86-89).
2. McCown (ed.), *Testament of Solomon*, pp. 68, 107.
3. Bornkamm, 'Heresy of Colossians', pp. 127-29.
4. R. Reitzenstein, *Hellenistic Mystery-Religions: Their Basic Ideas and Significance* (PTMS, 15; Pittsburgh: Pickwick, 1978), pp. 47-50, 200-208.

finds in this realization confirmation that the elements impart immortality and are themselves divine.

How likely is Bornkamm's understanding of the στοιχεῖα τοῦ κόσμου? The meaning of Tat's vision in the *Hermetica* is uncertain and can only be pressed into service if the interpreter accepts Reitzenstein's elaborate arguments which depend heavily on Iranian and Mandaean sources. Few have chosen to do so; Reitzenstein cannot claim much support. The so-called *Mithras Liturgy* seems to be clearer about the divinity of what could be called στοιχεῖα, but the Greek magical papyri, to which the *Liturgy* belongs, postdates Colossians by at least a century, perhaps two. Perhaps more disconcerting to those inclined toward Bornkamm's reading is the letter writer's failure to contest in any way the philosophy's claim of deification, which presumably would have been the goal of initiation into the στοιχεῖα cult at Colossae. It is inconceivable that the author would not have focused his attack on such an assertion, if it had actually been made.

A second flaw in the Jewish-Gnostic thesis lies in its failure to justify its identification of the στοιχεῖα with angels. H. Schlier's interpretation of the στοιχεῖα in Galatians presents the best argument for identification, in part because he relies on *1 Enoch,* a writing completed in all probability before Colossians.[1] Throughout *1 Enoch,* Schlier contends, one finds 'an especially close relationship between the stars and the elements, on the one hand, and the stars and angels or spirits, on the other'.[2] At 69.20-24, the heavenly bodies and the spirits of the water and the winds are grouped and personified as agents obedient to the Lord of the Spirits. At 60.11-24, as the angel informs the seer about the structure and the nature of the world, we are told

---

1. The most important passages for Schlier's argument come from the *Similitudes* (chs. 31–71), a section that may be late relative to the rest of *1 Enoch* but is still from the first century CE, according to Charlesworth (ed.), *Old Testament Pseudepigrapha*, I, p. 7. J. Milik's argument for a late (270 CE) Christian provenance for the *Similitudes* (*The Books of Enoch: Aramaic Fragments of Qumran Cave 4* [Oxford: Clarendon Press, 1976], p. 96) has found no support from scholars, most of whom consider it a first-century CE Jewish work (J. Charlesworth, 'The SNTS Pseudepigrapha Seminars at Tübingen and Paris on the Books of Enoch', *NTS* 25 [1978–79], p. 322).

2. H. Schlier, *Der Brief an die Galater* (MeyerK, 7; Göttingen: Vandenhoeck & Ruprecht, 11th edn, 1951), pp. 134-35.

that a spirit controls each of the natural phenomena, such as lightning, thunder, mist, and frost, all of which are also monitored by angels. These connections are evidence enough for Schlier to conclude that the various components of the natural world, what could loosely be called the στοιχεῖα, were regarded as ruling angelic or astral spirits.

The interpreter should not, however, mistake association for identification. True, at one point *1 Enoch* joins what it usually holds apart. At 60.17, the spirit of a natural phenomenon and the associated angel come together: 'The frost-wind [spirit] is its own angel and the hail-wind [spirit] is a kind of angel'. Nonetheless, the natural phenomena themselves are never portrayed as angels; *1 Enoch* never confuses the spirit *behind* a natural feature with the feature itself. And more important, *1 Enoch* never identifies any group of natural phenomena or features as the elements. This is a connection Schlier makes by pushing στοιχεῖα beyond its normal use as a reference to the basic constituents of the physical realm.

In Colossians, too, the elements and angels are associated, but the letter writer never identifies the στοιχεῖα with the ἄγγελοι. On the contrary, he gives the interpreter good reason for holding them apart. According to my exegesis, the use of στοιχεῖα τοῦ κόσμου in conjunction with κόσμος and the prepositions ἀπό and ἐν in Col. 2.20 indicates that the στοιχεῖα denote a sphere of existence or arena of activity formed and defined by the στοιχεῖα. Understood as cosmogonic or cosmological principles, the στοιχεῖα appear to have provided the intellectual basis of the Colossian philosophy. For the phrase φιλοσοφία κατὰ τὰ στοιχεῖα τοῦ κόσμου suggests that the στοιχεῖα are foundational and determinative for the philosophy; they are its epistemological principles. As such, the στοιχεῖα are not to be regarded as objects of worship. To exchange the στοιχεῖα for the ἄγγελοι is to ignore the letter writer's choice of φιλοσοφία κατὰ τὰ στοιχεῖα rather than φιλοσοφία τῶν στοιχείων, and θρησκεία τῶν ἀγγέλων, not θρησκεία κατὰ τοὺς ἀγγέλους.

Not only is the Jewish-Gnostic thesis's case for a στοιχεῖα/angel cult weak, its argument that the cult took the form of a mystery also lacks support. My exegesis considered the appearance of ἐμβατεύω (Col. 2.18b) as a reference to mystery initiation but rejected it for the following reason: taking ἐμβατεύω in its figurative sense—'investigating deeply'—saved the interpreter from extensive speculation about what one enters if ἐμβατεύω is taken literally. There is no good reason for classifying the Colossian philosophy as a mystery religion if the crucial piece of evidence for it is ambiguous, and another interpretation of that evidence lessens the need to speculate.

Lyonnet's criticism of Dibelius highlights the ambiguity of the term ἐμβατεύω both in and outside Colossians. That ἐμβατεύω appeared in Colossians was evidence enough for Dibelius that the Colossian philosophy practiced mystery initiation, because in Dibelius's opinion the term clearly referred to initiation in the second-century inscriptions at the Apollo oracle at Claros, a site close to Colossae.[1] But Lyonnet undermined the certainty of Dibelius's reasoning in his examination of the Claros inscriptions. He observed that ἐμβατεύω always appeared with μυέω or παραλαμβάνω τὰ μυστήρια at Claros.[2] In other words, ἐμβατεύω denoted initiation at Claros because it always occurred with language that unequivocally referred to initiation. This observation underscores the absence of language referring unequivocally to initiation or mystery at Colossae and thereby points to the great leap the interpreter must make in order to join Dibelius. It is not sound method to posit the existence of a mystery cult at Colossae on the basis of a word whose cultic, technical force is established only in conjunction with other words, words that fail to come from the letter writer's hand.

Placing στοιχεῖα worship against a Gnostic background constitutes the final and perhaps most serious weakness in the Jewish-Gnostic thesis. The difficulty began decades ago in the disagreement between the two major proponents of the thesis, Dibelius and Bornkamm, as to whether the στοιχεῖα were world-ruling tyrants (Gnostic archons) that demanded worship (Dibelius) or bearers of the divine fullness (Bornkamm). Making matters worse is that even with our increasing knowledge of Gnosticism, neither understanding of the στοιχεῖα can be located there. Simply put, in the Nag Hammadi documents the στοιχεῖα play neither the role of divinities nor world-ruling powers, positively or negatively understood.

The best that proponents of Bornkamm's position have been able to do is to argue that certain Nag Hammadi tractates do not cast the world-ruling powers in a hostile role.[3] The two documents Moyo

1. Dibelius, 'Isis Initiation', pp. 86-90.
2. Lyonnet, 'L'épître aux Colossiens', pp. 425-26. See also Nock, 'Vocabulary of the New Testament', p. 132.
3. Moyo, 'Colossian Heresy', p. 34.

3. Interpreting the Polemical Core in Colossians

cites, however, *Eugnostos the Blessed* and *Sophia of Jesus Christ*, hardly hold the cosmic powers in high regard. Even as *Eugnostos* describes the emanation of the perfect and good powers from the divine begetter, we learn that their procession from the divine 'revealed the defect of femaleness' (III, 3.85.5-10), an apparent reference to the genesis of evil through Sophia. *Sophia of Jesus Christ*, a later, Christianized version of the text on which *Eugnostos* is also based,[1] elaborates on the connection between divine emanation and the genesis of imperfection through the female element (III, 4.106.10-107.13). In this second text, the cosmic powers *arrogantly* and *ignorantly* claim to be gods (III, 4.118.20-25). This negative picture of the world-ruling powers in *Sophia of Jesus Christ* and the mixed picture of them in *Eugnostos*[2] hardly assure the interpreter that Moyo has found a correspondence in Gnostic material to the divinity-bearing στοιχεῖα of the Colossian philosophy.

Proponents of Dibelius's understanding of the στοιχεῖα/angels have had no better success in documenting their interpretation in the Nag Hammadi finds. Schenke joins Dibelius in regarding the στοιχεῖα/angels as archons, as evil cosmic rulers. True Gnostics, he argues, must resist them as enemies, but they may do so openly or covertly. The latter is what the Colossian philosophers have chosen to do, humiliating themselves (ταπεινοφροσύνη) before the archons as a means of camouflaging their true intent. Such is the letter writer's poor understanding of them that he sees and attacks only the superficial, that is, the worship of the στοιχεῖα/angels.[3]

To substantiate the twists and turns of his argument, Schenke attempts to find this feigned archon worship articulated in Gnostic thought. This turns out, however, to be a difficult task. Referring first to the Nag Hammadi material, Schenke cites a portion of the *Hypostasis of the Archons* (II, 4.92-93), where the arrogant Ruler claims his due service from Norea, the Gnostic protagonist of this tractate. As an overlord of this benighted realm, it was his prerogative to insist on subservience or worship from all those living in his realm, and Schenke makes much of it. But Norea's response expresses neither

---

1. J. Robinson (ed.), *The Nag Hammadi Library in English* (New York: HarperCollins, rev. edn, 1990), p. 220.
2. Kiley describes the view of the powers in *Eugnostos* as neutral (*Colossians as Pseudepigraphy*, p. 62).
3. Schenke, 'Widerstreit', p. 395.

submission nor obedience, feigned or otherwise. She refuses to serve the Ruler and cries instead for aid from the True God, a reaction that Schenke fails to mention.

Equally unconvincing is Schenke's argument that the well-known Gnostic libertinism would have made the worship of the archons likely. True, Gnosticism could engender a complete indifference to outward behavior, since it placed so much emphasis on knowledge and inner disposition and so greatly devalued the body. Irenaeus, for example, goes on at length about the reckless excesses of his opponents (*Adv. Haer.* 1.6.3; 1.24.5). Theoretically, then, Gnostics could indulge in any type of immoral or forbidden practice, even the worship of the despised powers of darkness, without endangering their real selves or their salvation. But Schenke cannot produce a single instance of a Gnostic group actually expressing its freedom in such worship. In other words, his argument substantiates a possibility but no more.

A more recent version of Schenke's argument comes from Pokorný, who recognizes a range of perspectives on the archons expressed in the Nag Hammadi treatises. Whatever the various Gnostic groups' dispositions toward them, he argues, the archons figured prominently in all Gnostic speculation, and this preoccupation with them might have been 'viewed from the outside and critically' as veneration of angels.[1] This interpretation skirts the difficulties in Schenke's and Moyo's interpretation of specific texts, but in doing so it rests on possibility, which makes it no more convincing than earlier efforts.

Hellenistic-Syncretistic Reconstructions. In the last two to three decades, several scholars loyal to the line of interpretation articulated by Dibelius and Bornkamm have dropped any argument for Gnostic influence at Colossae. No longer proponents of the full Jewish-Gnostic reconstruction, these scholars examine the Colossian philosophy as a product of Hellenistic syncretism. But although they bypass some of the problems troubling the Jewish-Gnostic thesis, their adherence to key portions of Dibelius's and Bornkamm's arguments makes them heirs to a host of interpretive problems.

Hegermann, for instance, makes no attempt at holding on to a Gnostic element in the philosophy, arguing instead that element worship precludes a Gnostic orientation. Nevertheless, he follows Dibelius in

1. Pokorný, *Colossians*, pp. 117-20.

3. Interpreting the Polemical Core in Colossians 87

finding a mystery religion focused on angel worship at Colossae. And in line with Bornkamm, he turns to the *Mithras Liturgy* as the document offering the closest parallels to the Colossian mystery, although he obviously no longer reads it as an example of Gnostic thought.[1] Because of this loyalty, he is subject to many of the criticisms of Dibelius and Bornkamm I have already presented. I mention only two: first, the equivocal ἐμβατεύω hardly provides a solid basis for supposing that the letter writer grapples with a mystery initiation at Colossae; and second, the *Mithras Liturgy* significantly postdates Colossians and describes the process of an initiate's deification that surely would have been combated by the letter writer, *if* the philosophy's piety had really mirrored such an initiation.

In addition to the shortcomings inherited from its intellectual predecessor, the Jewish-Gnostic reconstruction, the Hellenistic syncretism reading consistently fails, in all its versions, to account for how the particular blend of elements in the Colossian philosophy arose. Lähnemann, for instance, has little trouble locating possible sources for the philosophy's practices and character: its mystery religion structure came from Greece, its element worship from Persia, its Jewish practices from Palestine, and so forth.[2] But beyond presenting Colossae as the likely meeting place of Eastern and Western ideas, he does little to explain how elements from such diverse traditions made sense (and thus came) together. Nor does Lähnemann describe a social setting that would not simply have allowed contact but fostered a merger between various religions.

The same failing characterizes Kraabel's analysis.[3] In describing the Colossian philosophy as a syncretistic brand of Anatolian Judaism, he must do more than document the emergence of an angel cult in first-century Asia Minor. He must also explain why the Colossian Jews would have incorporated such a cult into their religious life. Given Judaism's monotheistic inclination, Kraabel's suggestion that the well-attested Jewish speculation about angels at that time would have engendered angel worship seems unlikely. L. Williams's very thorough turn-of-the-century study of angel worship could prove no such cause and effect, and L. Hurtado's recent review of the evidence reached the same conclusion. While angelology flourished, Jewish

1. Hegermann, *Vorstellung vom Schöpfungsmittler*, pp. 161, 163.
2. Lähnemann, *Kolosserbrief*, pp. 82-100.
3. Kraabel, 'Judaism in Western Asia Minor', pp. 141-48.

worship of angels was nonexistent.[1] Nevertheless, Kraabel's study is instructive because of the emphasis he places on local (Phrygian) religious tendencies for illuminating the Colossian philosophy.

An Analysis of Schweizer's Interpretation
In the writings of Schweizer, which include many articles and a commentary on Colossians,[2] the interpreter finds the most recent significant interpretation of the Colossian philosophy. The importance of his reconstruction lies in the fact that he introduces a bona fide alternative to both the purely Jewish and Jewish-Gnostic readings, an alternative he articulates in greater depth than any other scholar. In doing so he brings to the interpreter's attention a Hellenistic philosophical text whose focus on the στοιχεῖα, food regulations, proper worship, purification, and asceticism has much in common with the Colossian philosophy. Nevertheless, several weaknesses attend his interpretation of the Colossian philosophy as a form of Pythagoreanism, characterized by a legalistic and radically ascetic praxis formulated to free the philosopher from the στοιχεῖα and the dangerously chaotic world they define: first, he ignores the Jewish element in the Colossian philosophy; second, he too readily accepts the claim of ancient sources to represent Pythagoreanism; and third, the decidedly pessimistic philosophical world-view he finds dominating the NT period is not as pervasive as he insists.

Perhaps the most noticeable deficiency, if not the most problematic, is Schweizer's underestimation of Jewish influence on the Colossian philosophy,[3] a tendency his work shares with other German scholarship on the subject, such as the analysis of Dibelius. This failing is

1. L. Williams, 'The Cult of Angels at Colossae', *JTS* OS 10 (1909), p. 432; L. Hurtado, *One God, One Lord: Early Christian Devotion and Ancient Jewish Monotheism* (Philadelphia: Fortress Press, 1988), pp. 24-35.
2. E. Schweizer, 'Altes und Neues zu den "Elementen der Welt" in Kol 2,20; Gal 4,3.9', in K. Aland and S. Meurer (eds.), *Wissenschaft und Kirche: Festschrift für Eduard Lohse* (Texte und Arbeiten zur Bibel, 4; Bielefeld: Luther-Verlag, 1989), pp. 111-18; 'Askese nach Kol 1,24 oder 2,20?', in H. Merklein (ed.), *Neues Testament und Ethik: Für Rudolf Schnackenburg* (Freiburg: Herder, 1989), pp. 340-48; *Der Brief an die Kolosser*; 'Christ in the Letter'; 'Christianity of the Circumcised'; '"Elemente der Welt"'; *Letter to the Colossians*; 'Slaves of the Elements'; 'Versöhnung des Alls. Kol 1,20'; 'Zur neueren Forschung am Kolosserbrief (seit 1970)'.
3. Schweizer, *Letter to the Colossians*, p. 128.

3. Interpreting the Polemical Core in Colossians

striking since Schweizer depends on Philo's equation between angels and heroes or demons to bring the philosophy's Jewish-sounding θρησκεία τῶν ἀγγέλων into Hellenistic pagan parlance. What evidently led him to underplay Jewish influence is the polemic's attribution of the philosophy to *human* tradition and its regulations to *human* commands and teachings.[1] Yet, if my exegesis is correct, such a polemical line in the NT typically occurs in disputes between competing *religious* claims and says nothing accurate about the position under attack. This polemical assertion in Colossians does not, therefore, give grounds for locating the Colossian philosophy and its regulations in a philosophical rather than religious tradition.

Even in the mention of Sabbath observance (Col. 2.16) Schweizer finds no more than an isolated and vestigial reference to Judaism. Because the rigorous discipline depicted in ch. 2 matches so closely and completely that of his Pythagorean sources, Schweizer categorizes this lone reference to Jewish practice as an example of Pythagorized Judaism, what Ignatius later attacked as a 'Judaism of the uncircumcised' (*Phld.* 6.1).[2] But what Schweizer fails to note is that the *entire* list of holy days at 2.16 echoes the enumeration of Jewish holy days in the LXX (Hos. 2.13; 1 Chron. 23.31; 2 Chron. 2.3; 31.3), which indicates that Jewish practice is more central to the philosophy than Schweizer cares to admit.

If the Ignatian phrase 'Judaism of the uncircumcised' referred to a kind of pagan legalism, that would strengthen Schweizer's case for a philosophical legalism at Colossae. This expression and the mention of strange doctrines and old myths elsewhere in Ignatius (*Magn.* 8.1) Schweizer regards as unusual and unlikely references to Judaism.[3] Hence, he attributes these myths and doctrines to non-Jewish origins and finds behind the phrase 'uncircumcised Judaism' a non-Jewish tradition known for its strict discipline and legalism, namely, Pythagoreanism.[4] The contexts of these expressions hardly allow such a

---

1. Schweizer, *Letter to the Colossians*, p. 127.
2. Schweizer, 'Christianity of the Circumcised', pp. 245, 249.
3. Schweizer, 'Christianity of the Circumcised', p. 246.
4. Lending support to this conclusion would be M. Nilsson, who saw in Pythagoreanism a pronounced legalistic element (*Geschichte der griechischen Religion* [Handbuch der Altertumswissenschaft 5.2.1-2; 2 vols.; Munich: Beck, 3rd edn, 1967–74], I, pp. 707-708). See also W. Burkert, *Greek Religion* (Cambridge, MA: Harvard University Press, 1985), pp. 302-303.

reading, however. At *Magn.* 8.1 Ignatius is expressly engaged in warning his readers about Judaism, or more specifically, life according to Judaism. Elsewhere in early Christian literature, when writers sound the alarm over myths, the position combated appears to have a significant Jewish component (1 Tim. 1.3-7, esp. vv. 4 and 7; 4.7; 2 Tim. 4.4; Tit. 1.14; 3.9). As for *Phld.* 6.1, those whom Ignatius attacks appear to be Gentiles (the uncircumcised) who have adopted and now advocate certain Jewish practices and traditions.[1] Schweizer fails to make a case, therefore, for an early Christian problem with *pagan* legalism.

The need to correct Schweizer and supplement his proposed background for the philosophy with a Jewish component becomes even more pressing when the interpreter comes to grips with the term ταπεινοφροσύνη, which my exegesis placed at the center of the philosophy. The earliest Christians' high regard for humility rested in all probability on the positive attitude of Jewish tradition toward humility in general. In contrast to this, the term invariably had a negative connotation in Greek thought, where it referred to meanspiritedness (Epictetus, *Diss.* 3.24.56; cf. 2.8.15).[2] The latter background, therefore, does not provide much assistance in accounting for the term's positive and prominent place in the philosophy. Perhaps in order to avoid invoking a Jewish background, Schweizer identifies ταπεινοφροσύνη as fasting and thus can root it in a Greek tradition advocating such a practice.[3] Francis, too, made this equation, albeit for different reasons. Nowhere in the NT, however, does the term point to a specific practice, as my critique of Francis noted, so Schweizer must still face a term that is central to the philosophy but could not have come from a pagan background.

Making room in Schweizer's proposal for a Jewish component

1. L. Gaston, 'Judaism of the Uncircumcised in Ignatius and Related Writers', in S.G. Wilson (ed.), *Anti-Judaism in Early Christianity.* II. *Separation and Polemic* (Studies in Judaism and Christianity, 2; Waterloo: Wilfrid Laurier University, 1986), pp. 36-38; C. Roetzel, *The Letters of Paul* (Atlanta: John Knox, 1975), p. 54; C. Barrett, 'Jews and Judaizers in the Epistles of Ignatius', in Hamerton-Kelly and Scroggs (eds.), *Jews, Greeks and Christians*, pp. 220-34; W. Schoedel, *Ignatius of Antioch* (Hermeneia; Philadelphia: Fortress Press, 1985), p. 202.

2. W. Grundmann, 'ταπεινός, ταπεινόω, ταπείνωσις, ταπεινόφρων, ταπεινοφροσύνη', *TDNT*, VIII, pp. 5, 11; K. Wengst, *Humility: Solidarity of the Humiliated* (Philadelphia: Fortress Press, 1988), pp. 2, 4.

3. Schweizer, *Letter to the Colossians*, p. 127.

3. Interpreting the Polemical Core in Colossians 91

might not jeopardize his proposed interpretation, but a more intractable difficulty clings to his analysis of the philosophical climate contemporary with the NT and his classification of the Colossian philosophy as Pythagorean. The first hint of trouble appears in a close examination of the text upon which he places so much emphasis: the epitome of Pythagorean doctrine composed by Alexander Polyhistor in the first century BCE and preserved in Diogenes Laertius's *Lives of Eminent Philosophers* (8.25-33).[1] The text is called the *Hypomnemata* because it opens with Polyhistor's claim to be drawing from Pythagorean memoirs (ὑπομνήματα; *D.L.* 8.25). Schweizer's unreserved use of it as evidence for first-century BCE Pythagoreanism belies the longstanding and unresolved debate over its dating, composition, and philosophical orientation.

Schweizer's statements about the *Hypomnemata* reflect but one scholarly interpretation of the passage. To a great degree he follows the position argued by E. Zeller, M. Pohlenz, and others who placed it in the last quarter of the second century or in the first century BCE and thought it signaled the revival of Pythagoreanism at that time.[2] Schweizer clearly acknowledges the eclectic flavor that this line of scholarship attributed to Hellenistic philosophy and especially neo-Pythagoreanism when, in talking about the στοιχεῖα, he articulates a physics of the mundane realm with which all the schools came to grips. Moreover, he groups Pythagoreans and Platonists and links the adjectives Empedoclean and Pythagorean when he refers to this common view of the sublunar world.[3]

---

1. Schweizer regularly cites the text in the standard but less widely available edition, H. Diels and W. Kranz (eds.), *Die Fragmente der Vorsokratiker* (3 vols.; Berlin: Wiedmann, 6th edn, 1951–52), I, p. 448 l. 33 to p. 451 l. 19.

2. E. Zeller, *Die Philosophie der Griechen in ihrer geschichtlichen Entwicklung* (3 vols.; Leipzig: Reisland, 1920–23), III.2, pp. 92-108; M. Pohlenz, *Die Stoa: Geschichte einer geistigen Bewegung* (2 vols.; Göttingen: Vandenhoeck & Ruprecht, 1948–49), I, p. 386; Nilsson, *Geschichte der griechischen Religion*, II, pp. 415-16; A. Schmekel, *Die Philosophie der mittleren Stoa in ihrem geschichtlichen Zusammenhange* (repr.; New York: Olms, 1974 [1892]), pp. 428-34; I. Lévy, *Recherches sur les sources de la légende de Pythagore* (Bibliothèque de l'école des hautes études, sciences religieuses, 42; Paris: Leroux, 1926), pp. 75, 82, 148. At one point Schweizer departs from this line of thought when he notes that the first-century text reproduces fourth-century BCE Pythagorean material ('"Elemente der Welt"', p. 257 n. 70).

3. Schweizer, *Letter to the Colossians*, p. 133; 'Zur neueren Forschung am

Even if he could gather a consensus behind this understanding of neo-Pythagoreanism and the *Hypomnemata*, Schweizer would still face a serious complication in his interpretation. The line of scholarship he follows reaches conclusions regarding the *Hypomnemata* that undermine his basic assumption about the text: the centrality of Pythagorean thought in it. For, if the *Hypomnemata* is Hellenistic and represents neo-Pythagoreanism, then the text, like the age and school reborn at that time, is markedly eclectic. The composite nature of the *Hypomnemata* is nowhere more exhaustively detailed than in a lengthy article by A.-J. Festugière. He concludes that the passage draws from diverse sources, most of which are Platonic, but that there is no Pythagorean source behind the document at all.[1] These observations confirm Zeller's contention that neo-Pythagoreanism stood a great distance from traditional Pythagoreanism, and they support a history of Pythagoreanism which pictures it dying out in the fourth century BCE and re-emerging later only with a massive infusion of non-Pythagorean thought.[2]

Proponents and critics of this historical reconstruction both note the absence of salient Pythagorean features in a text that purports to summarize Pythagorean doctrine. In its discussion of first principles (*D.L.* 8.25) the *Hypomnemata* fails to mention the even and the odd, male and female, and limit and unlimited (πέρας, ἄπειρος), all important cosmogonic pairs in Pythagorean thought, according to Aristotle (*Metaph.* 1.5.5-6 [986a: 20-27]). When the epitome places the earth at the center of the universe (*D.L.* 8.25), this contradicts the Pythagorean notion of a central fire circled by the earth and an antiearth. In addition, the ascetic practices enjoined at the end of the passage (8.33) do not include some acknowledged Pythagorean prescriptions, such as celibacy, and do not strictly enforce others, such as the complete abstinence from meat.[3] Such observations place the

---

Kolosserbrief (seit 1970)', pp. 177, 179; 'Versöhnung des Alls. Kol 1,20', p. 498.

1. A.-J. Festugière, 'Les "mémoires pythagoriques" cités par Alexandre Polyhistor', *Revue des études grecques* 58 (1945), pp. 58-59. Festugière recommends that the *Hypomnemata* be removed from the category it occupies ('Pythagorean School') in Diels and Kranz (eds.), *Die Fragmente der Vorsokratiker*.

2. Zeller, *Philosophie der Griechen*, III.2, pp. 92, 107; *Outlines of the History of Greek Philosophy* (revised by W. Nestle; New York: Dover, 13th edn, 1980), p. 280. Unlike Festugière, Zeller sees Stoic thought dominating the *Hypomnemata*.

3. W. Burkert, *Lore and Science in Ancient Pythagoreanism* (Cambridge, MA:

3. Interpreting the Polemical Core in Colossians

Pythagorean character of the *Hypomnemata* into serious doubt.

A school of interpretation taking issue with Zeller's version of Pythagorean history and his view of the *Hypomnemata* exists, and it may in fact be more congenial with Schweizer's use of that text. But to refute Zeller, scholars must turn to testimonies of a relatively late date to verify that an idea is Pythagorean, an exercise that is decidedly perilous. Those attacking this practice, such as W. Burkert, point to the tendency among Greek writers beginning in the Hellenistic period to ascribe Aristotelian, Stoic, and especially Platonic and Academic doctrine to Pythagoras or his school. As a case in point, Burkert examines the provenance of the first principles in the *Hypomnemata*, the monad and the indefinite dyad. By the end of the second century CE, Sextus Empiricus could confidently assign the theory of the monad and indefinite dyad to Pythagoras himself (*Math.* 10.261). In contrast to this, Aristotle distinguishes Plato's position from the Pythagorean by attributing the supposition of a dyad solely to the former (*Metaph.* 1.6.6 [987b: 23-28]). With regard to the remainder of the opening section of the *Hypomnemata* (8.25), Burkert concludes: 'it is flagrantly contradictory to everything that Aristotle ascribes to the Pythagoreans... On the other hand, every aspect corresponds to the system of derivation which Aristotle ascribes to Plato and his pupils, in distinction from the Pythagoreans'. He is equally skeptical about a Pythagorean background for the other parts of the epitome he treats.[1]

Burkert's analysis is not without its detractors, but many of his observations and much of his method find ready support among scholars of ancient philosophy. W. Guthrie would agree with Burkert in his stress on the importance of Aristotle in establishing genuine Pythagorean thought and in his wariness about the reliability of later authorities.[2] As for the Pythagorizing tendencies of the Hellenistic and Roman periods, several scholars have noted the very same phenomenon.[3]

Harvard University Press, 1972), p. 58; A. Delatte (ed.), *La vie de Pythagore de Diogène Laërce: Edition critique avec introduction et commentaire* (Morals and Law in Ancient Greece; repr.; New York: Arno, 1979 [1922]), pp. 204, 232; Zeller, *Philosophie der Griechen*, III.2, p. 108; W. Guthrie, *A History of Greek Philosophy* (6 vols.; Cambridge: Cambridge University Press, 1962–1981), I, pp. 278–82.

1. Burkert, *Ancient Pythagoreanism*, pp. 35, 53-59, 73-75, 82.
2. Guthrie, *History of Greek Philosophy*, I, pp. 155-56.
3. For example, W. Ross, *Plato's Theory of Ideas* (Oxford: Clarendon Press,

If Burkert's analysis is essentially correct, then the line of scholarship that finds Pythagorean thought well represented in the *Hypomnemata* founders, and Zeller and Festugière are largely vindicated. When he composed the *Hypomnemata*, therefore, Alexander Polyhistor did not take care to preserve or summarize authentic Pythagorean ideas but followed the trend of his day by incorporating Platonic and other non-Pythagorean doctrine under the name of the Pythagoreans.

What impact does this understanding of the *Hypomnemata* have on Schweizer? Seemingly very little, since he openly acknowledges the eclectic flavor of Hellenistic philosophy and finds the notion of sublunar instability and the resulting struggle to overcome it alive in more than just Pythagorean thought. Plutarch, too, a good Platonist, could write that the four στοιχεῖα have produced a realm of continual becoming and destruction (*Is. et Os.* 63 [376D]) and that the soul that successfully escaped from this to the upper regions beyond the moon had returned home, as if from banishment (*Fac. Lun.* 28 [943C-D]). Hence, Schweizer could simply surrender his assessment of the *Hypomnemata* as Pythagorean. By doing so he would abandon the philosophical tradition most noted for its ascetic and legalistic tendencies[1] and thus most promising as the background for the Colossian philosophy's prescriptions. But if the *Hypomnemata* is Platonic, then Schweizer could presumably locate the Colossian philosophy in that tradition.

As troubling as Schweizer's incautious use of the *Hypomnemata* is his sweeping portrayal of the philosophical climate in the NT period.[2] Central to his interpretation of the Colossian philosophy and the *Hypomnemata* is his picture of a markedly pessimistic outlook that pervaded Hellenistic thought: apprehension about the chaotic nature of the mundane world, rooted in the notion of continual conflict among the στοιχεῖα, and prompting a flight from the realm of the στοιχεῖα to the stability and peace of the celestial realm. But do the *Hypomnemata* and the Colossian philosophy actually reflect this fear and rejection of the mundane realm? Do they encourage flight from it?

It is not at all clear in the *Hypomnemata* that the warring στοιχεῖα

1951), p. 187; J. Dillon, *The Middle Platonists: 80 BC to AD 220* (Ithaca, NY: Cornell University Press, 1977), pp. 37-38, 118-19.

1. Nilsson, *Geschichte der griechischen Religion*, I, pp. 707-708.
2. Schweizer, *Letter to the Colossians*, pp. 130-31. See also *idem*, '"Elemente der Welt"', pp. 252-56; 'Versöhnung des Alls. Kol 1,20', pp. 493-99.

have rendered the world so hopelessly chaotic that the only response that can be made is an unqualified rejection of, and flight from, it. Admittedly, the *Hypomnemata* gives hints of this severe pessimism: the inhabitants of the earth live in stagnant air and are mortal, but those of the uppermost air enjoy pure and healthy surroundings and are immortal (*D.L.* 8.26); the soul comes from an immortal source (8.28) and becomes bound to the body by veins, arteries, and sinews (8.31); and at death the pure are escorted to the uppermost region but the impure face bondage (8.31). On the other hand, at many points a very different picture emerges: the στοιχεῖα combine to produce an animate, intelligent, spherical universe in which the opposites are in equal proportion and are regularly in equilibrium (8.25-26); the heat and light of the divine realm penetrate to the depths of the cosmos and give life (8.27), an indication of continuity between the upper and lower realms; purification is undertaken not to separate oneself from the shackles of the body and the earth but in conjunction with the receipt of dreams and signs from the demons (8.32); and human life is to be spent winning the soul to good (8.32), which is hardly a clarion call for flight. Where are the menacing and soul-impeding στοιχεῖα? Where is a world so dangerously fragmented by strife that its very structure and existence is constantly threatened? They are nowhere to be found. While clearly lacking the order and perfection of the celestial realm, the mundane world of the *Hypomnemata* is not so inferior that it has gone out of control or lost its connections with the upper realm. While the *Hypomnemata* may have a dualistic outlook—soul versus body, sublunar world versus celestial world—that dualism is not nearly so antagonistic as Schweizer claims it to be. The soul need not take flight nor any other extraordinary action to ensure its safe ascent to the celestial world at death.

The Colossian philosophy also fails to give clear expression to the marked pessimism Schweizer finds dominating Hellenistic philosophy. The obvious importance of the στοιχεῖα τοῦ κόσμου to the philosophy, for instance, Schweizer understands to be an anxiety about them, because, in his reading of Col. 2.20, they chain humanity to this world.[1] Accordingly, Schweizer finds the Colossian philosophers seeking to escape from this world to a realm above, the latter being the unexpressed object of ἐμβατεύω at 2.18b.[2] But does the polemical

1. Schweizer, *Letter to the Colossians*, p. 127.
2. Schweizer, *Letter to the Colossians*, pp. 133, 161.

core really contain these motifs of apprehension and flight? No. The philosophers may have given great heed to the στοιχεῖα and been guided by them in formulating their praxis (2.8, 20), but there is no sign of enmity toward, or dread of, them. Rather, it is the letter writer who expresses alarm about the importance of the στοιχεῖα to the philosophy (2.8).[1] It is the letter writer who directs the philosophers to another realm when they still consider themselves to be living in this world (2.20; cf. 3.1-2). If the Colossian philosophers had really feared the στοιχεῖα and sought to overcome and flee them, the philosophers would presumably have formulated a φιλοσοφία κατὰ τῶν στοιχείων τοῦ κόσμου—*against* the elements of the world. Instead, the philosophers evidently regarded them as positive principles in the formulation of their thinking and action; theirs is a philosophy κατὰ τὰ στοιχεῖα—*according* to the στοιχεῖα. The pessimism that Schweizer finds in Colossians appears more in the thinking of the letter writer—an antagonism toward the world (2.15) and a pursuit of the realm above (3.2)—than in the scant evidence we have for the philosophy.

Conclusion
Such is my assessment of the previous major reconstructions of the Colossian philosophy. All have their shortcomings, the most significant of which I have now discussed. Several of the weaknesses in other interpretations act as a negative confirmation of the exegetical decisions I made: the failure of Francis and Lyonnet to achieve convincing reconstructions by reading θρησκεία τῶν ἀγγέλων as a subjective genitive makes the objective genitive option I favored that much more appealing, and the problem of finding in ἐμβατεύω clearcut initiation language adds to the probability that the word has the figurative sense I attributed to it.

Besides testing exegetical choices I have reached, this assessment of other reconstructions suggests a direction to any further analysis of the Colossian philosophy because not all the reconstructions are equally deficient. Some problems seem truly intractable. Providing a Gnostic background for the Colossian philosophy, for example, appears to be a hopeless cause. Less problematic, on the other hand, is Schweizer's reconstruction, despite the criticisms I made of it. The Hellenistic

---

1. Moyo, 'Colossian Heresy', p. 35. See also Lyonnet, 'Saint Paul et le gnosticisme', p. 548.

3. Interpreting the Polemical Core in Colossians

philosophical text so central to his interpretation, the *Hypomnemata*, describes a philosophy that corresponds to some extent to the Colossian philosophy. This observation holds even if the text says nothing reliable about Pythagoreanism. Accordingly, of the many exegetical conclusions I reached, those about φιλοσοφία, στοιχεῖα τοῦ κόσμου, the mind's investigative function, and the inevitability of physical dissolution—that they point to a philosophical provenance for the philosophy at Colossae—deserve further attention. Also important is the emphasis that the Hellenistic-syncretistic reconstructions, particularly Kraabel's, placed on the Anatolian setting of the Colossian philosophy.

Chapter 4

THE HISTORICAL AND SOCIAL SETTING OF THE
COLOSSIAN PHILOSOPHY

The exegesis of the polemical core and the critique of reconstructions just undertaken have left the interpreter with a firm grasp on the features of the philosophy and how they are most probably to be understood. Also emerging from the exegesis were indications as to the relative importance of each feature in constructing a coherent picture of the philosophy.

What belongs to the contents and contours of the Colossian philosophy? The most obvious feature of the Colossian philosophy is the praxis it imposes on its adherents: food and calendar regulations (Col. 2.16). Attention to such matters suggests a concern for purity, a preoccupation expressed aptly in the commands quoted from the philosophers in v. 21: '"Do not handle, do not taste, do not touch"'. That the pursuit of purity is instrumental in achieving other goals is suggested in the letter writer's comments on the commands in v. 23. Those commands constitute in part the philosophy's wisdom in achieving an asceticism of the body, correct religious service, and proper humility. The latter two objectives occupy a prominent place in the philosophy. Already in v. 18 we meet the letter writer's condemnation of the philosophy's insistence on θρησκεία τῶν ἀγγέλων and ταπεινοφροσύνη. Worship directed to angels and humility evidently lie at the heart of the philosophy.

Another term occurring twice in the course of the polemical core is τὰ στοιχεῖα τοῦ κόσμου (2.8, 20). Although this may be a phrase that the author of Colossians attaches to his opponents, it aptly describes a feature of the philosophy. The philosophers in some way take as their guiding principles the four elementary components of the cosmos: earth, air, water, and fire. Elsewhere in the polemical core the interpreter catches glimpses of other bases of, or warrants for, the philosophy's practices: first, its insistence on angel worship and

4. *The Historical and Social Setting of the Philosophy* 99

humility appears to rest on a vision or realization, enjoyed by the mind and achieved in the context of careful mental investigation (v. 18); and second, motivating the commands of v. 21 are the notions that all things in this cosmos are destined for corruption (v. 22) and that adherence to such regulations enables one to overcome the indulgence of the flesh (v. 23). Whatever importance these various warrants and reasonings have for the philosophers, the letter writer finds them all to be inadequate, for in each case the motivation for a practice does not come exclusively from Christ (2.19). Thus, he stigmatizes the philosophy as one according to human tradition (v. 8), even though the philosophy shows no evidence of making such a claim, and elsewhere he describes it in religious terms (2.18, 23).

The placement of this cluster of features in a specific historical and social setting—the next step in identifying the philosophers—was necessarily begun in the exegetical work of the previous chapters. In fact, I have already invoked several backgrounds for the proper understanding of the philosophy: (1) mention of the Sabbath assumes a Jewish perspective, (2) ταπεινοφροσύνη was a prized virtue among early Christians, and (3) interest in the στοιχεῖα τοῦ κόσμου understood as a reference to the four elemental constituents of the cosmos puts the interpreter in touch with Greek philosophy. But now undivided attention must be given to locating the probable background for the whole constellation of features deduced by my exegesis. Without this determination a reconstruction lacks plausibility. Even if the Colossian philosophy proves to be syncretistic, it is necessary to locate a context in which such a blending of traditions would have occurred.

The greatest strength of the more convincing reconstructions of the Colossian philosophy lay in their location of a single background for the many features of the philosophy they delineate. Schweizer's analysis in particular proved persuasive because he could locate the major features of the philosophy he isolated—human-based legalism, ascetic self-abasement, and fear of the στοιχεῖα—in one text, an epitome of Pythagorean thinking contemporary with the NT. In the previous chapter I aired my main criticisms of Schweizer's reconstruction, including my objections to his interpretation of that Pythagorean text and the philosophical climate of the NT period. Let me begin my pursuit of a background for the Colossian philosophy by returning to that discussion.

The Philosophical Climate in the New Testament Era

Left unfinished in my critique of Schweizer was an examination of the philosophical milieu at the time of Colossians, a task I will now undertake. Platonism figures prominently in any such presentation because, beginning in the first century BCE and particularly in the first century CE, it enjoyed a renewed vitality and importance in the philosophical culture.[1] This new phase of Platonism, called Middle Platonism, continued into the second century CE and was the chief influence on Plotinus, architect of neo-Platonism. For the two centuries prior to its revival, Platonism and the school representing it, the Academy, had faced rigorous competition from Aristotle and his legacy, the Peripatetics, and from two other schools of Greek thought, the Stoics and the Epicureans. In response to such challenges the Academy resorted to a thoroughgoing skepticism on philosophical issues and consequently fell into relative decline.[2]

The resurgence of Platonism took place for several reasons.[3] A trend in the first century BCE toward the reconciliation and partial harmonization of the various philosophical traditions encouraged a new appreciation of Plato's ideas and writings. Those outside the Academy, such as the Stoic Posidonius of Apamea (135–50 BCE), drew on the work of Plato in articulating and modifying their own traditions. Those within, such as Antioch of Ascalon (130–67 BCE), stressed the essential agreement between the great philosophers (Cicero, *Acad. Post.* 1.4 §17; *Acad. Pr.* 2.5 §15). A wide audience read Plato,

---

1. J. Whittaker, 'Platonic Philosophy in the Early Centuries of the Empire', *ANRW* II.36.1, pp. 81, 123.

2. J. Danielou, *A History of Christian Doctrine before the Council of Nicaea*. II. *Gospel Message and Hellenistic Culture* (Philadelphia: Westminster Press, 1973), p. 108; D. Rees, 'Platonism and the Platonic Tradition', in P. Edwards (ed.), *The Encyclopedia of Philosophy* (8 vols.; New York: Macmillan, 1967), VI, p. 337. H. Dörrie argues that the Academy had died out altogether. See his *Platonica Minora* (Studia et Testamonia Antiqua, 8; Munich: Fink, 1976), pp. 154-56; and *idem*, *Von Platon zum Platonimus: Ein Bruch in der Überlieferung und seine Überwindung* (Rheinisch-Westfälische Akademie der Wissenschaften, Geisteswissenschaften, Vorträge G211; Opladen: Westdeutscher Verlag, 1976).

3. Along with the reasons that follow, skeptical Platonism itself may have contributed to the rise of Middle Platonism. So argues H. Tarrant, *Scepticism or Platonism? The Philosophy of the Fourth Academy* (Cambridge Classical Studies; Cambridge: Cambridge University Press, 1985).

4. The Historical and Social Setting of the Philosophy 101

particularly the *Timaeus*, and subscribed to his ideas.[1] Alongside these specific explanations was an intangible yet more powerful cause, what E. Brehier called the rebirth of Athenian idealism in the opening centuries of the common era.[2] Reaching its full growth in neo-Platonism, the philosophical pursuit of the transcendent or the intelligible enjoyed new life in the intellectual culture of the first and second centuries CE.[3] This orientation fostered a markedly religious Platonism while signaling the demise of more materialistic traditions such as Epicureanism.[4]

Hand in hand with the growing ascendancy of the Platonic tradition went a tendency to present Platonic and Academic teachings uncritically and dogmatically.[5] Convinced that Plato had been a disciple of Pythagoras and that many had borrowed in turn from Plato, Middle Platonists made little effort to distinguish and eliminate Stoic and Aristotelian terminology or Pythagorean influences that had entered Academic thought.[6] At the same time, the widespread popularity and appreciation of Plato's writings brought them an unprecedented authority. As a consequence, interpretation of them in this period became systematic and grew increasingly scholastic and pedantic. Even as great literary figures, such as Plutarch and Apuleius, espoused Plato and his ideas and declared themselves Platonists, the understanding of him and his philosophy became rigid. Summaries of, and commentaries on, the *Timaeus* multiplied and that dialogue's cosmology commanded great respect.[7]

Concomitant with the revitalization of the Platonic tradition was the emergence of neo-Pythagoreanism, a school of thought drawing heavily on the dominant schools of Greek philosophy.[8] Along with

1. Dillon, *Middle Platonists*, p. 8; Zeller, *History of Greek Philosophy*, p. 285.
2. E. Brehier, *The History of Philosophy. II. The Hellenistic and Roman Age* (Chicago: University of Chicago Press, 1965), p. 148.
3. Brehier, *Hellenistic and Roman Age*, p. 170.
4. F. Brenk describes this development as a transition from immanentist to transcendentalist thinking. See his 'An Imperial Heritage: The Religious Spirit of Plutarch of Chaironeia', *ANRW* II.36.1, p. 249.
5. D. Runia, *Philo of Alexandria and the 'Timaeus' of Plato* (2 vols.; Amsterdam: Vrije Universiteit, 1983), I, pp. 32-33.
6. Whittaker, 'Platonic Philosophy', pp. 112-16.
7. Runia, *Philo and the 'Timaeus'*, I, pp. 37-38.
8. W. Guthrie, 'Pythagoras and Pythagoreanism', in Edwards (ed.), *Encyclopedia of Philosophy*, VII, p. 39; F. Copleston, *A History of Philosophy. I.*

Plato and other philosophers of classical Greece, Pythagoras fascinated the literate Hellenistic and Roman public, an interest stimulated in part by the presence of Pythagorean elements in Plato's increasingly popular writings. An intense demand for information about the shadowy Pythagoras coupled with a paucity of knowledge about him and his teachings generated a host of Pythagorean pseudepigrapha in the Hellenistic period. These writings freely combined Platonic, Academic, Stoic, Peripatetic, and old Pythagorean ideas under the name of Pythagoras or some early Pythagorean worthy.[1] These Pythagorica were but one product of a Pythagorizing tendency characteristic of many Hellenistic and Roman philosophers and writers. Since even those outside the neo-Pythagorean circle considered all Greek philosophers to be heirs of Pythagoras, many ancients accepted uncritically obvious amalgams of Greek philosophy as authentic Pythagorean thought. Also incorporated under the name of Pythagoras were significant amounts of esoteric, magical, and religious material. But these topics found their way into the writings of all the Hellenistic and Roman schools, not just the neo-Pythagoreans, for preoccupation with religion, magic, and the occult typified the age.[2]

Given the derivative character of both Hellenistic Pythagorean literature and neo-Pythagoreanism in general, it may well be wise to mention Pythagoreanism sparingly in a survey of Greco-Roman philosophy at the time of Colossians. Yet talk of Pythagorean influence at least *within* the Platonic tradition is not idle chatter, since Plato himself adopted certain Pythagorean ideas into his writings and the renewed interest in them brought Middle Platonists into contact with authentic Pythagorean material. Certain tendencies within Middle Platonism can usefully be described as exhibiting Pythagorean influence.[3] In such descriptions the Middle Platonist Eudorus of Alexandria, whose stress on divine transcendence resulted in a strongly dualistic

Greece and Rome (Westminster, MD: Newman, rev. edn, 1955), p. 446.

1. Guthrie, *History of Greek Philosophy*, I, p. 155; Dillon, *Middle Platonists*, pp. 38, 118-20.
2. Rees, 'Platonism', p. 337.
3. R. Berchman, *From Philo to Origen: Middle Platonism in Transition* (BJS, 69; Chico, CA: Scholars Press, 1984), pp. 23-25. See also Dillon, *Middle Platonists*, pp. 117-21; Whittaker, 'Platonic Philosophy', pp. 118-19; R. Witt, *Albinus and the History of Middle Platonism* (Cambridge Classical Studies; Cambridge: Cambridge University Press, 1937), pp. 23-25.

4. The Historical and Social Setting of the Philosophy

metaphysic, belongs to the Pythagorean-tinged wing of the school, whereas Antiochus of Ascalon, who saw a greater continuity between the cosmos and the divine, represents a more Stoic brand of Middle Platonism.[1]

The character of both Middle Platonism and neo-Pythagoreanism must be considered in any interpretation of the *Hypomnemata*, the text Schweizer finds so central to his reconstruction of the Colossian philosophy. The moment that he describes this text as a first-century BCE Pythagorean document, he must reckon with the eclectic nature of both neo-Pythagoreanism and Hellenistic Pythagorean texts. That he ignores those matters (and as a consequence concludes that the Colossian philosophy is Pythagorean) constituted one of my major criticisms of his work in the previous chapter. For despite the sober and reliable reputation of Alexander Polyhistor,[2] Diogenes Laertius's source for the *Hypomnemata*, and his claim to be drawing from Pythagorean memoirs, the text before us is clearly a composite, a feature acknowledged by even the most ardent proponents of a Pythagorean background for the text.[3] Encouraged by his contemporaries' interest in Pythagoreanism, Alexander evidently composed a text whose actual Pythagorean content is uncertain.

How Pythagorean is the *Hypomnemata*? In my criticism of Schweizer I referred to scholars who see *no* Pythagorean thought expressed there.[4] But perhaps more noteworthy is the tack taken by scholars who argue for a Pythagorean element in the *Hypomnemata*. For those portions of the text that show the greatest affinity to the Colossian philosophy—the part about the elements and their interplay (*D.L.* 8.25) and treatment of the soul's fate, demons, and purification (8.31-33)[5]—are the very parts shed by those scholars arguing for a Pythagorean core. Wiersma, for example, admits the Platonic flavor of section 8.25 while asserting that sections 8.26-30 constitute a

---

1. J. Glucker, *Antiochus and the Late Academy* (Hypomnemata, 56; Göttingen: Vandenhoeck & Ruprecht, 1978), p. 27.
2. C. Holladay (ed.), *Fragments from Hellenistic Jewish Authors*. I. *Historians* (SBLTT, 20; Chico, CA: Scholars Press, 1983), p. 8.
3. M. Wellmann, 'Eine pythagoreische Urkunde des IV. Jahrhundert v. Chr', *Hermes* 54 (1919), p. 226.
4. Festugière, '"Mémoires pythagoriques"', pp. 58-59; Burkert, *Ancient Pythagoreanism*, p. 35, 53-59, 73-75, 82.
5. According to Schweizer, *Letter to the Colossians*, p. 132.

Pythagorean kernel. Section 8.31 and following come from another source or sources, he argues, because at that point the epitome departs considerably from the sober and scientific approach of earlier sections. As a case in point, he notes that the demonic involvement in disease related in section 8.32 would not fit well with the explanation given for illness earlier (8.26).[1]

If the portions of the *Hypomnemata* most pertinent to the Colossian philosophy are those least likely to be Pythagorean, the question of whence Alexander Polyhistor drew this material becomes urgent.

Demonology in the Early Roman Empire

What is the likeliest source for the *Hypomnemata*'s demonology (8.32), a topic Schweizer finds key to understanding the Colossian devotion to the angels? Speculation about δαίμονες was a common and distinguishing feature of Middle Platonism.[2] Plutarch offers the best evidence of this, devoting parts of at least four essays to depicting the nature and function of demons and their relationship to the human soul. Much of his exposition is explanation of, or elaboration on, Plato;[3] he refers to Plato and the Academic Xenocrates frequently.

In *On the Sign of Socrates* (περὶ τοῦ Σωκράτους δαιμονίου), Plutarch attributes divine inspiration to the activity of demons, whose messages are available to all but are received only by those with a properly-ordered soul (20 [589D]; 22 [592C]). To explicate this matter Plutarch turns to the interpretation of a vision had by Timarchus (22 [590B-592E]). There the reader learns how and to what degree the soul intermingles with the body. Clearly drawing on Plato's *Timaeus* (90A), Plutarch explains that the part of the soul called the understanding remains unmixed with the body and is properly considered a demon. Those, like Socrates, whose demon rules the rest of the soul enjoy contact with the divine.

---

1. W. Wiersma, 'Das Referat des Alexandros Polyhistor über die pythagoreische Philosophie', *Mnemosyne*, series 3, 10 (1942), pp. 108-10.
2. Rees, 'Platonism', p. 337; Dillon, *Middle Platonists*, pp. 46-47; Burkert, *Ancient Pythagoreanism*, pp. 73-74.
3. Burkert, *Ancient Pythagoreanism*, p. 73; G. Soury, *La démonologie de Plutarque: Essai sur les idées religieuses et les mythes d'un platonicien éclectique* (Collection d'études anciennes; Paris: Société d'édition 'Les Belles Lettres', 1942), pp. 15, 22, 123, *passim*.

4. The Historical and Social Setting of the Philosophy

That demons serve as the link between the gods and human beings is a recurrent theme in Plutarch's other essays. His *Face on the Moon* describes demons descending from the moon to establish and administer oracles and religious initiations, to mete out divine punishment to evildoers, and to act as earthly saviors (30 [944C-D]). Similarly, in *Isis and Osiris* Plutarch turns to a theory about demons to account for sacred mythologies and religious rites and ceremonies of both Egypt and Greece (25-26 [360D-361C]). The *Obsolescense of Oracles*, too, gives the demons the same roles; they are guardians of sacred rites and avengers of injustice (13-14 [417A-D]).

Plutarch draws from several sources to articulate his sometimes inconsistent demonology, but none is more central to it than Plato's comments. Twice he makes obvious reference to a passage in the *Symposium* (202E-203A) that describes the demons as interpretive and ministering agents of the gods (*Is. et Os.* 26 [361C]; *Def. Orac.* 13 [416F]).[1] According to Plato, because the heavenly and earthly cannot mix, an intermediate class must act to facilitate communication between, and to unite, the two realms. Thus, the demons stand behind the prophetic and priestly arts. Clearly, these remarks were the chief stimulus for the Plutarchian demonology.

Plutarch's various presentations also reflect demonological speculation that occurred in later Platonic tradition. The Academic Xenocrates introduced evil demons to explain the origin of abhorrent religious practices (*Is. et Os.* 26 [361B]; cf. *Def. Orac.* 17 [419A]), and he formulated the demons' intermediate position between the gods and human beings in terms of various geometric figures (*Def. Orac.* 13 [416D]).[2]

Nowhere, on the other hand, is there solid evidence for a Pythagorean source behind Plutarch's demonology. He includes Pythagoras once in a list of authorities on demons (*Is. et Os.* 25 [360E]), but that same list appears elsewhere without Pythagoras (*Def. Orac.* 17 [419A]). Since Plato heads the list in both cases and Xenocrates, whose teaching was frequently attributed to Pythagoras, appears in both, many scholars consider the inclusion of Pythagoras in one of the

---

1. Soury, *Démonologie*, pp. 21-22.
2. Dillon, *Middle Platonists*, pp. 31-32; R. Heinze, *Xenokrates: Darstellung der Lehre und Sammlung der Fragmente* (repr.; Hildesheim: Olms, 1965 [1892]), pp. 78-123, 166-68 (frgs. 23-25).

lists an example of Pythagorizing tendencies.[1]

The *Hypomnemata*'s demonology, like Plutarch's, undoubtedly rests on Platonic, not Pythagorean, ground.[2] The demons (or heroes), according to that text, are situated in the air, midway between heaven and earth, conveying signs of future sickness and health to earth's creatures (*D.L.* 8.32). They serve other roles as well: 'and it is to them that purifications and lustrations, all divination, omens and the like, have reference'. None of these notions is foreign to Middle Platonic speculation. Plutarch locates the demons on the moon (*Fac. Lun.* 29 [944C]) and elsewhere compares the demons to the air, since it maintains the bond between earth and moon (*Def. Orac.* 13 [416E]). Inspiration for most of these notions comes from the *Symposium* (202E-203A), where Plato locates demons between gods and mortals, assigns them the task of envoys and interpreters, and puts them in charge of prophecy, divination, and initiation.

The context of the *Hypomnemata*'s demonology may well have come from Platonic soil as well. Just before its comments on demons, the epitome describes the fate of the soul at death (*D.L.* 8.31). The god Hermes collects all the souls, escorting the pure souls upwards (to their reward?) and turning the impure souls over to the Erinyes, the avengers of crime. That an exposition on demons ensues immediately should not surprise us, since they, like Hermes, are messengers of the gods and, like the Erinyes, administer the punishment of the unjust (Plutarch, *Fac. Lun.* 30 [944D]; *Def. Orac.* 13 [417B]). The connection between Hermes and demons is made even clearer in a short passage from another of Plato's dialogues. The *Phaedo* (107D-108C) relates how at death a guardian demon escorts the soul to the place of judgment and the other world. Like the *Hypomnemata*, Plato notes that the impure soul is strictly segregated from other souls. Such correspondences point unequivocally to a Platonic background for this portion of the *Hypomnemata*.

Whence comes the jumble of material following the *Hypomnemata*'s demonology? The portions relevant to the reconstruction of the Colossian philosophy according to Schweizer—the worship of heroes or demons and the requisite purification—were commonplace in Greco-Roman religion but were subjects of philosophy as well.

---

1. Dillon, *Middle Platonists*, p. 38; Burkert, *Ancient Pythagoreanism*, pp. 73, 129; Heinze, *Xenokrates*, p. 87.
2. Heinze, *Xenokrates*, p. 110.

4. The Historical and Social Setting of the Philosophy 107

Plutarch's discussion of demons (and heroes) includes recognition of their right to human devotion (σέβομαι; *Def. Orac.* 12 [416C]). And long before him, Plato recommended the worship of gods, demons, and heroes (*Resp.* 4.427B). In fact, much as the *Hypomnemata* ranks the gods as more deserving of worship than heroes (*D.L.* 8.33), Plato's *Laws* dictate the order in which gods, demons, and heroes deserve worship (4.717B).

What makes this demonological speculation in the Platonic tradition pertinent to the Colossian philosophy is the equation Philo of Alexandria draws between demons and heroes and the intermediaries of Jewish tradition, the ἄγγελοι. At several points in his writings he identifies the angels with the entities Greek philosophy calls heroes or demons (*Plant.* 4 §14; *Somn.* 1.22 §141; *Gig.* 4 §16; cf. *Conf. Ling.* 34 §171). In making this identification, Philo is well aware of Middle Platonic speculation:[1] the heroes or demons inhabit the air (*Plant.* 4 §14); and they exhibit a range of natures, both good and bad (*Gig.* 4 §16; *Somn.* 1.22 §140). In describing their function he relies on both biblical and Platonic traditions; they are ambassadors between heaven and earth, bringing tidings and blessings down and taking petitions upwards (*Plant.* 4 §14; *Somn.* 1.22 §141; *Gig.* 4 §16). Did the Colossian philosophy also know about Middle Platonic demonological speculation? Could the latter's advocacy of devotion to demons and heroes stand behind the former's devotion to angels? Earlier in this study I noted evidence of pagan speculation in southwestern Asia Minor about messenger or mediatorial figures, which came to expression in the form of inscriptions dedicated to the divine angel or angels.[2] While lack of evidence precludes any argument for direct Middle Platonic influence on those who composed these inscriptions, the angel or angels addressed in these inscriptions apparently functioned very much like the demons of Middle Platonism: as messengers and mediators between heaven and earth.

Philo may well have been the first to recognize this equivalency, but the connection between angels and demons becomes commonplace in

---

1. Dillon, *Middle Platonists*, pp. 172-74; D. Winston and J. Dillon, *Two Treatises of Philo of Alexandria: A Commentary on 'De Gigantibus' and 'Quod Deus Sit Immutabilis'* (BJS, 25; Chico, CA: Scholars Press, 1983), pp. 197-205.
2. Sokolowski, 'Sur le culte d'angelos', pp. 226-29; Nilsson, 'The High God and the Mediator', p. 116.

later thought.¹ On the one hand, Justin Martyr's telling of the birth of the Nephilim (Gen. 6.1-4) has the fallen angels begetting demons for children (*Apol.* 2.5). On the other hand, Celsus sets angels alongside demons and heroes and considers all worthy of worship (Origen, *Cels.* 7.68). Examples from later writers abound.²

The common function of angels and demons and the eventual equation made between them may provide the best background for understanding the Colossian philosophy's insistence on worship directed to angels. If angel worship is not well documented in the first century CE, the worship of demons certainly is. Demon worship constitutes an important part of the piety advocated by the philosophy epitomized by the *Hypomnemata* and by the philosophy at Colossae, whose proponents evidently equated angels with demons and expressed devotion to the latter in the Anatolian parlance of devotion to angels. However such devotion was expressed, both philosophies appear rooted in Platonism at this point.

Philosophical Purification

Discipline and Diet

In the closing section of the *Hypomnemata* (*D.L.* 8.33), following the description of how one should approach the gods and heroes or demons, comes a host of prescriptions for achieving the purity necessary for worship. Whereas the demonology of the *Hypomnemata* clearly belongs to Platonic tradition, the specific source for these prescriptions is not clear, although the command to avoid meat and beans and the detailed regulations in and of themselves point to Pythagoreanism, well known for its vegetarianism and legalistic outlook.³ But these prescribed lustrations and dietary restrictions were also typical of Hellenistic cultic practices, a fact made evident at the end of the epitome as the description of what accomplishes purification comes to a conclusion: 'Purification is by cleansing... and the other abstinences prescribed by those who perform mystic rites in the temples'.

If the regulations listed in the *Hypomnemata* have a strictly cultic

---

1. Heinze, *Xenokrates*, pp. 112-14.
2. Porphyry, *Ad Marcellam* 21.342-44; W. Bousset, 'Zur Dämonologie der späteren Antike', *ARW* 18 (1915), pp. 170-72.
3. Nilsson, *Geschichte der griechischen Religion*, I, pp. 705-708.

4. The Historical and Social Setting of the Philosophy 109

focus, the interpreter may have to turn elsewhere to locate the Colossian philosophy in its proper setting. For, as the exegesis of the polemical core revealed, the Colossian regulations and commands point to more than cultic purity. I concluded that the commands quoted by the letter writer in Col. 2.21, while they do prepare one for the proper θρησκεία, have as their goal humility and bodily asceticism (2.23). Moreover, although the letter writer denies that they are adequate for the task, the commands also constituted the antidote to the indulgence (πλησμονή) of the flesh.

The *Hypomnemata* may well be a crucial text for understanding the Colossian philosophy's θρησκεία τῶν ἀγγέλων, but the correspondence between the practices of each is not complete, Schweizer's arguments notwithstanding. Ostensibly, he includes baptism (based on Col. 2.12) as a distinguishing feature of the Colossian philosophy, even after disallowing 2.9-15 as a good source for a reconstruction, so that he can find a match for the *Hypomnemata*'s call for lustration.[1] But nothing in my exegesis of the polemical core points to baptism as a mark of the Colossian philosophy. In other words, neither the practices nor, more importantly, the reasons for them overlap wholly.

Another text may give the interpreter a better understanding of the Colossian philosophy's pursuit of purity: Timaeus Locrus's *On the Nature of the World and the Soul*. Thought in antiquity to be the source of Plato's *Timaeus*, modern scholarship has reversed that relationship, regarding Timaeus Locrus as post-Platonic.[2] Also viewed with skepticism is H. Thesleff's contention that it belongs to the Hellenistic Pythagorica and dates to 300 BCE.[3] A clear consensus of scholars places it in the first century BCE or first century CE and classifies it as an epitome of, or commentary on, Plato's *Timaeus*.[4] In

---

1. Schweizer, *Letter to the Colossians*, pp. 126, 133.
2. T. Tobin (ed.), *Timaios of Locri, 'On the Nature of the World and the Soul'* (SBLTT, 26; Chico, CA: Scholars Press, 1985), p. 3.
3. H. Thesleff, *An Introduction to the Pythagorean Writings of the Hellenistic Period* (Acta Academiae Åboensis, Humaniora, 24.3; Turku, Finland: Åbo Akademie, 1961), p. 115. He has since given up this early dating: 'On the Problem of Doric Pseudo-Pythagorica. An Alternative Theory of Date and Purpose', in K. von Fritz (ed.), *Pseudepigrapha I: Pseudopythagorica—Lettres de Platon, Littérature pseudépigraphique juive* (Entretiens sur l'antiquité classique, 18; Geneva: Fondation Hardt, 1972), p. 59.
4. Tobin (ed.), *Timaios of Locri*, p.19; M. Baltes (ed.), *Timaios Lokros, 'Über die Natur des Kosmos und der Seele'* (Philosophia Antiqua, 21; Leiden: Brill, 1972),

short, it is a typical product of Middle Platonism.

In Timaeus Locrus purification plays an essential role in ordering one's being properly and living well. The goal of philosophy is to strive for the correct balance within the soul, between soul and body, and among the various parts of the body (78 [103C]). Philosophy disciplines and educates the soul, enabling the rational mind to rule over the appetitive, irrational part of the soul and the body (82 [104A-B]). The edification and empowering of the mind Timaeus Locrus calls purification, for the mind is cleansed of false opinions (83 [104B-C]) and the hierarchy intended for the soul is restored (46 [99E]).

Vital to the soul's proper balance is a disciplined body. A body out of harmony and given to excess—desires (ἐπιθυμίαι) and pleasures (ἁδοναί)—has a dire effect on the soul, dragging it toward vice (72-74 [102E-103A]). Therefore, the philosophical life entails the discipline necessary for maintaining a harmoniously ordered body. This training includes a life outdoors, a simple diet, and a regimen of bodily exercise (76 [103B]; 80 [103D-E]). Purification, according to Timaeus Locrus, is the aim of this bodily discipline, too (81 [104A]).

Is there a connection between the Middle Platonic pursuit of purity and that of the Colossian philosophers? Apparently so. According to Timaeus Locrus, the philosophical pursuit of purity involves dietary matters, a subject of major importance to the Colossian philosophy (Col. 2.16, 21). This discipline in matters of food and drink was no inconsequential element in Platonic tradition but an essential part of it from its inception. In the fourth century BCE Xenophon recorded Socrates' lengthy remarks on the topic of self-control (ἐγκράτεια). The one trained to rule must be taught self-restraint in all matters: in eating (βρωτοῦ), drinking (ποτοῦ), sexual indulgence, and so forth (*Mem.* 2.1.1-6). Without this key virtue, one is enslaved to the pleasures of the body (ἡδοναὶ σώματος) and thus can accomplish nothing (1.5.1-6.2).

Plato himself offered good reasons for restraint in matters of food and drink and for an ascetic attitude toward the body. True philosophers focused all their efforts on the improvement of the soul, so that all matters pertaining to the body—the pleasure of food and drink—merited no attention (*Phaed.* 64D-E). To do otherwise, to attend to bodily desires, meant subordinating the soul to the body

pp. 20-26; F. Cornford, *Plato's Cosmology* (London: Routledge & Kegan Paul, 1937), p. 3.

4. The Historical and Social Setting of the Philosophy 111

(82C-D). Here, as in Timaeus Locrus centuries later, a clearly-defined hierarchical anthropology dictated that the soul rule the body and that the rational part of the soul reign over its appetitive, irrational side (*Resp.* 4.439A-E; *Tim.* 69C-70A). Loves, hungers, thirsts, and desires—everything arising from bodily impulse and the appetitive soul—had to be curbed (*Resp.* 4.439D; 9.585B). Only in that way could the soul be purified (*Phaed.* 67C).[1]

A similar anthropology, expressed in terms of body and soul symmetry, occupied Plato in the *Timaeus*, also generating a call to self-control (87C-88B). In this scheme, excessive pleasure and self-indulgence were to be avoided because they created an imbalance in the body and, in turn, brought disorder to the soul (86B-87A).

The pursuit of due proportion in one's life, following the well-ordered pattern of the cosmos, brought the soul and body into correct alignment. Concretely, this meant exercise of the body, to purify and unite it, and discipline of the soul, that is, a life according to reason (88C-89D).

This fully articulated rationale for philosophical purification and asceticism had a major impact on later philosophy, as Timaeus Locrus attests, and on the larger Greco-Roman culture. The student of philosophy catches glimpses of its influence on those in the Platonic tradition. The Academic Polemon (350–267 BCE), if the title of his lost book (*On the Life according to Nature*) is any indication, molded his life on the model of the universe. This undertaking included abstinence from meat (Clement of Alexandria, *Strom.* 7.32).[2]

Plutarch devotes two short treatises to the topic of eating meat. Considering the subject, one might expect Pythagorean or Empedoclean thinking to dominate. But at least one major line of argument taken by Plutarch has a Platonic rooting.[3] Throughout both treatises he contends that eating flesh runs contrary to the natural order (φύσις; *Carn. Es.* 1.5 [994F-995C]; 2.2 [997B]; *passim*). By eating flesh, we give in not to a natural hunger but to a desire for satiety and pleasure

---

1. R. Bluck (ed.), *Plato's 'Phaedo'* (London: Routledge & Kegan Paul, 1955), pp. 2-5, 47; B. Lohse, *Askese und Mönchtum in der Antike und in der alten Kirche* (Religion und Kultur der alten Mittelmeerwelt in Parallelforschungen, 1; Munich: Oldenbourg, 1969), pp. 48-51.
2. Dillon, *Middle Platonists*, p. 40.
3. D. Tsekourakis, 'Pythagoreanism or Platonism and Ancient Medicine? The Reasons for Vegetarianism in Plutarch's "Moralia"', *ANRW* II.36.1, pp. 388-91.

(ἡδονή; 2.2 [997B]), and thereby show our lack of control (2.1 [996E]). The imbalance in the body resulting from eating flesh perverts the soul (2.4 [988C]). Plutarch summarizes the matter nicely (1.6 [995D-E]): 'Note that the eating of flesh is not only physically against nature, but it also makes us psychically coarse and gross by reason of indulgence (πλησμονή) and surfeit'.

Besides the focus on diet they shared, the Middle Platonic and Colossian philosophy's pursuit of purity may have had other common elements. What little that can be gleaned from the polemical core about the objectives of the Colossian praxis points to an unsparing treatment of the body (ἀφειδία σώματος; Col. 2.23), which agrees with the Platonic tradition's call to keep a tight rein on the promptings of the body and to subject it to a regular discipline. Note, too, the danger both wish to avoid: surrender to the πλησμονή of the body or the flesh. If I read Col. 2.23 correctly, the Colossian philosophers believed that their practices brought a rigorous discipline to bear on the body and thus they kept themselves from indulging the flesh. Such a result is clearly the aim of Plutarch, when he decries a diet of meat, of Timaeus Locrus, when it recommends a simple diet and exercise to control desires and pleasures, and of Plato in the *Phaedo* and *Timaeus*.

Self-Control and Jewish Practices
Given these correspondences between the Middle Platonism and the Colossian philosophy, what is the interpreter to make of the significant Jewish elements in the latter? At some points the philosophers at Colossae have clearly drawn from Jewish tradition in framing their beliefs and practices. First, the entire list of holy days in Col. 2.16 (not just the Sabbath) echoes the enumeration of Jewish holy days in the LXX, which indicates that the philosophers follow the Jewish calendar (Hos. 2.13; 1 Chron. 23.31; 2 Chron. 2.3; 31.3). Also, one of the goals of the philosophy, ταπεινοφροσύνη, a prized Christian virtue, may have a Jewish background, since ταπεινός and related terms very seldom have a positive connotation in pagan traditions.[1]

Here it is important to reintroduce Philo, for he represents a bridge between Greek philosophy and Judaism. His essay *The Contemplative Life* merits attention because it describes a group called the Therapeutae who exhibit features of both Greek philosophy and

---

1. Grundmann, 'ταπεινός, κτλ', pp. 5, 11; Wengst, *Humility*, pp. 4-15. Typical is Plutarch's use of ταπεινόφρων in *Tranq. An.* 17 (475E).

Judaism. On the one hand, they are disciples of Moses, reading and interpreting the Law (3 §28), observing the Sabbath (3 §§30-33), and keeping Jewish festivals (8 §65). On the other hand, they are typical philosophers, devoted to freeing their souls from pleasures (ἡδοναί), desires (ἐπιθυμίαι), and all other passions and vices (1 §2). Key to their freedom is self-control (ἐγκράτεια; 4 §34); in matters of food and drink they refuse to give in to indulgence (πλησμονή) because of the danger it poses for the soul (4 §37). Accordingly, they maintain a very plain diet (4 §37) and fast regularly (4 §§34-35). Moreover, meat and wine have no place in their regimen, in order that the desires are not excited (9 §74). This is a familiar ascetic program; what the Therapeutae have undertaken clearly has much in common with the regimen of philosophical purity articulated by Plutarch, Timaeus Locrus, and Plato.

The Therapeutae give the interpreter an excellent model of how Jewish religious traditions and Greek philosophical interests came together. In fact, the two are so well integrated in this case that Jewish praxis becomes the vehicle for philosophical self-restraint; the religious gatherings and festivals sponsored by the Therapeutae are a showcase for their sobriety and moderation (8-10 §§64-82). In light of this example, it is quite possible that the unequivocally Jewish practices adhered to by the Colossian philosophy could have met philosophical goals. The calendar and food regulations (Col. 2.16) which the Colossian philosophers followed may well have aided them in achieving humility, a virtue prized in Christian piety. But those same practices may also have met philosophical goals: the achievement of bodily asceticism via the control of fleshly indulgence (πλησμονή; v. 23).

Another example from Philo offers striking verification of the dual purpose Jewish practices could have. Revealing is his description of Yom Kippur, a festival laden with religious significance (*Spec. Leg.* 2.32 §§193-95). The feast is, in fact, a fast, which points to the self-restraint (ἐγκράτεια) embodied in the rite. The Jews did not want their religious activities to be an occasion for ἐπιθυμία or ἡδονή, like the festivals of other people. Consequently, they avoided excess of any kind in their ceremonies.

This example gives the interpreter even better proof that a Jewish practice could be understood as a contribution to the philosophical life. With regard to the reconstruction of the Colossian philosophy, it means that the presence of Jewish features in that philosophy in no way hinders the argument that Middle Platonism was essential to the formulation of it. Moreover, the example indicates how elements from different traditions might combine to serve a common goal.

A Philosophy according to the World

There always exists some danger in drawing inferences from Philonic evidence, for Philo can serve the interpreter not as paradigm but only as an example of how Jewish and pagan philosophical traditions combined. Moreover, in the context of this study, an examination of how Platonic and Jewish elements might blend, it may be especially hazardous to invoke Philo because in the passages just cited from him he seems more Stoic then Platonic. When he writes about the control of desires and pleasures does he not depend on the Stoic doctrine of indifference to the four passions (πάθη), two of which are ἐπιθυμία and ἡδονή (cf. Cicero, *Fin.* 3.10 §35)? It is a doctrine he is clearly aware of (*Leg. All.* 2.25 §99). Are not the Therapeutae following Stoic thought when they turn to nature (φύσις) for instruction (*Vit. Cont.* 11 §90)? Is not Philo himself setting Judaism alongside Stoicism when he equates the observance of the Law with conformity to nature (*Op. Mund.* 1 §3; cf. *Abr.* 13 §60; *Vit. Mos.* 2.39 §211)? After all, life according to nature has always been connected with Stoic ethical thinking (*D.L.* 7.87).[1]

Nevertheless, Philonic evidence is for several reasons particularly illuminating as an example of how *Platonic* and Jewish ideas came together. First, whereas Philo undoubtedly relied on Stoicism in formulating some of his philosophical and theological positions, he rejected many of its basic tenets. Behind the Stoic call to follow nature lay a materialistic metaphysic which located the Divine *logos* in the cosmic order. Philo's belief in divine transcendence, rooted in Judaism and supported by Platonism, made this notion unacceptable.[2] On the whole, Philo belongs to the Platonic rather than the Stoic

---

1. W. Meeks, *The Moral World of the First Christians* (Library of Early Christianity, 6; Philadelphia: Westminster Press, 1986), p. 47.
2. E. Goodenough, *By Light, Light: The Mystic Gospel of Hellenistic Judaism* (New Haven: Yale University Press, 1935), p. 52; S. Sandmel, *Philo of Alexandria: An Introduction* (New York: Oxford University Press, 1979), pp. 121-22.

4. *The Historical and Social Setting of the Philosophy* 115

camp, an assessment reached by a consensus of scholars.[1]

Second, Philo's Stoic ideas may have come to him filtered through Middle Platonism. Already among members of the Academy we meet those whose ethic rests on the conformity to nature: Speusippus (cf. Clement of Alexandria, *Strom.* 2.133) and Polemon (*Strom.* 7.32). Cicero does not credit this notion to individuals only; he states that both the Old Academy and the Peripatetics made the goal of the good life conformity to nature (*Fin.* 2.11 §34).

More relevant to the evaluation of Philo is Antiochus of Ascalon (130–67 BCE), who stood at the beginning of the Middle Platonic era. The latitude of Middle Platonism, reflected in Antiochus's assertion that the Academy, Stoa, and Lyceum held much in common (cf. Cicero, *Acad. Pr.* 2.5 §15), allowed him to employ Stoic ideas in his formulation of Platonism.[2] Hence, he adopted the ethical goal of ἀπάθεια and along with it the Stoic passion theory (*Acad. Pr.* 2.44 §135).[3] He also subscribed to the long-held Academic, but originally Stoic, ethical program of life according to nature (*Acad. Post.* 1.5 §19; 6 §23). This evidence suggests that Philo's Stoic bent is nothing more than a typical Middle Platonic characteristic, at least as Platonism was articulated by Antiochus.

Antiochus's perspective on nature (φύσις) may prove illuminating to another issue: the significance of φιλοσοφία κατὰ τὰ στοιχεῖα τοῦ κόσμου (Col. 2.8). That phrase expresses a positive regard for the cosmos as a source of knowledge of how to conduct one's life (cf. 2.20). But the picture of how and what the world's elements teach the Colossian philosophers is incomplete; we know only that close mental scrutiny (ἐμβατεύω) produced or deciphered a revelatory vision or insight of some kind (v. 18), and the realization of the cosmos's finitude dictated food restrictions (vv. 21-22). Antiochus may offer some assistance here in that he, too, takes instruction from a specific

---

1. Dillon, *Middle Platonists*, pp. 138-83; Runia, *Philo and the 'Timaeus'*, I, pp. 16-17; Goodenough, *By Light, Light*, p. 235; T. Billings, *The Platonism of Philo Judaeus* (Ancient Philosophy, 3; repr.; New York: Garland, 1979 [1919]), p. 12; Meeks, *Moral World*, p. 8; Whittaker, 'Platonic Philosophy', pp. 121-23.

2. A. Graeser, *Plotinus and the Stoics: A Preliminary Study* (Philosophia Antiqua, 22; Leiden: Brill, 1972), p. 3; E. Ferguson, *Backgrounds of Early Christianity* (Grand Rapids: Eerdmans, 1987), p. 266; Glucker, *Antiochus*, pp. 27-31.

3. Dillon, *Middle Platonists*, pp. 77-78.

aspect of the cosmos. Antiochus's formulation of Platonism represents in part a reaction to the skepticism that had dominated the Academy until his time. In response to a theory of knowledge that affirmed only probability and mistrusted the sensible world totally, he argued that sensory perceptions, tested by the mind, formed the basis of knowledge and were essential to moral conduct (*Acad. Pr.* 2.7-8 §§19-23). Thus, he recommended that the philosopher seek in nature the proper ends of life.[1]

In one way this epistemology ran contrary to what is found in Platonism. Antiochus was well aware of the skepticism the Platonic tradition had towards perception. Sure knowledge came only from the contemplation of the forms. The senses produced nothing firmer than opinion because the objects of the senses were in constant flux (*Acad. Post.* 1.8 §§30-32). The theory is memorably expressed in Plato's allegory of the cave (*Resp.* 7.514A-521B).

But the intelligible world was not entirely separate from the world of appearances. The discourse that so dominated Middle Platonism, the *Timaeus*, described the creation of the mundane sphere on the model of the intelligible world (29A). The resulting copy, while inferior to the changeless upper realm, is an animate and relatively perfect sphere, enjoying good proportion and harmony among its components, the four elements (30A-34B).[2] The dualism implicit in Plato's epistemology and cosmology is tempered by the *Timaeus*'s high regard for the copy. It is a worthy reflection of the original.

Middle Platonism clearly regarded the *Timaeus*'s picture of the cosmos as definitive. The opening sections of the *Hypomnemata* describe the world as an animate, intelligent sphere, in which the opposites are in equal proportion and regularly in equilibrium (*D.L.* 8.25-26). So, too, in Timaeus Locrus we read that the world is a perfect, happy, and incorruptible place, blessed with the best proportion and balance between the four elements (7-14 [94C-95B]). And there is little doubt that Antiochus was profoundly affected by the *Timaeus*'s relatively positive assessment of the world. The continuity between the

---

1. Witt, *Middle Platonism*, pp. 47, 52; E. Des Places, *Etudes platoniciennes, 1929–1979* (EPRO, 90; Leiden: Brill, 1981), p. 275.

2. The fourth-century Christian commentator on the *Timaeus*, Calcidius, went so far as to claim that the four elements in and of themselves showed the imprint of the intelligible forms (J. Van Winden, *Calcidius on Matter: His Doctrine and Sources* [Philosophia Antiqua, 9; Leiden: Brill, 1959], p. 41).

4. *The Historical and Social Setting of the Philosophy* 117

intelligible and sensible worlds enunciated by the *Timaeus* lies at the heart of his affirmation of the senses and the natural order of the cosmos.[1]

The *Timaeus*'s cosmology was not lost on Philo either, nor was the thinking of Antiochus. Influenced as Philo was by the ideas of the Middle Platonist Eudorus—the radical transcendence of the divine and concomitant severe dualism—his physics and epistemology came from Antiochus.[2] *Who is the Heir of Divine Things* presents this theory of knowledge with some clarity. In it, Philo asserts that the senses, when they play their proper role, are servants of the mind and vehicles of knowledge (11 §53). For nature is not devoid of truth, and the senses can be used to find it (22 §§110-11).

What does the mind learn through the senses? The careful observer of nature finds a place of balance and perfection, a world in which the basic elements (στοιχεῖα) have been established in equal measure and have come together in a harmonious mixture (29 §§146-50; 41 §199). This order ultimately leads the philosopher to the orderer and sustainer of it: Divine Reason (23-24 §§115-19; 42 §206). Thus the knowledge the senses supply to the mind directs it upward to the contemplation of heavenly matters.

Who then is the heir of divine things? The true heir must learn to purify the mind by eliminating all earthly attachments and to focus it heavenward (13 §64). The senses and the sensible world are key to this education; they are the means by which the mind is directed upward. But presumably their role lessens in importance once the heir matures and undertakes the contemplative life (9 §48).[3] Much as we find in the Middle Platonism of the time (Timaeus Locrus 83 [104C]), Philo advocates a life of self-restraint and austerity so that the mind may become clear and pure and enjoy a vision of the divine realities.

This philosophy guided by the nature of the world, articulated by Philo of Alexandria and grounded in Antiochian Middle Platonism, may provide the interpreter with the closest parallel to the Colossian φιλοσοφία κατὰ τὰ στοιχεῖα τοῦ κόσμου (Col. 2.8). For in both

---

1. Berchman, *From Philo to Origen*, p. 27.
2. Berchman, *From Philo to Origen*, pp. 27, 172; Dillon, *Middle Platonists*, p. 143.
3. Antiochian Middle Platonism, according to Witt (*Middle Platonism*, p. 52), considers 'sensation... the first step of the ladder, of which the last step leads to philosophical knowledge'.

philosophies the cosmos is positively valued, so much so that it serves as the basis of their epistemologies.

For Philo, of course, knowledge ultimately comes from heaven. The true heirs of divine things learn from the careful examination of nature to turn heavenward, with the result that they shed earthly attachments, clear the mind, and enjoy a vision of the divine realm. This appears to be the perspective and program of the Colossian philosophers as well. Their pursuit of purity, directed by the στοιχεῖα (Col. 2.8, 20), has as its goals the control of the body and the curbing of fleshly indulgence (2.23). Perhaps this discipline, fostered by the close scrutiny (ἐμβατεύω) of the στοιχεῖα (2.18) and an understanding of cosmic corruptibility (2.22), was thought to free the mind to enjoy visionary access to divine knowledge (2.18).

The match between these philosophies is not exact, however. Antiochus and Philo delineated a philosophy according to nature (φύσις), the Colossian philosophy follows the στοιχεῖα. But this is hardly an insurmountable difference. After all, when Middle Platonists looked at nature they saw its order and beauty expressed in the balance among the στοιχεῖα (Timaeus Locrus 12-14 [95A-B]; cf. Philo, *Rer. Div. Her.* 29 §146). Moreover, Philo explicitly identifies the στοιχεῖα as the parts of nature (στοιχεῖα φύσεως; *Vit. Mos.* 2.46 §251; cf. *Spec. Leg.* 1.17 §97 and Josephus, *Ant.* 3.7.7 §§183-84), and at one point he notes that it is the order *of the parts* of the cosmos (later he discusses air, earth, and water) that gives us our apprehension of the First Cause (Philo, *Leg. All.* 3.32 §§97-99). In light of this evidence and the possibility that the φιλοσοφία κατὰ τὰ στοιχεῖα τοῦ κόσμου may be language introduced by the letter writer, however accurate, the subjects of the letter's polemic could have described their efforts as a philosophy according to the nature of the world.

The Social Location of the Colossian Philosophers

Despite the significant correspondences between Philo, Middle Platonism, and the Colossian philosophy, the analogies can be pressed only so far. The Jewish practices of the Colossian philosophy distinguish it from all other known types of Middle Platonism. Nor can the interpreter push the similarities between Colossae and Alexandria too far, for the Colossian philosophy exhibits none of the Theraputae's or

4. The Historical and Social Setting of the Philosophy

Philo's Torah-centeredness. Perhaps some at Colossae equated life according to nature with law obedience, as Philo did (*Op. Mund.* 1 §3; *Abr.* 13 §§60-61), but patchy evidence from Colossae makes this inference unwarranted. More certain is the gap between Philo and the Colossian philosophers: he would have condemned the worship they directed toward angels or demons.

This last incompatibility underscores the basic difference between Philo and the Colossian philosophy. As deeply as Philo embraced Greek philosophy, he was raised a Jew and remained loyal to Judaism. By contrast, the Colossian philosophers had a shallower rooting in Judaism; they engaged in practices foreign to Judaism even as they adopted a Jewish perspective and praxis. In other words, Philo and the Colossian philosophers cross paths at several points, but they are not headed in the same direction. In fact, to some degree they are headed in opposite directions: Philo was a Hellenizing Jew, the Colossian philosophers appear to have been Judaizing Gentiles. As a consequence, while both parties found substantial agreement between Judaism and Hellenistic philosophy, their attempts at integrating the two systems yielded different results. The Colossian philosophers achieved an integration of the two systems that was markedly more syncretistic: they were neither Hellenistic Jews nor entirely pagan philosophers.

What setting would have fostered this type of synthesis? Where would pagan Middle Platonists have encountered and been prompted to adopt Jewish practices? Geographical details about early Middle Platonism are few, but in general it thrived not in the west or even in Athens but farther east, in Alexandria and the cities of Asia Minor and Syria.[1] In some of these eastern cities Middle Platonists would undoubtedly have encountered Jewish colonies. For example, the second-century CE Platonist Numenius[2] of Apamea (on the Orontes)

---

1. Whittaker, 'Platonic Philosophy', p. 81; Glucker, *Antiochus*, pp. 135-38, 145, 225; D. Runia, 'Redrawing the Map of Early Middle Platonism', in A. Caquot, M. Hadas-Lebel, and J. Riaud (eds.), *Hellenica et Judaica* (Leuven: Peeters, 1986), pp. 85-104.

2. Reflecting Pythagorizing tendencies, the ancients called Numenius Pythagorean, but contemporary scholars consider him a Platonist. See for example Whittaker ('Platonic Philosophy', p. 119) and M. Stern ([ed.], *Greek and Latin Authors on Jews and Judaism* [3 vols.; Jerusalem: Israel Academy of Sciences and Humanities, 1974–84], II, p. 206).

had some familiarity with Judaism and wrote approvingly of it.[1] Clement of Alexandria quoted him as follows: 'For what is Plato, but Moses speaking Attic?' (*Strom.* 1.150). The Jews of Apamea (cf. Josephus, *War* 2.18.5 §479) or more likely the large colony in nearby Antioch evidently had enough prominence to draw Numenius's attention and even attract him.[2]

Whether Numenius adopted Jewish practices is unknown, but there is evidence that Judaism in the NT period enjoyed enough popularity in Hellenistic culture that some pagans even undertook Jewish practices. Josephus writes triumphantly about the widespread adoption of Sabbath observance, fasting, and dietary regulations by Gentiles (*Apion* 2.39 §282), and the complaint of Seneca only confirms Josephus's rosy picture: 'The ways of those dreadful people [the Jews] have taken deeper and deeper root and are spreading throughout the world. They have imposed their customs on their conquerors' (Augustine, *Civ. D.* 6.11). Certain Colossian Gentiles with philosophical interests appear to have been drawn to Judaism, as were many Gentiles of the time.

Besides indications of Gentile attraction to Judaism, there also exists evidence for variety in the degree of affiliation Gentiles could have with Judaism. This is an important matter in the case of the Colossian philosophy, whose angel or demon worship and limited allegiance to the Law could raise doubts about any possibility of affiliation. Affiliation appears, in fact, to have included many levels; assimilation to Judaism could be a process with many stages. The large Jewish colony at Antioch proved to be fertile ground for assimilation and conversion. Josephus reports that the pro-Jewish Gentiles there had 'in some manner' (τρόπῳ τινί) been incorporated into the Jewish community (*War* 7.3.3 §45). The exact level of affiliation goes unsaid in this text, but elsewhere Josephus goes into detail. The conversion of the Adiabene royal court began with the royal harem's adoption of Jewish worship, progressed to the queen mother's instruction in the Law, and culminated with the king's endorsement of Judaism and eventual circumcision (*Ant.* 20.2.1-4 §§17-48). Interestingly, this

---

1. Stern (ed.), *Authors on Jews*, II, pp. 206-16.
2. The history of Jewish settlement in and around ancient Antioch has been documented by W. Meeks and R. Wilken, *Jews and Christians in Antioch in the First Four Centuries of the Common Era* (SBLSBS, 13; Missoula, MT: Scholars Press, 1978).

4. *The Historical and Social Setting of the Philosophy* 121

same passage records the debate within Judaism over whether or not full conversion required circumcision (20.2.4 §§38-48).

Several stages of conversion to Judaism and levels of affiliation with the synagogue must have been common, for pagan writers with no sympathy for Judaism show familiarity with such phenomena. Juvenal describes a family's steady adoption of Judaism: the father's Sabbath and dietary observance leads to his son's circumcision (*Satire* 14.96-106). S. Cohen depicts the fluidity in the boundary between the Gentile world and Judaism in a list of seven possible relationships. Gentiles could associate with Judaism in the following ways: (1) admire some aspect of Judaism; (2) acknowledge the power of the God of the Jews, such as in the magical papyri; (3) benefit Jews or show friendliness to them; (4) engage in some or many Jewish practices; (5) venerate God alone; (6) join the Jewish community without conversion, such as a Gentile slave purchased by a Jew; or (7) become a full-fledged Jew observing the whole Law.[1]

Given this latitude in affiliation, the probable social location of the Colossian philosophy is clear. It would not have been unusual to have a group devoting itself to demons also taking instruction in the Jewish calendar and dietary regulations; this would have been a possible degree of affiliation. In fact, a situation corresponding to that at Colossae has now been documented in Aphrodisias, a site very near Colossae in southwestern Anatolia. The Jews of Aphrodisias solicited and received help from their fellow city dwellers for the construction of a building that evidently served as a Jewish soup kitchen, for an inscription from that site lists three groups, Jews, proselytes, and God-fearers (θεοσεβεῖς), as donors to that cause. This last category, composed of Greco-Roman names, includes nine city councilors whose duties would have included public worship of pagan gods.[2] In other words, a number of people in Aphrodisias—apparently Gentiles—had a foot in both the pagan and Jewish worlds.

What else can be said about these sympathizers with Judaism (θεοσεβεῖς) in Aphrodisias? The interpreter cannot generalize, for

---

1. S. Cohen, 'Crossing the Boundary and Becoming a Jew', *HTR* 82 (1989), pp. 15-30.
2. J. Reynolds and R. Tannenbaum, *Jews and God-Fearers at Aphrodisias* (Cambridge Philological Society, Supplementary Vol. 12; Cambridge: Cambridge University Press, 1987), pp. 47-58; R. Tannenbaum, 'Jews and God-Fearers in the Holy City of Aphrodite', *BARev* 12.5 (1986), pp. 55-57.

the term exhibits ambiguity in other inscriptions from Asia Minor. Synagogue donors at Sardis, who may have been either Jews or Gentiles, described themselves as θεοσεβής, which in this context may simply mean 'religious'.[1] An inscription at the Miletus theater, τόπος ειουδέων τῶν καὶ θεοσεβίον, continues to provoke disagreement as to whether a place has been reserved for Jews who are also called God-fearers or for two distinct groups, Jews and God-fearers.[2] In addition to this ambiguity, the interpreter should be wary of equating θεοσεβεῖς with the God-fearers mentioned in Acts (οἱ φοβούμενοι τὸν θεόν or οἱ σεβόμενοι τὸν θεόν; Acts 10.2; 13.16; 16.14, for example), for no archaeological evidence verifies the existence of a group with those exact names.[3] Nevertheless, the epigraphical evidence from Aphrodisias *is* unequivocal and, combined with the Jewish, Christian, and pagan literary evidence already cited, is sufficient to verify the existence of unconverted Gentiles affiliated in some way with Judaism, even if the portrait of God-fearers in Acts has limited historical accuracy and θεοσεβεῖς did not always have a precise, technical meaning.[4]

If anything tells against the relevance of the Aphrodisias inscription to this study it is the more than one hundred year gap between its likeliest date (210 CE) and the probable date of the letter to the Colossians. This gap highlights the problem of corroborating any reconstruction of the situation at ancient Colossae: the site has never been systematically excavated and as a consequence non-literary evidence is extremely meager.[5] At most, finds from the Colossae tell

---

1. L. Robert, *Nouvelles inscriptions de Sardes* (fasc. 1; Paris: Maisonneuve, 1964), pp. 37-45, esp. p. 39 (inscriptions #4, 5); B. Lifshitz, *Donateurs et fondateurs dans les synagogues juives* (CahRB, 7; Paris: Gabalda, 1967), pp. 24-26 (inscriptions #17, 18).

2. Robert, *Sardes*, pp. 41-42; E. Yamauchi, *The Archaeology of New Testament Cities in Western Asia Minor* (Baker Studies in Biblical Archaeology; Grand Rapids: Baker, 1980), p. 125; *CII*, II, pp. 14-15 (inscription #748).

3. R. MacLennan and T. Kraabel, 'The God-Fearers—A Literary and Theological Invention', *BARev* 12.5 (1986), pp. 49, 53.

4. T. Finn, 'The God-fearers Reconsidered', *CBQ* 47 (1985), pp. 83-84; L. Feldman, 'The Omnipresence of the God-fearers', *BARev* 12.5 (1986), pp. 59-63; P. Trebilco, *Jewish Communities in Asia Minor* (SNTSMS, 69; Cambridge: Cambridge University Press, 1991), pp. 145-66, esp. p. 164.

5. Yamauchi, *Cities in Western Asia Minor*, pp. 159-61; W. Buckler and W. Calder, (eds.), *Monumenta Asiae Minoris Antiqua. VI. Monuments and*

4. The Historical and Social Setting of the Philosophy   123

and vicinity verify that Colossae survived and even thrived after the devastating earthquake of 60/61 CE, which undercuts an argument for Paul's authorship of Colossians based on the rapid post-earthquake decline of Colossae.[1]

Literary evidence does, however, indicate that the social condition that fostered the situation in early third-century Aphrodisias had existed in southwestern Anatolia for several centuries, well before the time that Colossians was written. Jewish colonization of Asia Minor began at least as early as the third century BCE, when Antiochus III relocated 2000 Jewish families from Babylon to Phrygia (Josephus, *Ant.* 12.3.4 §147). These colonies evidently thrived because by the mid-first century BCE the half-shekel temple tax incumbent on Jewish males amounted to twenty pounds of gold at Laodicea (cf. Col. 4.15-16) and one hundred pounds at Apamea (cf. Cicero, *Flac.* 28 §68). These sums are the equivalent of 9000 and 45,000 half-shekels respectively, indication of a large Jewish adult male population in and around two cities very close to Colossae.[2]

Did this density of Jewish population hold for the rest of Asia Minor? S. Baron included Asia Minor in the 'Jewish belt', assigning it a population of one million.[3] But his estimates do not rest on entirely solid ground; he too readily accepts at face value the apologetically-motivated assertions of Jewish writers such as Philo, who claimed that half the human race knew the Jewish laws (*Vit. Mos.* 2.5 §27).

It is more accurate to conclude that a well-established and visible Jewish population lived in the cities of Phrygia, the region in which Colossae was located, and in all southwestern Anatolia. Support for this conclusion comes from the legislation regarding Jewish privileges in Asia Minor. When Josephus goes about illustrating the legal recognition of Jewish practices by the Romans, his examples come almost exclusively from the cities of western Anatolia: Ephesus, Sardis, Laodicea, Miletus, Pergamum, and Harlicarnasus (*Ant.* 14.10.10-25

Documents from Phrygia and Caria (Publications of the American Society for Archaeological Research in Asia Minor; Manchester: Manchester University Press, 1939), pp. 15-18, 142.

1. Schweizer, *Letter to the Colossians*, p. 19.
2. F. Bruce, 'Colossian Problems. Part 1: Jews and Christians in the Lycus Valley', *BSac* 141 (1984), p. 5.
3. S. Baron, *A Social and Religious History of the Jews*. I. *To the Beginning of the Christian Era* (New York: Columbia University Press, 2nd edn, 1952), p. 170.

§§219-64).¹ Rome's attention to the special needs of Jewish communities in Anatolia indicates that those communities enjoyed some degree of prominence; Jews there were not an insignificant or easily ignored minority.

Archaeological data confirm this situation, even though such data usually come from the second and later centuries. While one of Colossae's nearest neighbors, Laodicea on the Lycus, can provide no confirmation, as it remains largely unexcavated,² the nearby Hierapolis (Col. 4.13) provides clear evidence of a significant Jewish presence. Funerary inscriptions from the second and third centuries indicate Jewish membership in wool dyeing and weaving guilds, two key institutions of the city.³ In general the epigraphical evidence suggests that the Jewish colony there was the third major group in Hierapolis after Roman settlers and native Phrygians.⁴

The archaeological record of Sardis provides striking proof of the central place Jews might occupy in the urban centers of southwestern Anatolia. The city gave or sold the Jewish community in Sardis part of a huge Roman bath–gymnasium complex constructed during the first and second centuries CE, which the Jews remodeled into a synagogue in the third and early fourth centuries. Of immense size, centrally located, and lavishly decorated by donors with obvious means, the Sardis synagogue serves as architectural testimony to a well-established, prominent group.⁵ While this evidence is late relative

---

1. V. Tcherikover, *Hellenistic Civilization and the Jews* (New York: Atheneum, 1970), pp. 288-89.
2. G. Bean, *Turkey beyond the Maeander: An Archaeological Guide* (Totowa, NJ: Rowman & Littlefield, 1971), p. 247. A third-century CE fountain house has been excavated. See J. des Gagniers, P. Devambez, L. Kahil, and R. Ginouvès, *Laodicée du Lycos: Le Nymphée: Campagnes 1961-1963* (Université Laval, Recherches archéologiques, Series 1: Fouilles; Québec: Presses de l'Université Laval, 1969).
3. C. Humann, C. Cichorius, W Judeich and F. Winter (eds.), *Altertümer von Hierapolis* (Jahrbuch des kaiserlich deutschen archäologischen Instituts, 4th Supplement; Berlin: Reimer, 1898), pp. 46, 50-51, and inscriptions #69, 212, 342 on pp. 96-97, 138, 174. See also *CII*, II, pp. 35-38.
4. Humann, *Hierapolis*, p. 34.
5. F. Yegül, *The Bath-Gymnasium Complex at Sardis* (Archaeological Exploration of Sardis, Report 3; Cambridge, MA: Harvard University Press, 1986), p. xvii; A. Seager and T. Kraabel, 'The Synagogue and the Jewish Community', in G. Hanfmann (ed.), *Sardis from Prehistoric to Roman Times* (Cambridge, MA:

4. *The Historical and Social Setting of the Philosophy*   125

to the first century, it nonetheless speaks to this earlier period, for the Jews of Sardis must have thrived for some time in order to achieve such a high public profile by the third century.[1]

Perhaps the best evidence vis-à-vis the Colossian situation comes from Acmonia, a city situated like Colossae in the Phrygian interior and also much closer to Colossae than Sardis in size and importance. The relevant inscription, dating in all likelihood to the first century CE, describes the restoration of a synagogue that had originally been built from funds provided by a certain Julia Severa.[2] In other inscriptions we learn that she was a city magistrate and pagan high priestess.[3] The latter piece of information makes it unlikely that she was a Jew, yet she must have had a strong affinity with the local Jewish community to account for her incredible generosity to it. Here we have evidence not only of Jewish presence, even prominence, but also of the local pagan response: a socially important local pagan found the local Jewish community attractive and worthy enough to merit substantial support. Much more uncertain is the situation in Colossae; whether it had a synagogue or even a Jewish population has yet to be determined. Yet, if Colossae was anything like other Anatolian cities, it probably did have a Jewish community that by the first century CE could attract the attention, the interest, and perhaps even the favor of its pagan neighbors.

The letter to the Colossians indicates just how attractive Judaism was to some pagans at Colossae: philosophically-inclined pagans entering the Christian congregation maintained and advocated Jewish practices (2.16), even though the church there appears to have been wholly Gentile. The letter writer identifies his two co-workers from Colossae—Onesimus (4.9) and Epaphras (4.12)—as uncircumcised. Moreover, in addressing his readers he uses language that assumes their Gentile background: 'And when you were dead in trepasses and the uncircumcision of your flesh', (2.13); 'And you who were once

Harvard University Press, 1983), pp. 171-74, 183-85.

1. T. Kraabel, 'The Diaspora Synagogue: Archaeological and Epigraphical Evidence since Sukenik', *ANRW* II.19.1, pp. 487-88.

2. *CII*, pp. 27-28 (inscription #766); Lifshitz, *Donateurs*, pp. 34-36 (inscription #33).

3. Seager and Kraabel, 'Synagogue', p. 181; Trebilco, *Jewish Communities*, pp. 58-59; B. Brooten, *Women Leaders in the Ancient Synagogues* (BJS, 36; Chico, CA: Scholars Press, 1982), p. 144.

estranged and hostile in mind, doing evil deeds', (1.21);[1] 'To them [his saints] God chose to make known how great among the Gentiles are the riches of the glory of this mystery, which is Christ in you' (1.27).[2] Debates over the Law or circumcision—telltale signs of Torah-obedient missionary activity—do not appear in the letter. Rather, at Colossae we have pagans who have affiliated themselves to some extent with Judaism, joining the church—their advocacy of humility suggests this—and commending certain Jewish practices in their new setting. This situation corresponds to that found elsewhere in southwestern Anatolia. In writing to Philadelphia, Ignatius feels compelled to warn his readers about Judaism expounded by the uncircumcised, that is, by the Judaizing Gentile (*Phld.* 6.1).[3]

To summarize, no evidence about the social realities of the first century CE tells against the situation at Colossae as I reconstruct it. In fact, Colossae and other cities in southwestern Anatolia appear to have been likely places for the meeting and even joining of Jewish and pagan traditions. Both Jewish and pagan contemporary writers attest to Judaism's attractiveness to the Hellenistic world as a whole, and the well-established Jewish population of southwestern Anatolia meant that Judaism enjoyed relatively high visibility in that culture and region. Pagan interest in Judaism made association with it fairly common, and the relative latitude within Judaism permitted many levels to that relationship, such that a group exhibiting both Jewish and pagan features would have startled no one. While neither full converts nor even proselytes, the Colossian philosophers had an attachment to Judaism, an attachment significant enough that they did not shed their Jewish ties upon entering the Christian fold. On the contrary, they appear to have commended their Jewish practices to others even as they embraced the Christian tradition.

The Philosophers in the Colossian Congregation

Placing the Colossian philosophy in the Middle Platonic tradition and giving it a plausible social history and location lend credibility to my reconstruction of it, but there remains the important question of why

1. Lohse, *Colossians and Philemon*, pp. 62-63.
2. Schweizer, *Letter to the Colossians*, p. 106.
3. Gaston, 'Judaism of the Uncircumcised', pp. 37-38; Schoedel, *Ignatius of Antioch*, p. 202.

4. The Historical and Social Setting of the Philosophy

pagans *with philosophical interests* were drawn into the Christian community. The observation that Middle Platonism had a markedly religious disposition, while true, is too general an explanation to account fully for the specifics of the Colossian situation. A more thorough answer takes us back to Philo, for he provides an example of the way a religious tradition might be made appealing to the philosophically oriented.

Philo's understanding of Yom Kippur, cited earlier, bears repeating here (*Spec. Leg.* 2.32 §§193-95). He contrasts this Jewish festival with the revelry and excesses of other nations' festivals, noting that the Jews hold no banquet and indulge in no merriment. Rather, Yom Kippur is marked by fasting, which points to the self-restraint (ἐγκράτεια) fostered by the festival. With this interpretation Philo shows that Jewish praxis could meet philosophical goals: a Jewish festival, rather than encouraging pleasure (ἡδονή) and desire (ἐπιθυμία), could be a vehicle for philosophical self-restraint.

This manner of portraying Judaism had an obvious apologetic value; it could serve Hellenistic Jews well in making Judaism acceptable and appealing to philosophically-trained non-Jews. Not surprisingly, then, the theme appears elsewhere in Jewish literature of the Diaspora. *4 Maccabees*, whose place of origin may be Asia Minor,[1] defends Judaism against the charge of foolishness by insisting that following the Law enabled one to achieve temperance, courage, and justice—all traditional Greek philosophical virtues (5.22-24).

What actual impact this and similar presentations of Judaism had on philosophically-inclined Gentiles is difficult to assess. One cannot ignore the possibility that much Jewish apologetic was directed not to Gentiles but to Jews, as a way of encouraging loyalty to their religious tradition in the face of Hellenistic culture's dominance and attraction.[2] On the other hand, at one point Philo seems to have in mind the pro-Jewish philosopher when he writes that the true sojourner (proselyte) is one who circumcises not his foreskin but his pleasures, desires, and passions (*Quaest. in Exod.* 2.2). There is also the instance of Numenius I mentioned earlier, a second-century Platonist who acquainted himself to some degree with Jewish tradition and showed high regard for it. More generally, evidence does exist for the appeal

---

1. Charlesworth (ed.), *Old Testament Pseudepigrapha*, II, pp. 535-37.
2. V. Tcherikover, 'Jewish Apologetic Reconsidered', *Eos* 48 (1956), Fasc. 3, pp. 169-93.

that the oriental religions had on pagan philosophy in the NT period. Plutarch devotes an entire essay to a glowing portrayal of Egyptian religion. What inclined him favorably to the Egyptian rites were their promotion of moral and practical values, as opposed to the irrational or superstitious (*Is. et Os.* 8 [353E]), and their possession of wisdom, which was readily discerned in their various myths and legends (9 [354C]). Just as earlier Greek philosophers and sages—Solon, Thales, Plato, Pythagoras—had learned much from the Egyptian philosophy (10 [354E]), so now truth continued to be available from the Egyptian priests, whose reverent and philosophical interpretation of their tradition imparted an accurate picture of the gods and the world (11 [355C-D]). Plutarch endorsed Isis to a great degree because he saw an essential agreement between Egyptian wisdom and Greek philosophical truth.

Some of the philosophically inclined at Colossae found Eastern religion similarly attractive, first the Jewish tradition and then Christianity. The Colossian philosophers' adoption of certain Jewish practices evidently aided them in achieving a key philosophical goal, bodily asceticism (Col. 2.23). If Jewish festivals encouraged them to maintain self-control, as Philo thought they did (*Spec. Leg.* 2.32 §195), then their ascetic program could be furthered by following the Jewish calendar (Col. 2.16). If obedience to Jewish dietary law signaled the victory of the mind over the body or the successful control of pleasure (ἡδονή) and desire (ἐπιθυμία), as it did in *4 Maccabees* (1.33-35; 5.22-25), then adopting Jewish dietary regulations (Col. 2.16, 21) allowed the philosophers to maintain a proper balance in themselves and to avoid any fleshly indulgence (2.23; cf. Philo, *Vit. Cont.* 4 §§34-37; Plutarch, *Carn. Es.* 1.6 [995D-E]).

Entry into the Christian congregation at Colossae may also have aided or confirmed the Colossian philosophers in their philosophical pursuits. That entry was evidently smoothed by the common elements between Judaism and Christianity: the emphasis on humility in the Colossian church (Col. 3.12) would not have been entirely new to the philosophers. But something distinctive in Colossian Christianity must have drawn them to this new tradition. What was this distinctive element that proved so appealing to the Colossian philosophers? I suggest that they found support in the Christian congregation for their emphasis and reliance on the στοιχεῖα τοῦ κόσμου.

My exegesis of the Colossian polemical core concluded that the

4. The Historical and Social Setting of the Philosophy

στοιχεῖα, as the four constituents of the cosmos, were the positive guiding principles of the philosophy. How the στοιχεῖα could be the Colossian philosophy's epistemological foundation became clear later in my examination of Middle Platonism and Philo. Inspired by the appreciative view of the mundane realm in Plato's highly influential *Timaeus*, Platonists of the NT period regarded the balance and order among the στοιχεῖα as a source of knowledge, even divine knowledge. This interpretation of the Colossian philosophy and its background, indebted as it is to Schweizer, parts dramatically with him on the issue of the philosophy's regard for the στοιχεῖα. Schweizer read the philosophy's preoccupation with them differently, as evidence for a fear of them.[1] Already I have offered evidence for rejecting his view that the Colossian philosophers and Hellenistic philosophy monolithically advocated a flight from the στοιχεῖα-defined realm.

Nevertheless, Schweizer's position remains important as a reminder of a problem that Greek and later Hellenistic philosophy faced: the transitoriness of the sublunar realm. Whether expressed as Heraclitean flux, the Empedoclean strife among the elements, or Stoicism's periodic conflagration, all philosophies rooted in Greek thought acknowledged a world in constant change. The Colossian philosophy, too, seems aware of this perspective, if I correctly read its rationale for dietary regulations: dissolution (φθορά)—in this case via consumption—is the inevitable end of all foodstuffs (Col. 2.22).

Middle Platonism had no immunity to this outlook. Timaeus Locrus's *On the Nature of the Soul and the World* depicted a world in constant and potentially chaotic change—generation and dissolution (γενέσιας καὶ φθοράς; 38 [98E]). But even so that document insisted that the ratio among the στοιχεῖα remained in equilibrium (36-41 [98E-99B]), meaning that cosmic proportion and balance remained (14 [95B]).

Philo gave the same answer, but at times his response relied heavily on Jewish tradition. In a discourse on the Jewish New Year festival Philo draws an analogy between the destruction wrought by human warfare and the disorder produced by nature at war with itself:

---

1. Schweizer, *Letter to the Colossians*, pp. 127, 131; 'Slaves of the Elements', p. 464.

> And there is another war not of human agency when nature is at strife with herself, when her parts make onslaught one on another and her law-abiding sense of equality is vanquished by the greed for inequality. Both these wars work destruction on the face of the earth... While the forces of nature use drought, rainstorms, violent moisture-laden winds, scorching sun-rays, intense cold accompanied by snow, with regular harmonious alternations of the yearly seasons turned into disharmony... (*Spec. Leg.* 2.31 §§190-91).

In the face of this disharmony and imbalance among the parts—the στοιχεῖα (*Spec. Leg.* 1.17 §97)—of nature, Philo asserted that the well-proportioned cosmos would remain intact because God would sustain and regulate the created order. The very purpose of the New Year feast was to offer thanks to God as 'peacemaker (εἰρηνοποιοῦ) and peace keeper, who destroys faction both in cities and in the various parts of the universe (παντός)' (*Spec. Leg.* 2.31 §192).

A question related to this matter appears elsewhere in Philo, in his discourses on priestly vestments: who invokes God to maintain harmony and sustain the cosmic order he established? The answer is the high priest, an answer made obvious in Philo's symbolic interpretation of the high priest's garb. The priest's vestments represent the various parts of the cosmic realm (*Vit. Mos.* 2.24-26 §§117-35; *Spec. Leg.* 1.16-17 §§84-97; cf. *Quaest. in Exod.* 2.118), so that when the priest goes to the altar he bears with him the whole universe (*Vit. Mos.* 2.26 §§133, 135). Accordingly, the high priest offers prayers and thanks 'not only on behalf of the whole human race but also for the parts of the universe, earth, water, air, fire' (*Spec. Leg.* 1.17 §97).[1]

How widespread Philo's interpretation of the high priest was outside of Alexandria we cannot say, although Josephus writes in a similar vein about the symbolic meaning of the high priest's apparel (*Ant.* 3.7.7 §§184-87). Anatolian Judaism may not have known any connection between the high priest and the στοιχεῖα. But Philo's understanding of God as peacemaker in the universe must have had some currency there because the notion appears in the letter to the Colossians (1.20). Widely acknowledged to be a piece of tradition employed by the letter writer,[2] the Colossian hymn (1.15-20) ends

---

1. Schweizer discusses these matters fully in 'Versöhnung des Alls. Kol 1, 20', p. 492-93.

2. B. Vawter, 'The Colossians Hymn and the Principle of Redaction', *CBQ* 33 (1971), p. 67. The historical development of this consensus is presented in

with the declaration that God[1] has reconciled the universe (τὰ πάντα) to himself by making peace (εἰρηνοποιήσας) through Jesus Christ (vv. 19-20). Besides the thematic similarity, the shared vocabulary between *Spec. Leg.* 2.31 §192 and the hymn make the correspondence between the two strong, particularly since εἰρηνοποιέω is a *hapax legomenon* in the NT and εἰρηνοποιός is a *hapax legomenon* in Philo.[2] This connection with Philonic or similar Hellenistic Jewish interpretation means that the hymn was evidently in touch with the problem of cosmic disruption arising from the strife between the cosmic elements, even though the hymn says nothing explicit about such strife.

Did the hymn reflect a theology that was current among the Colossian Christians? That the letter writer cites the hymn and incorporates it into his address to the Colossians suggests it: what better point of departure for his arguments (1.21ff.) than a formulation that had some authority, that would strike a responsive chord with his readers?[3] If this is the case, what attracted the Colossian philosophers to the Christian community becomes evident. For those who sought guidance from the ordering and balance among the στοιχεῖα, an assurance that God maintained peace in the cosmos would have been good news indeed. Even if the Jews of Colossae could offer the same assurance of God's sustaining the cosmic order, the Colossian Christians could counter with a better offer: cosmic peace has been established *once and for all time* through the Christ-event.

Conclusion

It would go beyond the meager evidence available from the Colossian polemical core to conclude that at Colossae a group of Middle Platonists had found their way into the Christian congregation and were advocating their ideas to others. Nevertheless, many features

---

H. Gabathuler, *Jesus Christus, Haupt der Kirche—Haupt der Welt* (ATANT, 45; Zurich: Zwingli-Verlag, 1965).

1. The apparent subject of the action. See Lohse, *Colossians and Philemon*, pp. 56-59.
2. S. Lyonnet, 'L'hymne christologique de l'épître aux Colossiens et la fête juive du nouvel an', *RSR* 48 (1960), p. 99.
3. Vawter, 'Colossians Hymn', p. 80; Lohse, *Colossians and Philemon*, p. 46; Pokorný, *Colossians*, p. 29; Schweizer, *Letter to the Colossians*, p. 133.

gleaned from the polemical core can be documented in Hellenistic philosophy of the NT period, particularly in Middle Platonism. Demon or angel worship, control of the body through asceticism, and an epistemological interest in the ordering of the στοιχεῖα τοῦ κόσμου can all be located in sources with a Middle Platonic perspective. Moreover, these features cohere around a common philosophical theme: the pursuit and acquisition of divine knowledge. The philosophers at Colossae pursued that wisdom in many ways: through the στοιχεῖα τοῦ κόσμου; via purification (asceticism) of the body so that the mind could receive and understand visions from above; and probably even through the demons or angels, because they acted as messengers between heaven and earth. From what the polemical core tells us, the Colossian philosophers exhibited none of the philosophical sophistication of Philo or Antiochus of Ascalon. Theirs was a simple, more popular form of philosophy. But even in its simplicity it is recognizably Middle Platonic.

The philosophy at Colossae also embodied a Jewish outlook. Since Torah obedience is not an issue in the letter and the philosophers have not given up the abhorrent practice of demon or angel worship, they hardly appear to be proselytes of Judaism. But their calendar observance reveals their Jewish orientation. Evidently, the Colossian philosophers were affiliated at some level with the Colossian Jewish community, a common phenomenon in the NT period, particularly in areas of significant and well-established Jewish population, such as the region around Colossae.

What attracted those philosophers to Judaism is indicated by the Hellenistic Jewish interpretation of Jewish tradition vis-à-vis Greek philosophy. Philo and others presented Jewish practices as a vehicle for philosophical goals. Jewish calendar and food regulations could help the philosopher to overcome the indulgence of the flesh (Col. 2.23) and thus to achieve philosophical purification. The Hellenistic Jewish presentation of Judaism suggests how the Colossian philosophers produced a synthesis between traditions: Jewish practices served philosophical ends and the Colossian philosophy had a markedly Jewish outlook.

Added to the synthesis was a Christian component, for the Colossian philosophy's emphasis on humility suggests contact with Christianity. What would have drawn the philosophers to, and even into, the Christian community at Colossae? The special appeal of Colossian

4. The Historical and Social Setting of the Philosophy

Christianity lay in the assurances it could bring to a philosophy so focused on the στοιχεῖα for guidance. The philosophers joined others at Colossae in celebrating Christ as the one who brought peace to the cosmic order (Col. 1.20). By doing so they could follow that cosmic order without anxiety.

Chapter 5

THE CONTROVERSY IN COLOSSIANS

The important steps in reconstructing the Colossian philosophy have now been completed: first, other reconstructions have been presented and assessed; second, the Colossian polemical core has been identified and exegeted, and that exegesis defended; and third, the resulting picture of the philosophy has been socially and historically located. What remains to be accomplished in this study is to verify the accuracy of this reconstruction by testing it against the letter to the Colossians as a whole. In other words, does this interpretation of the Colossian philosophy, based as it is on the polemical core of Colossians, ring true with the remainder of the letter?

This question arises in part from the methodological conservatism that guided my exegetical work. For reasons enunciated at the beginning of Chapter 3, I narrowed the scope of this investigation to the polemical core of Colossians and restricted that core to Col. 2.8, 16-23. At this point, however, it would be artificial to maintain this narrow a perspective, particularly since other verses in the letter may have been important to the letter writer's polemic, even if they say little about the philosophy itself. Assessing what role other portions of Colossians played in the polemic expressed in Col. 2.8, 16-23 will reveal not only how consonant my reading of the polemic is with the rest of the letter but also where the polemic fits in the logic and structure of the whole letter.

Another important question may be resolved by gauging the place of the polemic in the letter as a whole: the importance the letter writer placed on his correction of the Colossian philosophy. If the philosophy's potential or actual disruption of the Colossian congregation is the reason or one of the primary reasons for writing the letter, then polemic-related material should abound and extend throughout and even beyond ch. 2. Francis showed overconfidence when he began his

5. *The Controversy in Colossians*

study of the Colossian controversy by asserting that the interpretation of Col. 2.18 was crucial to determining the occasion of the letter.[1] But this assertion may have merit if significant portions of the letter contribute to the effectiveness of the letter writer's polemic.

So unavoidable is an examination of the whole letter that even as I have restricted myself to Col. 2.8, 16-23 in reconstructing the Colossian philosophy, I have frequently turned to other parts of the letter in conducting my exegesis, assessing other reconstructions, and relating the philosophy to the Colossian church. Already I have examined σάρξ (2.18) in light of its occurrences in 1.22 and 2.11, ταπεινοφροσύνη in 2.18, 23 and 3.12, and so forth. Moreover, information I gathered about the nature of the Colossian congregation—its theological perspective and Gentile composition—came from outside the polemical core.

The Polemical Core in its Epistolary Context

The search for polemic-related material in Colossians need not go far afield. This study has largely neglected the immediate context of the polemical core, paying scant attention even to 2.9-15, a passage bracketed by Col. 2.8, 16-23. One would expect to find some anticipation of the polemic in that passage, perhaps even polemical elements, although that passage and others were judged to be of little value for reconstructing the features of the Colossian philosophy.

Col. 2.9-15 deserves the attention of the interpreter for several reasons, not just because it sits squarely between portions of the polemical core. As noted earlier, the style and content of 2.9-15 distinguish it dramatically from the surrounding verses; the straightforward warnings and directions of 2.8 and 2.16-23 contrast markedly with the hymnic or liturgical flavor of 2.9-15. While these features make the passage a poor hunting ground for information about the Colossian philosophy, they prompt a question whose answer would give the interpreter insight into the letter writer's purpose at this point in the letter. Why the contrast between 2.8, 16-23 and 2.9-15? Most scholars account for the distinctiveness of 2.9-15 by noting that the letter writer has relied heavily on traditional material in these verses.[2] By explaining why the letter writer introduces tradition into

1. Francis, 'Colossian Controversy', pp. 6-7.
2. J. O'Neill, 'The Source of the Christology in Colossians', *NTS* 26

his composition here, the interpreter would have a clue to the letter writer's purpose in writing.

Col. 2.9-15 belongs to the author's commentary on the christological hymn of Col. 1.15-20; he introduces tradition to interpret the hymnic tradition he introduced earlier.[1] Apart from the context he provides for the hymn (1.13-14) and possible changes he makes in the hymn itself,[2] the letter writer begins his interpretation of the hymn immediately after its appearance in the letter. In 1.21-22 he draws out the implications of the universal reconciliation (ἀποκαταλλάσσω) mentioned in the hymn (1.20) for the human congregation.[3] This interpretive work intensifies in 2.9-15. Verses 9 and 10 take the reader back to the hymn by repeating important vocabulary from it. In that repetition the author offers his interpretation of the hymn. In 2.9 the author qualifies and emphasizes the fullness that was pleased to dwell in Christ (1.19): the fullness *of the deity* (θεότητος) dwells in him bodily (σωματικῶς). Verse 10 spells out the implication of this indwelling for believers: 'and you have come to fullness of life in him'.[4]

The letter writer's interpretation of the hymn continues in the remainder of the passage; the latter half of v. 10 through v. 15 clarify Christ's relationship to the principalities and powers (ἀρχαὶ καὶ ἐξουσίαι; 1.16; 2.10, 15). Tradition plays a prominent part here, for vv. 11-13 reflect baptismal formulae[5] and vv. 14 and 15 turn to confessional material, a transition marked by the shift from second to

---

(1979–80), p. 95; Cannon, *Traditional Materials*, pp. 11, 37-49; Bujard, *Kolosserbrief*, p. 227; Lähnemann, *Kolosserbrief*, p. 20.

1. Kiley, *Colossians as Pseudepigraphy*, p. 78; Bujard, *Kolosserbrief*, pp. 81-86; O'Neill, 'Source of Christology', pp. 97-99; Lohse, *Colossians and Philemon*, pp. 99-101.

2. Vawter, 'Colossians Hymn', pp. 75-76; Lohse, *Colossians and Philemon*, pp. 42-45; J. Robinson, 'A Formal Analysis of Colossians 1.15-20', *JBL* 76 (1957), pp. 281, 284-87; J. Sanders, *The New Testament Christological Hymns* (SNTSMS, 15; Cambridge: Cambridge University Press, 1971), pp. 12-14.

3. W. Meeks, 'In One Body: The Unity of Humankind in Colossians and Ephesians', in Jervell and Meeks (eds.), *God's Christ and His People*, p. 211.

4. Lohse, *Colossians and Philemon*, pp. 99-101; Schweizer, *Letter to the Colossians*, pp. 137-40.

5. Lohse, *Colossians and Philemon*, pp. 101-105; Meeks, 'In One Body', pp. 210-11.

5. *The Controversy in Colossians* 137

first person plural in v. 13.[1] The hymn says that all things, including the ἀρχαί and ἐξουσίαι (1.16), were created in Christ, and that in Christ God reconciled all things by his peacemaking efforts (1.20). The letter writer defines what Christ's agency in creation means with regard to the cosmic powers: he is the head of every ἀρχή and ἐξουσία (2.10). As for God's reconciliation for all things in Christ, that was achieved by conquering and humiliating the ἀρχαί and ἐξουσίαι (2.15).

This interpretation clarifies certain ambiguities in the hymn. Unarticulated in 1.15-20 is the way in which the cosmic harmony celebrated in the hymn's opening lines was lost, such that reconciliation became necessary.[2] The second strophe of the hymn begins with the phrase πρωτότοκος ἐκ τῶν νεκρῶν (1.18), which only hints at the way in which the original universal order failed: death entered the cosmic realm. In that same verse we learn that Christ has gained lordship over death. But how did this come about? Must not death be conquered (cf. 1 Cor. 15.26; Rev. 21.4)? The letter writer asserts that the reconciling and peacemaking actions that gave Christ lordship over all creation (Col. 1.18) should be understood as the *conquest* of cosmic forces (2.15).

In this clarification of the hymn the letter writer casts the ἀρχαί and ἐξουσίαι in a decidedly negative role.[3] The hymn includes them in the cosmic order created and sustained by God through Christ (1.16). That order is maintained by God's reconciling and peace-making efforts (1.20). But in the letter writer's interpretation the hymn's image of reconciliation and peacemaking gives way to military imagery. The grammar of 2.15 lacks clarity, for the subject of the verse could be either God or Christ and the final words of the verse (ἐν αὐτῷ) could mean 'in him', presumably Christ, or 'in it', that is, the cross. Yet such grammatical ambiguity does not obscure the actions and object in the verse: the peacemaking that established or restored Christ's headship over the principalities and powers (cf. 1.16, 18; 2.10) entailed disarming or stripping (απεκδύομαι) these cosmic

---

1. Lohse, *Colossians and Philemon*, p. 106. His full treatment of this passage appears in 'Ein hymnisches Bekenntnis in Kol 2,13c-15', in A. Descamps and A. de Halleux (eds.), *Mélanges bibliques en hommage au R.P. Béda Rigaux* (Gembloux: Duculot, 1970), pp. 430-35.
2. Vawter, 'Colossians Hymn', p. 76.
3. Meeks, 'In One Body', p. 211.

powers, exposing them to public ridicule (δειγματίζω ἐν παρρησίᾳ), and leading them as one would captives in a triumphal procession, or simply triumphing over them (θριαμβεύω).[1] Such language makes it impossible to regard the cosmic powers as neutral or positive; the letter writer thought they were inimical to God's rule and thus had to be conquered (cf. 1 Cor. 15.24).[2]

The purpose of putting a tradition-laden interpretation of the hymn between polemical portions of the letter should now be clear. Such a juxtaposition suggests, first of all, that the hymn had some degree of authority among the recipients of the letter, including the Colossian philosophers.[3] If not, there would be little reason to interrupt the polemic of ch. 2 and remind readers of the hymn. The return to the hymn at this point also indicates why the letter writer included the hymn in the letter: to anticipate the polemic of ch. 2.[4] But to serve the letter writer's purposes well, the hymn had to be interpreted so that it would unequivocally support his polemic. To be persuasive, the letter writer shrouded his interpretation in traditional language. He used such language to eliminate any positive reading of the powers that belong to the cosmic realm. That the hymn allows such an understanding[5] but the letter writer's interpretation does *not* attest to his success in preparing for his assault on the στοιχεῖα-guided philosophy. By putting this spin on 1.15-20, 2.9-15 anticipates and

1. BAGD, pp. 83, 172, 363; Lohse, *Colossians and Philemon*, pp. 111-13; Wink, *Naming the Powers*, pp. 55-60; R. Yates, 'Christ and the Powers of Evil in Colossians', in E. Livingstone (ed.), *Studia Biblica 1978: III. Papers on Paul and Other New Testament Authors* (JSNTSup, 3; Sheffield: JSOT Press, 1980), pp. 364-66.
2. W. Carr has argued for a more positive understanding of the cosmic powers in 2.15 (*Angels and Principalities: The Background, Meaning and Development of the Pauline Phrase hai archai kai hai exousiai* [SNTSMS, 42; Cambridge: Cambridge University Press, 1981], pp. 52-66), an argument that has persuaded R. Yates ('Colossians 2.15: Christ Triumphant', *NTS* 37 [1991], pp. 573-91), but Sappington notes several problems with Carr's interpretation (*Revelation and Redemption*, pp. 208-13, esp. p. 213 n. 2).
3. Pokorný, *Colossians*, p. 29; Schweizer, *Letter to the Colossians*, p. 133; 'Versöhnung des Alls. Kol 1,20', pp. 499-500.
4. W. Rollins, 'Christological *Tendenz* in Colossians 1.15-20: A *Theologia Crucis*', in R. Berkey and S. Edwards (eds.), *Christological Perspectives* (New York: Pilgrim Press, 1982), p. 131.
5. N. Wright, 'Poetry and Theology in Colossians 1.15-20', *NTS* 36 (1990), pp. 451-52.

undergirds the polemical core surrounding it. As Moyo says of the passage:

> Paul is in fact polemicising against a positive understanding of the elements when he stresses Christ's victory over the principalities and powers (cf. 2:15). He wants to demonstrate the superiority of Christ over the powers and consequently insists that they be negatively understood.[1]

Moyo also notes that in the letter writer's negative portrayal of the principalities and powers a dualistic outlook has entered the letter. The letter writer, not the Colossian philosophers, set Christ and the powers of the world in opposition.[2] Others have observed this phenomenon elsewhere in the letter, particularly Lyonnet, who made great use of it in his criticism of the Jewish-Gnostic reconstructions of the philosophy.[3] That the dualistic language comes from the letter writer and that it pervades the letter is clear: we find the oppositions light/darkness (1.12-13), dead/alive (2.12-13), things that are above/things that are on the earth, and old self/new self (3.9-10).

But what is the purpose of these antinomies? If their function in 2.9-15 is any indication, the letter writer's dualistic categories provide a basis for his polemic against the Colossian philosophy, for this dualistic perspective allows the author to attack any attachment to the old order. A logic based on this orientation clearly stands behind the question he poses the philosophers and their sympathizers in 2.20: 'If you died with Christ, parted from the elements of the world, why do you submit to rules as if living in the world?' In other words, if you died to the worldly στοιχεῖα, why do they still guide you in your new life? This is a reasonable question from the letter writer, given his dualistic outlook, and it is a question that Paul himself might have raised, since he maintained that the believer had been crucified to the world (Gal. 6.14). But the logic prompting this question is not shared by the Colossian philosophers. They, too, have a dualistic outlook, but they see little of the danger and discontinuity the letter writer associates with that dualism. Proper discipline can control the body and the promptings of the flesh, so that the mind is not lost on fleshly things (cf. Col. 2.18, 23). The στοιχεῖα of this world can be relied on to convey knowledge of the things above. In the grammar of the question

---

1. Moyo, 'Colossian Heresy', p. 35.
2. Moyo, 'Colossian Heresy', pp. 34-35.
3. Lyonnet, 'Saint Paul et le gnosticisme', p. 548.

at 2.20 the letter writer reveals the position of the philosophers; the ὡς + participle construction sets forth the basis on which the philosophers act: they submit to rules imagining that they *do* live in the world.[1] As much as they believe this, however, the letter writer's question and the perspective implied by the question make the philosophers' affirmation seem untenable. Simply put, the antinomies sprinkled throughout Colossians appear to provide a point of view that makes the polemical question of 2.20 especially damaging. Moreover, they may be the basis for the alternative to the philosophy's praxis that the letter writer expresses in the paraenesis of ch. 3. For there dualistic language in the opening verses (3.2; 3.9-10) serves as the basis for the distinctions the letter writer draws between types of orientation and behavior.

This first foray into the epistolary context of the polemical core shows the central place that the letter writer's attack on the philosophy occupies in the letter. While by no means a direct attack on the philosophy, 2.9-15 undergirds the polemic in the surrounding verses. Moreover, because 2.9-15 intentionally reintroduces the christological hymn, the hymn itself seems to have been included in the letter to set the stage for the polemic.[2] The same seems to be true of the letter's antinomies. Whatever other function(s) the letter writer's dualistic perspective may have had, with regard to the letter's polemic it served admirably as a basis for the assault on the philosophy. Language full of antinomies was bound to undercut a philosophy that saw strong continuity between this world and the divine.

A Debate over Knowledge

Perhaps other features of the letter contributed to the effectiveness of the writer's polemic against the Colossian philosophy. One of the letter's most prominent features, its Christology, merits the interpreter's attention, particularly since many reconstructions of the philosophy have placed a christological debate at the center of the Colossian controversy.[3] In his critique of such interpretations Francis

---

1. Smyth, *Greek Grammar*, §2086a-b. *Contra* Francis, 'Christological Argument', p. 206.
2. Robinson, 'Formal Analysis', p. 283.
3. Francis describes such reconstructions in 'Christological Argument', pp. 194-96.

5. *The Controversy in Colossians* 141

examined the christological statements of Colossians and concluded that the philosophy's Christology was not the bone of contention at Colossae.[1] In support of Francis, my reconstruction of the Colossian philosophy found no grounds for describing the debate between the letter writer and the Colossian philosophy as a battle of Christologies.

Yet if the letter writer's concern to undercut the philosophy triggered his writing, the interpreter would expect the letter's prominent Christology to be connected in some way with the polemic. Such is the case with the passages just treated, 2.9-15 and 1.15-20, verses laden with christological language and laying the groundwork for the letter writer's polemic. Other passages, too, abound with christological affirmations, and, like 2.9-15, express the letter writer's elaboration of the christological hymn. According to W. Schenk, much of this christological reflection on the hymn revolves around the issue of revelation. Thus, in the language of Col. 1.25-28 and 2.2-3, where Christ is associated with and even identified as God's mystery, Schenk finds the letter writer exploring the hymn as an affirmation of Christ as the locus of God's revelation to humankind.[2] In these verses Christ has become the source of all knowledge and basis for all teaching:

> It is he whom we proclaim... teaching everyone in all wisdom (1.28)

> I want their hearts to be encouraged and united in love, so that they may have all the riches of assured understanding and have knowledge of God's mystery, that is, Christ himself, in whom are hidden all the treasures of wisdom and knowledge (2.2-3).

Such an epistemology had an ethical corollary, notes Schenk.[3] If the hymn proclaims Christ as the sole unveiling of God's mystery, then he becomes the guiding principle for all ethics and praxis: 'You have stripped off the old self with its practices and have clothed yourselves with the new self, which is being renewed in knowledge according to the image [εἰκών; cf. Col. 1.15] of its creator' (3.9-10).

The connection between the letter writer's emphasis on Christology and his polemic should now be clear. His Christocentric understanding of revelation has clear implications for the question I placed at the center of the dispute between the letter writer and the Colossian

---

1. Francis, 'Christological Argument', pp. 196-207.
2. W. Schenk, 'Christus, das Geheimnis der Welt, als dogmatisches und ethisches Grundprinzip des Kolosserbriefes', *EvT* 43 (1983), pp. 147-51.
3. Schenk, 'Christus, das Geheimnis der Welt', pp. 151-55.

philosophers: how does one acquire divine knowledge?[1] My exegesis of the Colossian polemical core revealed that the letter writer invariably moved from condemnation of the discipline enjoined by the philosophers to rejection of their authority and disparagement of the bases for their practices and authority. Throughout the polemic the letter writer points to inadequate foundations: (1) a philosophy based on human tradition, not on Christ (2.8, 22); (2) a life regulated by principles (στοιχεῖα) that have no bearing on the believer (2.20); (3) a guiding insight or vision received and investigated by a *fleshly* mind (2.18); and (4) a wisdom that is illusory and inadequate to the task of checking the indulgence of the flesh (2.23). The rebuttal and distortion built into this polemic have an obvious aim, which is to undermine the philosophy's claim to have wisdom and the sources of that wisdom.

In taking this tack the letter writer has focused his polemic accurately. As my reconstruction of the Colossian philosophy indicated, the various features of the philosophy cohere around a single pursuit, the acquisition of divine knowledge. Such knowledge the philosophers acquired in several ways: through the στοιχεῖα τοῦ κόσμου, whose proportion and harmony reflected a divine ordering; via asceticism of the body, so that the mind would be free to receive and understand revelatory insight from above; and from the demons or angels, who passed information from heaven to earth. The letter writer's polemic expresses a rejection of all these avenues of knowledge, and the effectiveness of this polemical line rests in part on the theology of revelation enunciated in the christological affirmations outside the polemical core. A philosophy not according to Christ (2.8) is one devoid of an epistemological base, for in Christ 'are hidden *all* the treasures of wisdom and knowledge' (2.3). For the letter writer, the identification of Christ as God's mystery means not only that divine knowledge is available through Christ, but also that all other reputed sources of it are in fact worthless. The argument at work in the polemical core assumes precisely such exclusivity: apart from Christ no source of wisdom exists.

That the subject under debate at Colossae is wisdom is not a novel observation; even interpreters representing opposing reconstructions of the Colossian philosophy have reached the same conclusion. Both Moyo and Lyonnet, for example, placed wisdom at the center of the

1. H. Lona, *Die Eschatologie im Kolosser- und Epheserbrief* (FB, 48; Würzburg: Echter Verlag, 1984), pp. 233-34.

5. *The Controversy in Colossians*

Colossian controversy, but the former turned to the Nag Hammadi finds to explain this preoccupation with knowledge, the latter to the Dead Sea Scrolls.[1] Both introduced promising backgrounds for their reconstructions. But what they failed to account for, even when they observed it, was that the letter writer himself, particularly in the themes of God's hidden mystery and wisdom (Col. 1.26; 2.3) and pronounced dualism, came closer to the thought of the Dead Sea Scrolls[2] or Gnosticism[3] than did the Colossian philosophy. Thus, I have introduced an altogether different background for understanding the philosophers' pursuit of wisdom, that of Middle Platonic philosophy. In doing so I have tried to take Lyonnet seriously when he asserts that it is insufficient merely to say that knowledge was the subject of the conflict at Colossae. One also has to specify the context in which the debate over knowledge was conducted.[4]

Yet to specify the Colossian philosophy's epistemology as Middle Platonic provides an incomplete background for the debate reflected in Colossians. If it were the full context, the interpreter could coordinate the dispute at Colossae with broad developments in Hellenistic philosophy. In this framework, reliance on the στοιχεῖα places the Colossian philosophy in the Stoic-Antiochian wing of the school and marks it as immanentist in thinking, as I have already argued; the world-wary author of Colossians expresses the Pythagorean-Eudorian perspective within Middle Platonism and represents the transcendental or idealist mode of thinking that came to characterize Platonism and much of ancient philosophy in the Roman Empire.[5] This analysis, however, obscures the background out of which the letter writer frames his polemic: apocalyptic thought. The letter writer's negative portrayal of this-worldly powers (2.15), his use of antinomies (1.12-13; 2.12-13; 3.2; 3.9-10), and his emphasis on the hiddenness of wisdom (1.26; 2.3) all bespeak an outlook typical of the more explicitly apocalyptic sections of Paul's letters (for example, 1 Cor. 2.6-8;

---

1. Moyo, 'Colossian Heresy', pp. 35-37; Lyonnet, 'Paul's Adversaries', pp. 151-53.
2. Congdon, 'False Teachers', p. 268.
3. R. Grant, *Gnosticism and Early Christianity* (New York: Columbia University Press, 2nd edn, 1966), p. 160.
4. Lyonnet, 'Saint Paul et le gnosticisme', p. 540.
5. Brenk, 'Imperial Heritage', p. 249; Witt, *Middle Platonism*, pp. 23-25.

15.24-28).[1] Moreover, the distinctive language the letter writer uses to express this apocalyptic perspective, such as 'treasures of wisdom' in 2.3, may find its strongest parallels in *2 Bar.* 44.14 and 54.13, and the antinomies of Col. 3.1-6 may best be understood by reference to *2 Bar.* 48.42–52.7.[2] Whatever the nature of these latter correspondences,[3] the letter writer shows his Pauline pedigree by framing his response to crisis according to an apocalyptic perspective, much as Paul did.[4] Admittedly, the letter writer articulates an eschatology that differs from Paul's.[5] Still, very much like Paul, the letter writer employs apocalyptic language to sanction what he regards as normative behavior (ch. 3) and to support a polemic designed to correct deviant beliefs and practices disrupting the community he addresses.[6]

This second foray into the epistolary context of the polemical core confirms the finding of the first: significant passages of the letter outside the polemic, such as 2.9-15 and 1.15-20, and major thematic emphases of the letter, such as Christology, revelation, and dualism, share the common goal of laying a foundation for the letter's polemic. This partnership between core and context reveals itself most clearly in the midst of battle: at points, such as Col. 2.20, the polemic assumes the claims and perspective articulated in key non-polemical portions of the letter.

This correspondence between the polemical core and several dominant features in Colossians constitutes certain evidence that the

---

1. H. Conzelmann, *1 Corinthians* (Hermeneia; Philadelphia: Fortress Press, 1975), pp. 56-63, 269-75; C. Beker, *Paul the Apostle: The Triumph of God in Life and Thought* (Philadelphia: Fortress Press, 1980), p. 145.

2. Bandstra, 'Colossian Errorists', pp. 340-43; J. Levison, '2 Apoc. Bar. 48.42–52.7 and the Apocalyptic Dimension of Colossian 3.1-6', *JBL* 108 (1989), pp. 96-104, 107-108.

3. An argument for the literary dependence of Colossians on *2 Baruch* would face a dating problem, as the relevant portions of the latter may have reached their present form decades (around 110 or 120 CE) after Colossians. See Charlesworth (ed.), *Old Testament Pseudepigrapha*, I, pp. 616-17.

4. E. Käsemann, 'On the Subject of Primitive Christian Apocalyptic', in *New Testament Questions of Today* (Philadelphia: Fortress Press, 1969), p. 133.

5. Compare for instance the different understandings of baptism in Col. 2.12 and Rom. 6.3-11 (Lona, *Eschatologie*, pp. 163-64).

6. W. Meeks, 'Social Functions of Apocalyptic Language in Pauline Christianity', in D. Hellholm (ed.), *Apocalypticism in the Mediterranean and the Near East* (Tübingen: Mohr, 1983), p. 700.

5. The Controversy in Colossians

threat posed by the Colossian philosophy was a major reason for composing the letter. In fact, it may have been *the* occasion for writing. The wide-ranging christological affirmations of chs. 1 and 2, begun in the hymn and continued in the letter writer's interpretation of the hymn, are most coherent if understood as prelude to the polemic of Col. 2.8, 16-23. The rich christological language is not the product of unfocused or unmotivated reflection; much of it coheres around a Christocentric theology of knowledge, the obvious stimulus of which was the Colossian philosophy's wisdom claims.

Epilogue

THE COLOSSIAN PHILOSOPHY AND THE CONFLICT AT COLOSSAE TODAY

Whether or not the letter to the Colossians had the effect intended by its author is not known now and will probably never be known with certainty, although the Council of Laodicea's prohibition of angel worship (canon 35) indicates continuing problems in western Anatolia with practices reminiscent of the Colossian philosophy's. Whatever its intended and actual effect, because of its inclusion in the New Testament Colossians has had a profound effect on generations of Christians throughout the world. There is no need to chronicle here its impact over the centuries. Its importance is obvious: quite apart from its value as a mirror of early theological developments, especially Christology, the letter provides an instructive picture of the origins and dynamics of conflict, a condition which characterizes Christian communities of all times and places.

Valuable lessons often illuminate and warn, often instruct both by positive and negative examples, and such seems to be the case with Colossians. For the letter has preserved for all generations an early hymn that shines light on early Christian worship, specifically the Christocentric focus of early Christian liturgy. Moreover, if my reconstruction of the Colossian philosophy and the conflict at Colossae is correct, the Christian community at Colossae and all parties in conflict recognized the hymn. In other words, as language of worship and as an affirmation about Christ, the hymn may preserve what the Colossians Christians and the letter writer held in common.

The hymn brought people together, but it also divided them. In his commentary on Colossians, J. Burgess critiques contemporary theological claims based on the hymn by noting how easily it may be misunderstood and even misused:

1:15-20 is a hymn, not a series of doctrinal propositions... It focused totally on Christ as the only Lord and Savior, not the nature of the cosmos or its inhabitants. The hymn did not intend or imply a theology (Christology) of nature, and only an over-reading of the text will find a theology of nature in it.[1]

Ironically, what Burgess faults in contemporary interpretations of the hymn occurred already in the first century. According to my reconstruction of the situation at Colossae, the Colossian philosophers were drawn to Christianity precisely because they understood the community there to proclaim a savior that had restored peace to an unstable, threatening cosmos. Hence, they could fearlessly rely on the elements of the world to guide them. The letter writer also over-read the hymn when he appropriated it for his polemic, for what I described in the last chapter as his elimination of ambiguity in the hymn may also be seen as a misapplication of the hymn. If Col. 2.15 was the letter writer's interpretation of what Christ's peacemaking implied for the cosmos—the conquest and humiliation of the cosmic powers—then 2.15 turned the hymn into a theology of nature. Doxology became dogma within Colossians itself. The hymn, to the extent that it was a basis for the letter writer's polemic, became a weapon of division.

The letter to the Colossians also teaches a lesson as it relates to the apostle Paul. The contemporary Christian would do well to follow the example of the author of Colossians, whose allegiance to Paul did not express itself in a rigid, literal application of Paul to the crisis he faced. L. Keck and V. Furnish characterize the approach in this way: 'Clearly, he [the writer] does not regard the Pauline tradition as something inert, to be boxed up and saved in the church's theological attic like a family heirloom. He receives it rather as a living tradition, which grows and develops as it is interpreted and applied'.[2]

No example is perfect, however. Anyone who claims to speak for Paul, as the author of Colossians did, bears a heavy responsibility, especially if the pursuit of victory in a dispute, or perhaps control of a community, results in a distortion of Paul's thought, which seems to be the case in Colossians. In opposing Christ to the elements of the world (2.8) and devaluing the latter entirely (2.20), the letter writer did not do full justice to Paul's theology. Paul was well aware of

1. Burgess, 'Letter to the Colossians', p. 58.
2. L. Keck and V. Furnish, *The Pauline Letters* (Interpreting Biblical Texts; Nashville: Abingdon Press, 1984), p. 124.

worldly powers inimical to God's rule, but he expected reconciliation to entail more than conquest; he awaited the ultimate transformation and redemption of *all* creation (Rom. 8.18-25).

The letter writer's caricature of Paul has not always served later generations of Christians well; it deserves correction. Perhaps nowhere is this task more effectively accomplished in recent years than in the scholarship of W. Wink. His three-volume study of power does not limit itself to Colossians, Paul, or even the NT, yet it focuses on the Pauline conception of the cosmic powers.[1] In the introduction to the final volume Wink summarizes the thesis of the entire work: the powers are good but they are fallen, so they must be redeemed.[2] He finds this thesis especially well captured in the christological hymn of Colossians, but even as he appreciatively explores the hymn, he implies the inadequacy of the letter writer's understanding of it:

> The Jesus who died at the hands of the Powers died every bit as much for the Powers as he died for the people. The statement in Col. 1:20 that God was pleased to reconcile to himself all things, whether on earth or in heaven, by making peace through the blood of the cross, cannot apply just to people, since we are not in 'heaven'. It must mean the Powers referred to in v. 16, in both their visible and invisible aspects, as the reiteration of the phrase 'on earth or in heaven' (1:16, 20) makes clear. It is these Powers that Christ reconciles to God through his death on the cross. That death is not, then, merely an unmasking and exposure of the Powers for what they are (Col. 2:15), but an effort to transform the Powers into what they are meant to be.[3]

To set the elements of the world in unqualified opposition to Christ, as the author of Colossians did, is to limit and distort what Christ's triumph means. As Wink notes, 'Christ makes all things subject to himself, not by coercion, but by healing diseased reality and restoring its balance and integrity'.[4]

The letter writer also misrepresented Paul's epistemology. Paul himself regarded the world as a source of knowledge about God

---

1. Wink, *Naming the Powers*; *Unmasking the Powers: The Invisible Forces that Determine Human Existence* (Philadelphia: Fortress Press, 1986); *Engaging the Powers: Discernment and Resistance in a World of Domination* (Minneapolis: Fortress Press, 1992).
2. *Engaging the Powers*, p. 10.
3. *Engaging the Powers*, p. 82.
4. *Engaging the Powers*, p. 83.

Epilogue *The Colossian Philosophy*

(Rom. 1.19-20), even though humankind consistently fails to respond to this insight and even distorts this truth (1.18, 21-23), but the author of Colossians located God's wisdom narrowly, entirely in Christ (Col. 1.26; 2.2-4), to the apparent exclusion of all else (2.8, 20). Because the letter writer claimed the authority of Paul, it is perhaps understandable that when M. Daly attacks what she perceives as Paul's total denigration of the cosmos and the elements of the world, she quotes largely from Colossians.[1] This reliance on Colossians invalidates some of her claims about Paul. Nevertheless, her critique of, and counterproposal to, Christianity merit attention for two reasons. First, the alternative she proposes is a way of life uncannily—or perhaps *not* unexpectedly—like the Colossian philosophy, at least as I have reconstructed it. Daly calls for women to tap their elemental potency, that is, to reclaim their 'capacity to receive inspiration, truth from the elements of the natural world'.[2] To overcome what she regards as false distinctions and antinomies, such as that of spirit versus matter, Daly recommends a return to the angelic, demonic and elemental as the guides to true being.[3] Second, Daly's elemental feminist philosophy takes issue with Christianity on the same subject that fueled the Colossian controversy: wisdom and how one gets it.

The conflict that raged at Colossae is bound to arise again and again because the issue of how and to what degree divine wisdom comes to expression in the world remains disputed among Christian thinkers. Given the lack of unanimity over the centuries, it would probably be fair to conclude that Christian theology recognizes a complex and dynamic relationship between God and the world. Unfortunately, the author of Colossians could not tolerate such ambiguity, attempting instead to silence the party to the conversation at Colossae representing the view in tension with his. This is not to say that the Colossian philosophy did not deserve criticism. It probably did. Perhaps Daly does, too. But ideally, then as now, those criticisms should be raised in the course of a conversation among participants in a community, not in a polemic meant to end discussion.

---

1. M. Daly, *Pure Lust: Elemental Feminist Philosophy* (New York: Harper-Collins, 1984), pp. 8-9, 178-81.
2. *Pure Lust*, p. 169.
3. *Pure Lust*, pp. 11, 19, 155, 291-93.

BIBLIOGRAPHY

Baltes, M. (ed.), *Timaios Lokros, 'Über die Natur des Kosmos und der Seele'* (Philosophia Antiqua, 21; Leiden: Brill, 1972).
Bandstra, A.J., 'Did the Colossian Errorists Need a Mediator?', in R.N. Longenecker and M.C. Tenney (eds.), *New Dimensions in New Testament Study* (Grand Rapids: Zondervan, 1974), pp. 329-43.
—*The Law and the Elements of the World: An Exegetical Study in Aspects of Paul's Teaching* (Kampen: Kok, 1964).
Baron, S.W., *A Social and Religious History of the Jews*. I. *To the Beginning of the Christian Era* (New York: Columbia University Press, 2nd edn, 1952).
Barrett, C.K., 'Jews and Judaizers in the Epistles of Ignatius', in R. Hamerton-Kelly and R. Scroggs (eds.), *Jews, Greeks and Christians: Religious Cultures in Late Antiquity: Essays in Honor of W.D. Davies* (Leiden: Brill, 1976), pp. 220-44.
Bean, G.E., *Turkey beyond the Maeander: An Archaeological Guide* (Totowa, NJ: Rowman & Littlefield, 1971).
Beasley-Murray, G.R., 'The Second Chapter of Colossians', *RevExp* 70 (1973), pp. 469-79.
Behm, J., and E. Würthwein, 'νοέω, νοῦς, κτλ', *TDNT*, IV, pp. 948-1022.
Beker, J.C., *Paul the Apostle: The Triumph of God in Life and Thought* (Philadelphia: Fortress Press, 1980).
Berchman, R.M., *From Philo to Origen: Middle Platonism in Transition* (BJS, 69; Chico, CA: Scholars Press, 1984).
Betz, H.D. (ed.), *Plutarch's Theological Writings and Early Christian Literature* (SCHNT, 3; Leiden: Brill, 1975).
Bianchi, U. (ed.), *The Origins of Gnosticism: Colloquium of Messina 13–18 April 1966* (Studies in the History of Religions, Numen Supplement, 12; Leiden: Brill, 1967).
Billings, T., *The Platonism of Philo Judaeus* (Ancient Philosophy, 3; repr.; New York: Garland, 1979 [1919]).
Blinzler, J., 'Lexikalisches zu dem Terminus τὰ στοιχεῖα τοῦ κόσμου bei Paulus', in *Studiorum Paulinorum Congressus Internationalis Catholicus 1961* (AnBib, 17–18; 2 vols.; Rome: Pontificio Instituto Biblico, 1963), II, pp. 429-43.
Bluck, R.S. (ed.), *Plato's 'Phaedo'* (London: Routledge & Kegan Paul, 1955).
Bornkamm, G., *Das Ende des Gesetzes: Paulusstudien* (BEvT, 16; Munich: Chr. Kaiser Verlag, 1952).
—'Die Häresie des Kolosserbriefes', *TLZ* 73 (1948), pp. 11-20.
—'The Heresy of Colossians', in Francis and Meeks (eds.), *Conflict at Colossae*, pp. 123-45.
Bousset, W., 'Zur Dämonologie der späteren Antike', *ARW* 18 (1915), pp. 134-72.
Box, G.H. (ed.), *Apocalypse of Abraham* (Translations of Early Documents, Series 1: Palestinian Jewish Texts; London: SPCK, 1918).

Braun, H., *Qumran und das Neue Testament* (2 vols.; Tübingen: Mohr, 1966).
Brehier, E., *The History of Philosophy*. II. *The Hellenistic and Roman Age* (Chicago: University of Chicago Press, 1965).
Brenk, F.E., 'An Imperial Heritage: The Religious Spirit of Plutarch of Chaironeia', *ANRW* II.36.1, pp. 248-349.
—'In the Light of the Moon: Demonology in the Early Imperial Period', *ANRW* II.16.3, pp. 2068-145.
Brooten, B.J., *Women Leaders in the Ancient Synagogue: Inscriptional Evidence and Background Issues* (BJS, 36; Chico, CA: Scholars Press, 1982).
Brown, R.E., *The Churches the Apostles Left Behind* (New York: Paulist Press, 1984).
Bruce, F.F., 'Colossian Problems. Part 1: Jews and Christians in the Lycus Valley', *BSac* 141 (1984), pp. 3-15.
—'Colossian Problems. Part 3: The Colossian Heresy', *BSac* 141 (1984), pp. 195-208.
Buckler, W.H., and W.M. Calder, *Monumenta Asiae Minoris Antiqua*. VI. *Monuments and Documents from Phrygia and Caria* (Publications of the American Society for Archaeological Research in Asia Minor; Manchester: Manchester University Press, 1939).
Bujard, W., *Stilanalytische Untersuchungen zum Kolosserbrief* (SUNT, 11; Göttingen: Vandenhoeck & Ruprecht, 1973).
Burgess, J., 'The Letter to the Colossians', in G. Krodel (ed.), *Ephesians, Colossians, 2 Thessalonians, the Pastoral Epistles* (Proclamation Commentaries; Philadelphia: Fortress Press, 1978), pp. 41-71.
Burkert, W., *Greek Religion: Archaic and Classical* (Cambridge, MA: Harvard University Press, 1985).
—*Lore and Science in Ancient Pythagoreanism* (Cambridge, MA: Harvard University Press, 1972).
Caird, G.B., *Paul's Letters from Prision (Ephesians, Philippians, Colossians, Philemon)* (New Clarendon Bible; Oxford: Oxford University Press, 1976).
Cannon, G.E., *The Use of Traditional Materials in Colossians* (Macon: Mercer University Press, 1983).
Carr, W., *Angels and Principalities: The Background, Meaning and Development of the Pauline Phrase hai archai kai hai exousiai* (SNTSMS, 42; Cambridge: Cambridge University Press, 1981).
Charles, R.H. (ed.), *The Ascension of Isaiah* (Translations of Early Documents, Series 1: Palestinian Jewish Texts; London: SPCK, 1917).
Charlesworth, J.H. (ed.), *The Old Testament Pseudepigrapha* (2 vols.; Garden City, NY: Doubleday, 1983–85).
—*The Pseudepigrapha and Modern Research with a Supplement* (SBLSCS, 7S; Chico, CA: Scholars Press, 1981).
—'The SNTS Pseudepigrapha Seminars at Tübingen and Paris on the Books of Enoch', *NTS* 25 (1978–79), pp. 315-23.
Cohen, S.J.D., 'Crossing the Boundary and Becoming a Jew', *HTR* 82 (1989), pp. 13-33.
Cohn, L., and P. Wendland (eds.), *Philonis Alexandrini opera quae supersunt* (7 vols.; Berlin: Reimer, 1962–63).
Congdon, L.M., 'The False Teachers at Colossae: Affinities with Essene and Philonic Thought' (PhD dissertation, Drew University, 1968).

Conzelmann, H., 'Der Brief an die Kolosser', in J. Becker, H. Conzelmann, and G. Friedrich (eds.), *Die Briefe an die Galater, Epheser, Philipper, Kolosser, Thessalonicher und Philemon* (NTD, 8; Göttingen: Vandenhoeck & Ruprecht, 15th edn, 1981), pp. 176-202.
—*1 Corinthians* (Hermeneia; Philadelphia: Fortress Press, 1975).
Copleston, F., *A History of Philosophy*. I. *Greece and Rome* (Westminster, MD: Newman, rev. edn, 1955).
Cornford, F.M., *Plato's Cosmology* (International Library of Psychology, Philosophy and Scientific Method; London: Routledge & Kegan Paul, 1937).
Cramer, A.W., *Stoicheia tou kosmou: Interpretatie van een nieuwtestamentische term* (Nieuwkoop: de Graaf, 1961).
Cumont, F., 'Les anges du paganisme', *RHR* 72 (1915), pp. 159-82.
Daly, M., *Pure Lust: Elemental Feminist Philosophy* (New York: HarperCollins, 1984).
Danielou, J., *A History of Christian Doctrine before the Council of Nicaea*. II. *Gospel Message and Hellenistic Culture* (Philadelphia: Westminster Press, 1973).
Darling, R.A., 'TAPEINOSIS and Typology in the Study of Early Christian Asceticism: A Consideration of Method' (paper presented at Annual Meeting of the SBL, Boston, December 5, 1987).
Davies, W.D., *Christian Origins and Judaism* (London: Darton, Longman & Todd, 1962).
—'Paul and the Dead Sea Scrolls: Flesh and Spirit', in K. Stendahl (ed.), *The Scrolls and the New Testament* (New York: Harper, 1957), pp. 157-82.
Dean-Otting, M., *Heavenly Journeys: A Study of the Motif in Hellenistic Jewish Literature* (Judentum und Umwelt, 8; New York: Peter Lang, 1984).
Delatte, A. (ed.), *La vie de Pythagore de Diogène Laërce: Edition critique avec introduction et commentaire* (Morals and Law in Ancient Greece; repr.; New York: Arno, 1979 [1922]).
Delling, G., 'στοιχέω, συστοιχέω, στοιχεῖον', *TDNT*, VII, pp. 666-87.
DeMaris, R.E. '"According to the Elements of the World" (Colossians 2.8): The Colossian Opponents' Wisdom and the Sapiential Tradition in Hellenistic Judaism' (paper presented at Annual Meeting of the SBL, Kansas City, November 25, 1991).
—'Element, Elemental Spirit', *ABD*, II, pp. 444-45.
—'Philosophy', *ABD*, V, p. 346.
—'Whence Comes Wisdom? The Crux of Conflict at Colossae' (paper presented at Annual Meeting of the SBL, New Orleans, November 17, 1990).
Des Places, E., *Etudes platoniciennes, 1929–1979* (EPRO, 90; Leiden: Brill, 1981).
Dibelius, M., *Die Geisterwelt im Glauben des Paulus* (Göttingen: Vandenhoeck & Ruprecht, 1909).
—'The Isis Initiation in Apuleius and Related Initiatory Rites', in Francis and Meeks (eds.), *Conflict at Colossae*, pp. 61-121.
—'Die Isisweihe bei Apuleius und verwandte Initiations-Riten', in G. Bornkamm and H. Kraft (eds.), *Botschaft und Geschichte* (2 vols.; Tübingen: Mohr, 1953–56), II, pp. 30-79.
Dibelius, M., and H. Conzelmann, *The Pastoral Epistles* (Hermeneia; Philadelphia: Fortress Press, 1972).
Dibelius, M., and H. Greeven, *An die Kolosser, Epheser, an Philemon* (HNT, 12; Tübingen: Mohr, 3rd edn, 1953).

Diels, H., and W. Kranz (eds.), *Die Fragmente der Vorsokratiker* (3 vols.; Berlin: Weidmann, 6th edn, 1951–52).
Dillon, J., *The Middle Platonists: 80 BC to AD 220* (Ithaca, NY: Cornell University Press, 1977).
Dörrie, H., *Platonica Minora* (Studia et Testimonia Antiqua, 8; Munich: Fink, 1976).
—*Von Platon zum Platonismus: Ein Bruch in der Überlieferung und seine Überwindung* (Rheinisch-Westfälische Akademie der Wissenschaften, Geisteswissenschaften, Vorträge G211; Opladen: Westdeutscher Verlag, 1976).
Eitrem, S., 'ΕΜΒΑΤΕΥΩ. Note sur Col 2, 18', *ST* 2 (1948), pp. 90-94.
Evans, C.A., 'The Colossian Mystics', *Bib* 63 (1982), pp. 188-205.
Feldman, L.H., 'The Omnipresence of the God-fearers', *BARev* 12.5 (1986), pp. 58-63.
Ferguson, E., *Backgrounds of Early Christianity* (Grand Rapids: Eerdmans, 1987).
Festugière, A.-J., 'Les "mémoires pythagoriques" cités par Alexandre Polyhistor', *Revue des études grecques* 58 (1945), pp. 1-65.
Finn, T.M., 'The God-fearers Reconsidered', *CBQ* 47 (1985), pp. 75-84.
Foerster, W., 'Die Irrlehrer des Kolosserbriefes', in W. van Unnik and A. van der Woude (eds.), *Studia Biblica et Semitica: T.Ch. Vriezen [Festschrift]* (Wageningen: Veenman, 1966), pp. 71-80.
Francis, F.O., 'The Background of EMBATEUEIN (Col 2.18) in Legal Papyri and Oracle Inscriptions', in Francis and Meeks (eds.), *Conflict at Colossae*, pp. 197-207.
—'The Christological Argument of Colossians', in J. Jervell and W. Meeks (eds.), *God's Christ and His People: Studies in Honour of Nils Alstrup Dahl* (Oslo: Universitetsforlaget, 1977), pp. 192-208.
—'Humility and Angelic Worship in Col 2.18', in Francis and Meeks (eds.), *Conflict at Colossae*, pp. 163-95. Originally published in *ST* 16 (1962), pp. 109-34.
—'A Re-Examination of the Colossian Controversy' (PhD dissertation, Yale University, 1965).
—'Visionary Discipline and Scriptural Tradition at Colossae', *Lexington Theological Quarterly* 2 (1967), pp. 71-81.
Francis, F.O., and W.A. Meeks (eds.), *Conflict at Colossae* (SBLSBS, 4; Missoula, MT: Scholars Press, rev. edn, 1975).
Gabathuler, H.J., *Jesus Christus, Haupt der Kirche—Haupt der Welt* (ATANT, 45; Zurich: Zwingli-Verlag, 1965).
Gagniers, J. des, P. Devambez, L. Kahil, and R. Ginouvès, *Laodicée du Lycos: Le Nymphée: Campagnes 1961–1963* (Université Laval, Recherches archéologiques, Series 1: Fouilles; Québec: Presses de l'Université Laval, 1969).
Gaston, L., 'Judaism of the Uncircumcised in Ignatius and Related Writers', in S.G. Wilson (ed.), *Anti-Judaism in Early Christianity. II. Separation and Polemic* (Studies in Judaism and Christianity, 2; Waterloo: Wilfrid Laurier University, 1986), pp. 33-44.
Glucker, J., *Antiochus and the Late Academy* (Hypomnemata: Untersuchungen zur Antike und zu ihrem Nachleben, 56; Göttingen: Vandenhoeck & Ruprecht, 1978).
Gnilka, J., *Der Kolosserbrief* (HTKNT, 10.1; Freiburg: Herder, 1980).
Goodenough, E.R., *By Light, Light: The Mystic Gospel of Hellenistic Judaism* (New Haven: Yale University Press, 1935).

Goppelt, L., 'πίνω, πόμα, πόσις, πότος, ποτήριον, καταπίνω, ποτίζω', *TDNT*, VI, pp. 135-60.
Graeser, A., *Plotinus and the Stoics: A Preliminary Study* (Philosophia Antiqua, 22; Leiden: Brill, 1972).
Grant, R.M., *Gnosticism and Early Christianity* (New York: Columbia University Press, 2nd edn, 1966).
Griffiths, J.G., *Apuleius of Madauros: The Isis-Book ('Metamorphoses', Book XI)* (EPRO, 39; Leiden: Brill, 1975).
Grundmann, W., 'ταπεινός, ταπεινόω, ταπείνωσις, ταπεινόφρων, ταπεινοφροσύνη', *TDNT*, VIII, pp. 1-26.
Grundmann, W., G. von Rad and G. Kittel, 'ἄγγελος, ἀρχάγγελος, ἰσάγγελος', *TDNT*, I, pp. 74-87.
Gunther, J.J., *St. Paul's Opponents and their Background* (NovTSup, 35; Leiden: Brill, 1973).
Guthrie, W.K.C., *A History of Greek Philosophy* (6 vols.; Cambridge: Cambridge University Press, 1962-81).
—'Pythagoras and Pythagoreanism', in P. Edwards (ed.), *The Encylopedia of Philosophy* (8 vols.; New York: Macmillan, 1967), VII, pp. 37-39.
Hanssler, B., 'Zu Satzkonstruktion und Aussage in Kol 2,23', in H. Feld and J. Nolte (eds.), *Wort Gottes in der Zeit: K.H. Schelkle Festschrift* (Düsseldorf: Patmos-Verlag, 1973), pp. 143-48.
Harder, G., 'φθείρω, φθορά, φθαρτός, κτλ', *TDNT*, IX, pp. 93-106.
Hegermann, H., *Die Vorstellung vom Schöpfungsmittler im hellenistischen Judentum und Urchristentum* (TU, 82; Berlin: Akademie Verlag, 1961).
Heinze, R., *Xenokrates: Darstellung der Lehre und Sammlung der Fragmente* (repr.; Hildesheim: Olms, 1965 [1982]).
Holladay, C.R. (ed.), *Fragments from Hellenistic Jewish Authors*. I. *Historians* (SBLTT, 20; Chico, CA: Scholars Press, 1983).
Hollenbach, B., 'Col. II.23: Which Things Lead to the Fulfilment of the Flesh', *NTS* 25 (1978-79), pp. 254-61.
Hooker, M.D., *From Adam to Christ: Essays on Paul* (Cambridge: Cambridge University Press, 1990).
—'Were there False Teachers in Colossae?', in B. Lindars and S. Smalley (eds), *Christ and Spirit in the New Testament: In Honour of C.F.D. Moule* (Cambridge: Cambridge University Press, 1973), pp. 315-31.
House, H.W., 'Doctrinal Issues in Colossians. Part 1: Heresies in the Colossian Church', *BSac* 149 (1992), pp. 45-59.
Humann, C., C. Cichorius, W. Judeich and F. Winter (eds.), *Altertümer von Hierapolis* (Jahrbuch des kaiserlich deutschen archäologischen Instituts, 4th Supplement; Berlin: Reimer, 1898).
Hurtado, L.W., *One God, One Lord: Early Christian Devotion and Ancient Jewish Monotheism* (Philadelphia: Fortress Press, 1988).
Johnson, S.L., 'Beware of Philosophy', *BSac* 119 (1962), pp. 302-11.
Käsemann, E., 'On the Subject of Primitive Christian Apocalyptic', in *New Testament Questions of Today* (Philadelphia: Fortress Press, 1969), pp. 108-37.
Keck, L.E., and V.P. Furnish, *The Pauline Letters* (Interpreting Biblical Texts; Nashville: Abingdon Press, 1984).

Kehl, N., *Der Christushymnus im Kolosserbrief: Eine motivegeschichtliche Untersuchung zu Kol 1,12-20* (SBM, 1; Stuttgart: Katholisches Bibelwerk, 1967).
—'Erniedrigung und Erhöhung in Qumran und Kolossä', *ZKT* 91 (1969), pp. 364-94.
Kiley, M., *Colossians as Pseudepigraphy* (The Biblical Seminar, 4; Sheffield: JSOT Press, 1986).
Kraabel, A.T., 'The Diaspora Synagogue: Archaeological and Epigraphical Evidence since Sukenik', *ANRW* II.19.1, pp. 477-510.
—'Judaism in Western Asia Minor under the Roman Empire with a Preliminary Study of the Jewish Community at Sardis, Lydia' (PhD dissertation, Harvard Divinity School, 1968).
Lähnemann, J., *Der Kolosserbrief: Komposition, Situation und Argumentation* (SNT, 3; Gütersloh: Gerd Mohn, 1971).
Lampe, G.W.H. (ed.), *A Patristic Greek Lexicon* (Oxford: Clarendon Press, 1961).
Levison, J.R., '2 Apoc. Bar. 48.42–52.7 and the Apocalyptic Dimension of Colossians 3.1-6', *JBL* 108 (1989), pp. 93-108.
Lévy, I., *Recherches sur les sources de la légende de Pythagore* (Bibliothèque de l'école des hautes études, sciences religieuses, 42; Paris: Leroux, 1926).
Liddel, H.G., and R. Scott, *A Greek–English Lexicon* (ed. H.S. Jones; Oxford: Clarendon Press, rev. edn, 1940).
Lifshitz, B., *Donateurs et fondateurs dans les synagogues juives* (CahRB, 7; Paris: Gabalda, 1967).
Lightfoot, J.B., 'The Colossian Heresy', in Francis and Meeks (eds.), *Conflict at Colossae*, pp. 13-59.
—*St. Paul's Epistles to the Colossians and to Philemon* (London: Macmillan, 3rd edn, 1879).
Lindemann, A., *Der Kolosserbrief* (Züricher Bibelkommentare NT, 10; Zurich: Theologischer Verlag, 1983).
Lohmeyer, E., *Die Briefe an die Philipper, an die Kolosser und an Philemon* (MeyerK, 9.2; Göttingen: Vandenhoeck & Ruprecht, 11th edn, 1956).
Lohse, B., *Askese und Mönchtum in der Antike und in der alten Kirche* (Religion und Kultur der alten Mittelmeerwelt in Parallelforschungen, 1; Munich: Oldenbourg, 1969).
Lohse, E., *Colossians and Philemon* (Hermeneia; Philadelphia: Fortress Press, 1971).
—'Ein hymnisches Bekenntnis in Kol. 2,13c-15', in A. Descamps and A. de Halleux (eds.), *Mélanges bibliques en hommage au R.P. Béda Rigaux* (Gembloux: Duculot, 1970), pp. 427-35.
Lona, H.E., *Die Eschatologie im Kolosser- und Epheserbrief* (FB, 48; Würzburg: Echter Verlag, 1984).
Lyonnet, S., 'L'épître aux Colossiens (Col. 2.18) et les mystères d'Apollon Clarien', *Bib* 43 (1962), pp. 417-35.
—'L'étude du milieu littéraire et l'exégèse du Nouveau Testament', *Bib* 37 (1956), pp. 1-38.
—'L'hymne christologique de l'épître aux Colossiens et la fête juive du nouvel an', *RSR* 48 (1960), pp. 93-100.
—'Paul's Adversaries in Colossae', in Francis and Meeks (eds.), *Conflict at Colossae*, pp. 147-61.
—'Saint Paul et le gnosticisme: L'épître aux Colossiens', in Bianchi (ed.), *The Origins of Gnosticism*, pp. 538-51.

Macgregor, G.H.C., 'Principalities and Powers: The Cosmic Background of Paul's Thought', *NTS* 1 (1954–55), pp. 17-28.
MacLennan, R.S., and A.T. Kraabel, 'The God-Fearers—A Literary and Theological Invention', *BARev* 12.5 (1986), pp. 46-53.
Marshall, P., *Enmity in Corinth: Social Conventions in Paul's Relations with the Corinthians* (WUNT, 2.23; Tübingen: Mohr, 1987).
Martin, R.P., *Colossians: The Church's Lord and the Christian's Liberty* (Grand Rapids: Zondervan, 1973).
McCown, C.C. (ed.), *The Testament of Solomon* (UNT, 9; Leipzig: Hinrichs, 1922).
Meeks, W.A., 'In One Body: The Unity of Humankind in Colossians and Ephesians', in J. Jervell and W. Meeks (eds.), *God's Christ and His People: Studies in Honour of Nils Alstrup Dahl* (Oslo: Universitetsforlaget, 1977), pp. 209-21.
—*The Moral World of the First Christians* (Library of Early Christianity, 6; Philadelphia: Westminster Press, 1986).
—'Social Functions of Apocalyptic Language in Pauline Christianity', in D. Hellholm (ed.), *Apocalypticism in the Mediterranean World and the Near East* (Tübingen: Mohr, 1983), pp. 687-705.
Meeks, W.A., and R.L. Wilken, *Jews and Christians in Antioch in the First Four Centuries of the Common Era* (SBLSBS, 13; Missoula, MT: Scholars Press, 1978).
Meyer, H.A.W., *Kritisch Exegetisches Handbuch über die Briefe Pauli an die Philipper, Kolosser und Philemon* (MeyerK, 9; Göttingen: Vandenhoeck & Ruprecht, 5th edn, 1886).
Michel, O., 'φιλοσοφία, φιλόσοφος', *TDNT*, IX, pp. 172-88.
Milik, J.T., *The Books of Enoch: Aramaic Fragments of Qumran Cave 4* (Oxford: Clarendon Press, 1976).
Moffatt, J., *An Introduction to the Literature of the New Testament* (International Theological Library; New York: Charles Scribner's Sons, 3rd edn, 1925).
Moyo, A.M., 'The Colossian Heresy in the Light of Some Gnostic Documents from Nag Hammadi', *Journal of Theology for Southern Africa* 48 (1984), pp. 30-44.
Nilsson, M.P., *Geschichte der griechischen Religion* (Handbuch der Altertumswissenschaft, 5.2.1-2; 2 vols.; Munich: Beck, 3rd edn, 1967–74).
—'The High God and the Mediator', *HTR* 56 (1963), pp. 101-20.
Nock, A.D., 'The Vocabulary of the New Testament', *JBL* 52 (1937), pp. 131-39.
Nock, A.D., and A.-J. Festugière (eds.), *Corpus Hermeticum* (2 vols.; Paris: Société d'edition 'Les Belles Lettres', 1945).
Odeberg, H. (ed.), *3 Enoch or the Hebrew Book of Enoch* (repr.; New York: Ktav, 1973 [1928]).
O'Neill, J.C., 'The Source of the Christology in Colossians', *NTS* 26 (1979–80), pp. 87-100.
Percy, E., *Die Probleme der Kolosser- und Epheserbriefe* (Acta Regiae Societatis Humaniorum Litterarum Lundensis, 39; Lund: Gleerup, 1946).
Perrin, N., *The New Testament: An Introduction* (New York: Harcourt Brace Jovanovich, 1974).
Pohlenz, M., *Die Stoa: Geschichte einer geistigen Bewegung* (2 vols.; Göttingen: Vandenhoeck & Ruprecht, 1948–49).
Pokorný, P., *Colossians: A Commentary* (Peabody, MA: Hendrickson, 1991).
Preisendanz, K. (ed.), *Papyri graecae magicae* (2 vols.; Stuttgart: Teubner, 2nd edn, 1973).

Preisker, H., 'ἐμβατεύω', *TDNT*, II, pp. 535-36.
Ramsay, W.M., *The Cities and Bishoprics of Phrygia* (2 vols.; Oxford: Clarendon Press, 1895–97).
Rees, D. 'Platonism and the Platonic Tradition', in P. Edwards (ed.), *The Encyclopedia of Philosophy* (8 vols.; New York: Macmillan, 1967), VI, pp. 333-41.
Reitzenstein, R., *Hellenistic Mystery-Religions: Their Basic Ideas and Significance* (PTMS, 15; Pittsburgh: Pickwick, 1978).
Reynolds, J., and R. Tannenbaum, *Jews and God-Fearers at Aphrodisias* (Cambridge Philological Society, Supplementary Vol. 12; Cambridge: Cambridge University Press, 1987).
Robert, L., *Nouvelles inscriptions de Sardes* (fasc. 1; Paris: Maisonneuve, 1964).
Robinson, J.M., 'A Formal Analysis of Colossians 1.15-20', *JBL* 76 (1957), pp. 270-87.
Robinson, J.M. (ed.), *The Nag Hammadi Library in English* (New York: HarperCollins, rev. edn, 1990).
Roetzel, C.J., *The Letters of Paul: Conversations in Context* (Atlanta: John Knox, 1975).
Rollins, W.G., 'Christological *Tendenz* in Colossians 1:15-20: A *Theologia Crucis*', in R. Berkey and S. Edwards (eds.), *Christological Perspectives: Essays in Honor of Harvey K. McArthur* (New York: Pilgrim Press, 1982), pp. 123-38.
Rongy, H., 'Les erreurs combattues dans l'épître aux Colossiens. II,16-19', *Revue ecclésiastique de Liège* 30 (1938–39), pp. 245-49.
—'La réfutation des erreurs de Colosses. Col. II, 8-15', *Revue ecclésiastique de Liège* 31 (1939–40), pp. 216-26.
Ross, W.D., *Plato's Theory of Ideas* (Oxford: Clarendon Press, 1951).
Roueché, C., *Aphrodisias in Late Antiquity: The Late Roman and Byzantine Inscriptions* (*Journal for Roman Studies* Monograph, 5; London: Society for the Promotion of Roman Studies, 1989).
Rowland, C., 'Apocalyptic Visions and the Exaltation of Christ in the Letter to the Colossians', *JSNT* 19 (1983), pp. 73-83.
Runia, D.T., *Philo of Alexandria and the 'Timaeus' of Plato* (2 vols.; Amsterdam: Vrije Universiteit, 1983).
—'Redrawing the Map of Early Middle Platonism', in A. Caquot, M. Hadas-Lebel, and J. Riaud (eds.), *Hellenica et Judaica: Hommage à Valentin Nikiprowetzky* (Leuven: Peeters, 1986), pp. 85-104.
Rusam, D., 'Neue Belege zu den στοιχεῖα τοῦ κόσμου (Gal 4,3.9; Kol 2,8.20)', *ZNW* 83 (1992), pp. 119-25.
Sanders, E.P., 'Literary Dependence in Colossians', *JBL* 85 (1966), pp. 28-45.
Sanders, J.T., *The New Testament Christological Hymns: Their Historical Religious Background* (SNTSMS, 15; Cambridge: Cambridge University Press, 1971).
Sandmel, S., *Philo of Alexandria: An Introduction* (New York: Oxford University Press, 1979).
Sappington, T.J., *Revelation and Redemption at Colossae* (JSNTSup, 53; Sheffield: JSOT Press, 1991).
Saunders, E.W., 'The Colossian Heresy and Qumran Theology', in B. Daniels and J. Suggs (eds.), *Studies in the History and Text of the New Testament: In Honor of K.W. Clark* (SD, 29; Salt Lake City: University of Utah Press, 1967), pp. 133-45.
Schenk, W., 'Christus, das Geheimnis der Welt, als dogmatisches und ethisches Grundprinzip des Kolosserbriefes', *EvT* 43 (1983), pp. 138-55.

—'Der Kolosserbrief in der neueren Forschung (1945–1985)', *ANRW* II.25.4, pp. 3327–64.
Schenke, H.-M., 'Der Widerstreit gnostischer und kirchlicher Christologie im Spiegel des Kolosserbriefes', *ZTK* 61 (1964), pp. 391-403.
Schlier, H., *Der Brief an die Galater* (MeyerK, 7; Göttingen: Vandenhoek & Ruprecht, 11th edn, 1951).
—*Principalities and Powers in the New Testament* (QD; New York: Herder & Herder, 1961).
Schmekel, A., *Die Philosophie der mittleren Stoa in ihrem geschichtlichen Zusammenhange* (repr.; New York: Olms, 1974 [1892]).
Schoedel, W., *Ignatius of Antioch* (Hermeneia; Philadelphia: Fortress Press, 1985).
Schulz, S., 'σκιά, ἀποσκίασμα, ἐπισκιάζω', *TDNT*, VII, pp. 394-400.
Schweizer, E., 'Altes und Neues zu den "Elementen Der Welt" in Kol 2,20; Gal 4,3.9', in K. Aland and S. Meurer (eds.), *Wissenschaft und Kirche: Festschrift für Eduard Lohse* (Texte und Arbeiten zur Bibel, 4; Bielefeld: Luther-Verlag, 1989), pp. 111-18.
—'Askese nach Kol 1,24 oder 2,20?', in H. Merklein (ed.), *Neues Testament und Ethik: Für Rudolf Schnackenburg* (Freiburg: Herder, 1989), pp. 340-48.
—*Der Brief an die Kolosser* (EKKNT; Zurich: Benzinger Verlag; Neukirchen–Vluyn: Neukirchener Verlag, 1976).
—'Christianity of the Circumcised and Judaism of the Uncircumcised: The Background of Matthew and Colossians', in R. Hamerton-Kelly and R. Scroggs (eds.), *Jews, Greeks and Christians: Religious Cultures in Late Antiquity: Essays in Honor of W.D. Davies* (Leiden: Brill, 1976), pp. 245-60.
—'Christ in the Letter to the Colossians', *RevExp* 70 (1973), pp. 451-67.
—'Die "Elemente der Welt" Gal. 4,3.9; Kol. 2,8.20', in O. Böcher and K. Haacker (eds.), *Verborum Veritas: Festschrift für Gustav Stählin* (Wuppertal: Brockhaus, 1970).
—*The Letter to the Colossians* (Minneapolis: Augsburg, 1982), pp. 245-59.
—'Slaves of the Elements and Worshipers of Angels: Gal 4.3, 9; Col 2.8, 18, 20', *JBL* 107 (1988), pp. 455-68.
—'Versöhnung des Alls. Kol 1,20', in G. Strecker (ed.), *Jesus Christus in Historie und Theologie: Neutestamentliche Festschrift für Hans Conzelmann zum 60. Geburtstag* (Tübingen: Mohr, 1975), pp. 487-501.
—'Zur neueren Forschung am Kolosserbrief (seit 1970)', in J. Pfammatter and F. Furger (eds.), *Theologische Berichte 5* (Zurich: Benziger Verlag, 1976), pp. 163-91.
Seager, A.R., and A.T. Kraabel, 'The Synagogue and the Jewish Community', in G.M.A. Hanfmann (ed.), *Sardis from Prehistoric to Roman Times* (Cambridge, MA: Harvard University Press, 1983), pp. 168-90.
Smyth, H.W., *Greek Grammar* (Cambridge, MA: Harvard University Press, 1920).
Sokolowski, F., 'Sur le culte d'angelos dans le paganisme grec et romain', *HTR* 53 (1960), pp. 225-29.
Soury, G., *La démonologie de Plutarque: Essai sur les idées religieuses et les mythes d'un platonicien éclectique* (Collection d'études anciennes; Paris: Société d'édition 'Les Belles Lettres', 1942).
Stern, M. (ed.), *Greek and Latin Authors on Jews and Judaism* (3 vols.; Jerusalem: Israel Academy of Science and Humanities, 1974–84).

Stewart, J.S., 'A First-Century Heresy and its Modern Counterpart', *SJT* 23 (1970), pp. 420-36.
Tabor, J.D., *Things Unutterable: Paul's Ascent to Paradise in its Greco-Roman, Judaic, and Early Christian Contexts* (Studies in Judaism; Lanham, MD: University Press of America, 1986).
Tannenbaum, R., 'Jews and God-Fearers in the Holy City of Aphrodite', *BARev* 12.5 (1986), pp. 54-57.
Tarrant, H., *Scepticism or Platonism? The Philosophy of the Fourth Academy* (Cambridge Classical Studies; Cambridge: Cambridge University Press, 1985).
Tcherikover, V., *Hellenistic Civilization and the Jews* (New York: Atheneum, 1970).
—'Jewish Apologetic Reconsidered', *Eos* 48 (1956) Fasc. 3, pp. 169-93.
Thesleff, H., *An Introduction to the Pythagorean Writings of the Hellenistic Period*. Acta Academiae Åboensis, Humaniora, 24.3; Turku, Finland: Åbo Akademie, 1961).
—'On the Problem of Doric Pseudo-Pythagorica: An Alternative Theory of Date and Purpose', in K. von Fritz (ed.), *Pseudepigrapha I: Pseudopythagorica—Lettres de Platon, Littérature pseudépigraphique juive* (Entretiens sur l'antiquité classique, 18; Geneva: Fondation Hardt, 1972), pp. 57-102.
Tobin, T. (ed.), *Timaios of Locri, 'On the Nature of the World and the Soul'* (SBLTT, 26; Chico, CA: Scholars Press, 1985).
Trebilco, P.R., *Jewish Communities in Asia Minor* (SNTSMS, 69; Cambridge: Cambridge University Press, 1991).
Tsekourakis, D., 'Pythagoreanism or Platonism and Ancient Medicine? The Reasons for Vegetarianism in Plutarch's "Moralia"', *ANRW* II.36.1, pp. 366-93.
Van Winden, J.C.M., *Calcidius on Matter: His Doctrine and Sources* (Philosophia Antiqua, 9; Leiden: Brill, 1959).
Vawter, B., 'The Colossians Hymn and the Principle of Redaction', *CBQ* 33 (1971), pp. 62-81.
Wahl, O. (ed.), *Apocalypsis Esdrae, Apocalypsis Sedrach, Visio Beati Esdrae* (PVTG, 4; Leiden: Brill, 1977).
Weiss, H., 'The Law in the Epistle to the Colossians', *CBQ* 34 (1972), pp. 294-314.
Wellmann, M., 'Eine pythagoreische Urkunde des IV. Jahrhundert v. Chr', *Hermes* 54 (1919), pp. 225-48.
Wengst, K., *Humility: Solidarity of the Humiliated* (Philadelphia: Fortress Press, 1988).
White, J.L., *The Form and Function of the Body of the Greek Letter* (SBLDS, 2; Missoula, MT: Scholars Press, 2nd edn, 1972).
Whittaker, J., 'Platonic Philosophy in the Early Centuries of the Empire', *ANRW* II.36.1, pp. 81-123.
Wicker, K.O. (ed.), *Porphyry, the Philosopher, 'To Marcella'* (SBLTT, 28; Atlanta: Scholars Press, 1987).
Wiersma, W., 'Das Referat des Alexandros Polyhistor über die pythagoreische Philosophie', *Mnemosyne*, series 3, 10 (1942), pp. 97-112.
Williams, A.L., 'The Cult of Angels at Colossae', *JTS* OS 10 (1909), pp. 413-38.
Wilson, R., *Gnosis and the New Testament* (Philadelphia: Fortress Press, 1968).
Wink, W., *Engaging the Powers: Discernment and Resistance in a World of Domination* (Minneapolis: Fortress Press, 1992).
—*Naming the Powers: The Language of Power in the New Testament* (Philadelphia: Fortress Press, 1984).

—*Unmasking the Powers: The Invisible Forces that Determine Human Existence* (Philadelphia: Fortress Press, 1986).
Winston, D., *The Wisdom of Solomon* (AB, 43; Garden City, NY: Doubleday, 1979).
Winston, D., and J. Dillon, *Two Treatises of Philo of Alexandria: A Commentary on 'De Gigantibus' and 'Quod Deus Sit Immutabilis'* (BJS, 25; Chico, CA: Scholars Press, 1983).
Witt, R.E., *Albinus and the History of Middle Platonism* (Cambridge Classical Studies; Cambridge: Cambridge University Press, 1937).
Wright, N.T., 'Poetry and Theology in Colossians 1.15-20', *NTS* 36 (1990), pp. 444-68.
Yamauchi, E., *The Archaeology of New Testament Cities in Western Asia Minor* (Baker Studies in Biblical Archaeology; Grand Rapids: Baker, 1980). This book has also been published under the title *New Testament Cities in Western Asia Minor*.
—'Qumran and Colossae', *BSac* 121 (1964), pp. 141-52.
Yates, R., 'Christ and the Powers of Evil in Colossians', in E.A. Livingstone (ed.), *Studia Biblica 1978: III. Papers on Paul and Other New Testament Authors* (JSNTSup, 3; Sheffield: JSOT Press, 1980), pp. 461-68.
—'Colossians and Gnosis', *JSNT* 27 (1986), pp. 49-68.
—'Colossians 2.15: Christ Triumphant', *NTS* 37 (1991), pp. 573-91.
—' "The Worship of Angels" (Col. 2.18)', *ExpTim* 97 (1985), pp. 12-15.
Yegül, F.K., *The Bath-Gymnasium Complex at Sardis* (Archaeological Exploration of Sardis, Report 3; Cambridge, MA: Harvard University Press, 1986).
Zeller, E., *Outlines of the History of Greek Philosophy* (revised by W. Nestle; New York: Dover, 13th edn, 1980).
—*Die Philosophie der Griechen in ihrer geschichtlichen Entwicklung* (3 vols.; Leipzig: Reisland, 1920–23).

INDEXES

INDEX OF REFERENCES

OLD TESTAMENT

Genesis		Joshua		Psalms	
6.1-4	108	19.49	64	34.13-14	75
		19.51	64		
Exodus				Isaiah	
19–20	31	Judges		29.13	50
34.28	56	13.14	56	58.3	75
				58.5	75
Leviticus		1 Chronicles			
11.1-47	56	15.24	43	Daniel	
		23.31	56, 89, 112	1.8	57
Numbers				1.12	57, 58
6.2-4	56	2 Chronicles			
		2.3	56, 89, 112	Hosea	
Deuteronomy		31.3	56, 112	2.13	56, 89, 112
9.9	56	31.3	89		
9.18	56			Amos	
114.3-20	56			2.12	56

APOCRYPHA

Wisdom		1 Maccabees		15.40	64
7.17	52	12.25	64		
14.18	60	13.20	64	2 Maccabees	
14.27	60	14.31	64	2.30	28, 64, 65
19.18	52				

NEW TESTAMENT

Matthew		Mark		Luke	
15.1-20	50	7.1-23	50	14.11	59, 75
15.6-9	50	7.7	50	18.14	59, 75
18.4	59, 75	7.8	50		
23.12	59, 75	7.19	57	Acts	
				10.2	122

13.16	122	*Galatians*				75, 78, 89,
16.14	122	3.4	67			134, 138, 145
20.19	75	3.23–4.7	54	2.1-5		42
26.5	60	4.1	54	2.1		68
		4.3	28, 54	2.2-4		20, 32, 149
Romans		4.5	54	2.2-3		141
1.18	149	4.8	54	2.2		21
1.19-20	149	4.9-10	54	2.3		32, 66, 143,
1.21-23	149	4.9	28, 54			144
4.24	43	4.11	67	2.5		42, 68
6.3-11	144	6.8	69	2.6–4.1		42
6.4	43	6.14	139	2.6-23		42, 43, 44
7.25	68			2.6-8		43, 44
8.3	54	*Ephesians*		2.6-7		41, 44, 51
8.18-25	148	1.21	81	2.6		42, 43, 50
8.21	69	4.2	75	2.8		7, 12, 13, 15,
13.4	67	6.12	81			16, 21, 23, 24,
14	57, 58					29, 41-50, 52,
14.2	57, 58	*Philippians*				53, 55, 62, 66,
14.3	57	2.3	59, 75			69, 72, 73, 96,
14.5-6	58					98, 99, 115,
14.14	57	*Colossians*				117, 118, 134,
14.20	57	1	41, 145			135, 142, 145,
14.21	57	1.1-23	42			147, 149
		1.1	50	2.9-15		43, 109,
		1.11	51			135, 136,
1 Corinthians		1.12-13	139, 143			138-41, 144
2.6-8	143	1.13-14	136	2.9-10		20, 23, 24
4.6	67	1.15-20	7, 11, 14,	2.9		136
4.18	67		130, 136-	2.10		21, 29, 43,
4.19	67		38, 141, 144			136, 137
5.2	67	1.16	20, 21, 136,	2.11-23		28
8.1	67		137	2.11-13		136
10.23–11.1	57	1.18	137	2.11		19, 23, 29,
10.23	57	1.19-20	131			68, 135
10.26	57	1.19	20, 136	2.12-13		43, 139, 143
13.4	67	1.20	130, 133,	2.12		38, 109, 144
15.2	67		136, 137	2.13		68, 125, 137
15.24-25	144	1.21-22	136	2.14		23, 43, 53,
15.24	138	1.21	126, 131			78, 136
15.26	137	1.22	29, 68, 135	2.15		20, 21, 29,
15.42	69	1.24	42, 68			61, 96, 136,
15.50	69	1.25-28	141			137, 143,
8.1-13	57	1.26-28	19			147
		1.26	21, 143, 149	2.16-23		44, 45, 47,
2 Corinthians		1.27	21, 126			134, 135,
10.1	59	1.28	141			145
11.7	59	2	24, 39, 41-44,	2.16		15-17, 19,
11.14	61					

Index of References

Ref	Pages	Ref	Pages	Ref	Pages
	22, 23, 35, 38, 41-43, 47, 49, 56-58, 63, 89, 98, 110, 112, 113, 125, 128		47, 49-51, 58, 69-72, 75, 99, 118, 129	*2 Timothy*	
				4.4	90
		2.23	16, 17, 20, 21, 36, 47, 49, 58, 59, 68-72, 77, 98, 99, 109, 112, 113, 118, 128, 132, 135, 139, 142	*Titus*	
				1.10	50
				1.14	50, 90
2.17-18	38			3.9	50, 90
2.17	23, 47, 63, 64			*Hebrews*	
				5.12	52
2.18-23	46			8.5	63
2.18-19	63			10.1	63
2.18	15, 17, 20-23, 29-31, 33, 38, 41-43, 47, 59, 61-65, 67, 68, 72, 73, 77, 79, 83, 95, 98, 99, 115, 118, 135, 139	2.9-15	44	*James*	
		3	41, 42, 140, 144	1.26-27	60
				4.10	59, 75
		3.1-6	144		
		3.1-2	96	*1 Peter*	
		3.1	42, 43	3.8	59
		3.2	96, 140, 143	3.22	61
		3.5	42	5.5	59, 75
		3.9-10	139-41, 143	5.6	59
		3.12	42, 59, 71, 128, 135	*2 Peter*	
2.19	66, 67, 99				
2.20	13, 16, 21, 23, 29, 37, 43, 46, 52, 53, 55, 72, 73, 78, 83, 95, 96, 98, 115, 118, 139, 140, 144, 147, 149	3.16	20	1.4	69
		3.19-20	51	2.12	69
		3.21	75	2.19	69
		3.22	68	3.10	53
		4.3	21	3.12	53
		4.7-18	42	2.4	61
		4.9	125		
		4.12	125	*Revelation*	
		4.13	124	1.20	61
2.21-22	55, 115	4.15-16	123	4.1-2	77
2.21	15, 23, 35, 41, 47, 51, 58, 69-72, 75, 98, 99, 109, 110	5.12	51	7.1	61
				9.15	61
		1 Timothy		9.20	62
		1.3-7	90	12.7	61
		1.4	90	21.4	137
2.22-23	63, 68, 69	1.7	90		
2.22	16, 43, 46,	4.7	90		

PSEUDEPIGRAPHA

Ref	Page	Ref	Page	Ref	Page
1 Enoch		40.9	61	60.16-22	61
6.2-7	61	47.2	61	60.17	83
14	77	53.3	61	61.10	61
19.1	61	60.11-24	82	69.2	61

69.20-24	82	9.23-25	31, 58	2.7-11	76
99.3	61	12.51–13.1	31	6.1–11.4	76
		12.51	58	7	76
2 Baruch				5.1-14	76
5.7	31	*4 Maccabees*			
9.2–10.1	31	1.1	48	*Gk Apoc. Ezra*	
12.5–13.1	31	1.33-35	128	1.3-7	75
21.1	31	5.7	60		
43.3	31	5.11	48	*T. Isaac*	
44.14	32, 144	5.13	60	4.1-6	76
47.2	31	5.22-25	128	5.4	76
48.42–52.7	144	5.22-24	48, 127	6.1	76
54.13	32, 144	12.13	52		
				T. Sol.	
3 Enoch		*Apoc. Abr.*		8.1-2	80
15B	76	9	76	8.2	81
15B.2	75	12	76	8.3-4	80
		15	76	18.2	81
4 Ezra				20.15	81
5.13-20	31	*Asc. Isa.*			
6.31	31	1.1-3.12	76		
6.35	31				

QUMRAN

1QH		*1QSb*		1QpHab	
3.20-22	31	4.25-26	31	9.2	29, 68
11.13-14	31				

PHILO

Abr.		*Fug.*		*Plant.*	
13 §§60-61	119	7 §41	60	4 §14	38, 61, 107
13 §60	114			19 §80	65
		Gig.			
Aet. Mund.		4 §16	61, 107	*Quaest. in Exod.*	
21 §§107-108	54			2.2	127
		Leg. All.		2.118	130
21 §109	53	2.25 §99	114		
		3.32 §§97-99	118	*Rer. Div. Her.*	
Conf. Ling.				9 §48	117
34 §171	107	*Leg. Gai.*		11 §53	117
		37 §298	60	13 §64	117
Dec.				22 §§110-11	117
12 §58	69	*Migr. Abr.*		23–24	
17 §82	63	2 §12	63	§§115-19	117
				29 §§146-50	117
Det. Pot. Ins.		*Op. Mund.*		29 §146	118
7 §21	60	1 §03	114, 119	41 §99	117

42 §206	117	2.32		4 §§34-37	128
		§§193-95	113	8-10 §64-82	113
Somn.		3.32 §178	69		
1.22 §140	107			*Vit. Mos*	
1.22 §141	107	*Virt.*		2.39	
		11 §73	53	§§211-16	48
Spec. Leg.				2.39 §211	48
2.32 §195	128	*Vit. Cont.*		2.39 §216	48
1.16-17		1 §02	113	2.46 §251	53
§§84-97	130	3 §28	113	2.24-26	
1.17 §97	118, 130	3 §§30-33	113	§§117-35	130
1.58 §315	60	4 §§34-35	113	2.26 §133	130
2.31		4 §34	113	2.26 §135	130
§§190-91	130	4 §37	113	2.39 §211	114
2.31 §192	130, 131	8 §65	113	2.46 §251	118
2.32		9 §74	113	2.5 §27	123
§§193-95	127	11 §90	114		

JOSEPHUS

Ant.		20.2.1-4		*Apion*	
116.4.3 §115	60	§§17-48	120	2.39 §282	120
12.3.4 §147	123	20.2.4			
12.5.4 §253	60	§§38-48	121	*Flacc.*	
14.10.10-25		3.7.7		15 §125	53
§§219-64	123	§§184-87	130		
17.9.3 §214	60	3.7.7		*War*	
18.1.2 §11	48	§§183-84	118	2.18.5 §479	120
18.1.3-5		4.8.44 §306	60	2.8.2 §119	48
§§12-22	49	8.8.4 §225	60	4.5.2 §324	60
19.5.2 §283	60			7.3.3 §45	120
2.12.1 §265	64				

CHRISTIAN AUTHORS

1 Clement		Hermas		*Phld.*	
45.7	60	*Sim.*		6.1	38, 89, 90, 126
		5.3.7	75		
Augustine					
Civ. D.		*Vis.*		Irenaeus	
6.11	120	3.10.6	75	*Adv. Haer.*	
		3.13.3	53, 54	1.24.5	86
Clement of Alexandria				1.6.3	86
Strom.		Ignatius			
1.150	120	*Magn.*			
2.133	115	8.1	89, 90		
7.32	111, 115				

Justin Martyr		Origen	
Apol.		*Cels.*	
2.5	108	7.68	108

GREEK AND LATIN AUTHORS

Apuleius		8.27	95	90A	104
Metamorphoses		8.28	95		
2.28	80	8.31	95, 104, 106	Plutarch	
11.4	80	8.31-33	103	*Carn. Es.*	
11.23	21, 79	8.32	95, 104, 106	1.5 (994F-	
11.25	80	8.33	92, 107, 108	995C)	111
				1.6 (995D-E)	112, 128
Aristotle		Epictetus		2.1 (996E)	112
Metaph.		*Diss.*		2.2 (997B)	111, 112
1.5.5-6	92	2.8.15	90	2.4 (988C)	112
1.6.6	93	3.24.56	90		
				De Facie in Orbe Lunae	
Cicero		Juvenal		28(943C-D)	94
Acad. Post.		*Satire*		29(944C)	106
1.4 §17	100	14.96-106	121	30(944C)	106
1.5 §19	115			30(944C-D)	105
1.8 §§30-32	116	Plato			
6 §23	115	*Laws*		*Def. Orac.*	
		4.717B	107	12(416C)	107
Acad. Pr.				13(416D)	105
2.44 §135	115	*Phaedo*		13(416E)	106
2.5 §15	100, 115	64D-E	110	13(416F)	105
2.7-8		82C-D	111	13(417B)	106
§§19-23	116	107D-108C	106	13-14	
				(417A-D)	105
Fin.		*Resp.*		17(419A)	105
2.11 §34	115	4.427B	107	40(432C)	68
3.10 §35	114	4.439A-E	111		
		4.439D	111	*De Gen. Soc.*	
Flac.		7.514A-521B	116	20(588D)	68
28 §68	123	9.585B	111	20(589D)	104
				22(590B-	
Diodorus Siculus		*Symposium*		592E)	104
2.29.1-4	48	202E-203A	105, 106	22(592C)	104
Diogenes Laertius		*Tim.*		*Is. et Os.*	
7.87	114	29A	116	8(353E)	128
8.25	91-93, 103	30A-34B	116	9(345E)	128
8.25-26	95, 116	69C-70A	111	25(360E)	105
8.25-33	37, 91	86B-87A	111	25-26(360D-	
8.26	95, 104	87C-88B	111	361C)	105
8.26-30	103	88C-89D	111	26(361B)	105

Index of References

26(361C)	105	*Timaeus Locrus*		78(103C)	110
63(376D)	69, 94	7-14		80(103D-E)	110
		(94C-95B)	116	81(104A)	110
Tranq. An.		12-14		82(104A-B)	110
17(475E)	112	(95A-B)	118	83 (104C)	117
		14(95B)	129	83(104B-C)	110
Porphyry		36-41			
Ad Marcellam		(98E-99B)	129	Xenophon	
21.342-44	108	38(98)	129	*Mem.*	
		46(99E)	110	1.4.1-19	48
Sextus Empiricus		72-74(102E-		1.5.1-6.2	110
Math.		103A)	110	2.1.1-6	110
10.261	93	76(103B)	110		

OTHER ANCIENT LITERATURE

Corpus Hermeticum		*Hyp. Arch.*		PGM 4.507	81
13.11	81	II 4.92-93	85		
13.20	81			*Soph. Jes. Chr.*	
		Mithras Liturgy		4.106.10-	
Eugnostos		PGM		107.13	85
III 3.85.5-10	85	4.475ff.	81	4.118.20-25	85

INDEX OF AUTHORS

Bandstra, A.J. 29-32, 40, 52, 55, 144
Baron, S.W. 27, 123
Barrett, C.K. 90
Bean, G.E. 124
Beasley-Murray, G.R. 24, 44
Behm, J. 68
Beker, J.C. 144
Berchman, R.M. 117
Bianchi, U. 19
Billings, T. 115
Blinzler, J. 30, 52
Bluck, R.S. 111
Bornkamm, G. 22-24, 33-35, 40, 41, 73, 79, 81, 82, 84, 86, 87
Bousset, W. 108
Box, G.H. 76
Braun, H. 29
Brehier, E. 101
Brenk, F.E. 62, 101, 143
Brooten, B.J. 125
Brown, R.E. 7, 11
Bruce, F.F. 32, 33, 123
Buckler, W.H. 122
Bujard, W. 11, 12, 43, 136
Burgess, J. 11, 146, 147
Burkert, W. 89, 92-94, 103, 104, 106

Caird, G.B. 36
Calder, W.M. 122
Cannon, G.E. 42, 43, 136
Carr, W. 138
Charles, R.H. 76
Charlesworth, J.H. 75, 76, 81, 82, 127, 144
Cichorius, C. 124
Cohen, S.J.D. 121
Cohn, L. 65

Congdon, L.M. 12, 30, 44, 143
Conzelmann, H. 22, 50, 144
Copleston, F. 101
Cornford, F.M. 110
Cramer, A.W. 29, 30, 52, 55
Cumont, F. 62

Daly, M. 149
Danielou, J. 100
Darling, R.A. 75
Davies, W.D. 28, 29, 68
DeMaris, R.E. 7
Dean-Otting, M. 76
Delling, G. 52, 55
Des Places, E. 116
Devambez, P. 124
Dibelius, M. 20-25, 27, 28, 33-35, 40, 50, 65, 73, 79-81, 84-88
Dillon, J. 94, 101, 102, 104-107, 111, 115, 117
Dörrie, H. 100

Eitrem, S. 22
Evans, C.A. 32

Feldman, L.H. 122
Ferguson, E. 115
Festugière, A.-J. 92, 94, 103
Finn, T.M. 122
Foerster, W. 29
Francis, F.O. 12, 18, 30-33, 40, 44, 45, 66, 73-79, 90, 96, 134, 135, 140, 141
Furnish, V.P. 147

Gabathuler, H.J. 131
Gagniers, J. des 124

Index of Authors

Gaston, L. 90, 126
Ginouvès, R. 124
Glucker, J. 103, 115, 119
Gnilka, J. 22, 35
Goodenough, E.R. 114, 115
Goppelt, L. 56
Graeser, A. 115
Grant, R.M. 143
Greeven, H. 80
Griffiths, J.G. 80
Grundmann, W. 61, 90, 112, 119
Gunther, J.J. 18, 29, 41, 44
Guthrie, W.K.C. 93, 101, 102

Hanssler, B. 70
Harder, G. 69
Hegermann, H. 33, 34, 87
Heinze, R. 106, 108
Holladay, C.R. 103
Hollenbach, B. 70
Hooker, M.D. 39
House, H.W. 40
Humann, C. 124
Hurtado, L.W. 87, 88

Johnson, S.L. 27
Judeich, W. 124

Kahil, L. 124
Käsemann, E. 144
Keck, L.E. 147
Kehl, N. 29, 30, 75, 76
Kiley, M. 12, 85, 136
Kittel, G. 61
Kraabel, A.T. 35, 87, 88, 97, 122, 124, 125

Lähnemann, J. 34, 42-44, 87, 136
Levison, J.R. 144
Lifshitz, B. 122, 125
Lightfoot, J.B. 18-20, 24-26
Lindemann, A. 24
Lohmeyer, E. 22
Lohse, B. 12, 22, 111
Lohse, E. 42, 52, 125, 126, 131, 136, 137, 138
Lona, H.E. 142
Lyonnet, S. 27-30, 33, 39, 40, 65, 73, 74, 77-79, 84, 96, 131, 139, 142, 143

MacLennan, R.S. 122
Macgregor, G.H.C. 22
Marshall, P. 15, 67
Martin, R.P. 24
McCown, C.C. 81
Meeks, W.A. 18, 45, 74, 114, 115, 120, 136, 137, 144
Meyer, H.A.W. 36
Michel, O. 47
Milik, J.T. 82
Moffatt, J. 19, 36
Moyo, A.M. 25, 40, 84-86, 96, 139, 142, 143

Nilsson, M.P. 62, 89, 91, 94, 108
Nock, A.D. 66, 84

O'Neill, J.C. 135, 136
Odeberg, H. 76

Percy, E. 36, 43, 44
Perrin, N. 11
Pohlenz, M. 91
Pokorný, P. 12, 25, 42, 86, 138
Preisker, H. 65, 66

Rad, G. von 61
Ramsay, W.M. 62
Rees, D. 100, 104
Reitzenstein, R. 81, 82
Reynolds, J. 121
Robert, L. 122
Robinson, J.M. 85, 136, 140
Roetzel, C.J. 90
Rollins, W.G. 138
Rongy, H. 33
Ross, W.D. 93
Roueché, C. 62
Rowland, C. 32, 33
Rusam, D. 53

Sanders, E.P. 43
Sanders, J.T. 136
Sandmel, S. 114
Sappington, T.J. 12, 33, 44, 138

Saunders, E.W. 26
Schenk, W. 11, 25, 33, 141
Schenke, H.-M. 40, 85, 86
Schlier, H. 22, 82, 83
Schmekel, A. 91
Schoedel, W. 90, 126
Schulz, S. 63
Schweizer, E. 12-14, 36-38, 40, 44, 55, 73, 88-90, 92-96, 99, 100, 103, 104, 106, 109, 123, 126, 129-31, 136, 138
Seager, A.R. 124, 125
Smyth, H.W. 43, 70, 140
Sokolowski, F. 62, 107
Soury, G. 104, 105
Stern, M. 119, 120
Stewart, J.S. 40

Tabor, J.D. 76
Tannenbaum, R. 121
Tarrant, H. 100
Tcherikover, V. 124
Thesleff, H. 109
Tobin, T. 109

Trebilco, P.R. 122, 125
Tsekourakis, D. 111

Van Winden, J.C.M. 116
Vawter, B. 130, 131, 136, 137

Wahl, O. 75
Weiss, H. 78
Wellmann, M. 103
Wendland, P. 65
Wengst, K. 90, 112
White, J.L. 42, 44
Whittaker, J. 100, 102, 115, 119
Wiersma, W. 103, 104
Wilken, R.L. 120
Williams, A.L. 87, 88
Wink, W. 52, 148
Winston, D. 52, 107
Winter, F. 124
Witt, R.E. 102, 116, 117
Wright, N.T. 138

Yamauchi, E. 26, 27, 122
Yates, R.

JOURNAL FOR THE STUDY OF THE NEW TESTAMENT

Supplement Series

5 THE PEOPLE OF GOD
  Markus Barth
6 PERSECUTION AND MARTYRDOM IN THE THEOLOGY OF PAUL
  John S. Pobee
7 SYNOPTIC STUDIES:
  THE AMPLEFORTH CONFERENCES OF
  1982 AND 1983
  Edited by C.M. Tuckett
8 JESUS ON THE MOUNTAIN:
  A STUDY IN MATTHEAN THEOLOGY
  Terence L. Donaldson
9 THE HYMNS OF LUKE'S INFANCY NARRATIVES:
  THEIR ORIGIN, MEANING AND SIGNIFICANCE
  Stephen Farris
10 CHRIST THE END OF THE LAW:
   ROMANS 10.4 IN PAULINE PERSPECTIVE
   Robert Badenas
11 THE LETTERS TO THE SEVEN CHURCHES OF ASIA IN THEIR LOCAL
   SETTING
   Colin J. Hemer
12 PROCLAMATION FROM PROPHECY AND PATTERN:
   LUCAN OLD TESTAMENT CHRISTOLOGY
   Darrell L. Bock
13 JESUS AND THE LAWS OF PURITY:
   TRADITION HISTORY AND LEGAL HISTORY IN MARK 7
   Roger P. Booth
14 THE PASSION ACCORDING TO LUKE:
   THE SPECIAL MATERIAL OF LUKE 22
   Marion L. Soards
15 HOSTILITY TO WEALTH IN THE SYNOPTIC GOSPELS
   Thomas E. Schmidt
16 MATTHEW'S COMMUNITY:
   THE EVIDENCE OF HIS SPECIAL SAYINGS MATERIAL
   Stephenson H. Brooks
17 THE PARADOX OF THE CROSS IN THE THOUGHT OF ST PAUL
   Anthony Tyrrell Hanson
18 HIDDEN WISDOM AND THE EASY YOKE:
   WISDOM, TORAH AND DISCIPLESHIP IN MATTHEW 11.25-30
   Celia Deutsch

19 JESUS AND GOD IN PAUL'S ESCHATOLOGY
    L. Joseph Kreitzer
20 LUKE
    A NEW PARADIGM (2 Volumes)
    Michael D. Goulder
21 THE DEPARTURE OF JESUS IN LUKE–ACTS:
    THE ASCENSION NARRATIVES IN CONTEXT
    Mikeal C. Parsons
22 THE DEFEAT OF DEATH:
    APOCALYPTIC ESCHATOLOGY IN 1 CORINTHIANS 15 AND ROMANS 5
    Martinus C. de Boer
23 PAUL THE LETTER-WRITER
    AND THE SECOND LETTER TO TIMOTHY
    Michael Prior
24 APOCALYPTIC AND THE NEW TESTAMENT:
    ESSAYS IN HONOR OF J. LOUIS MARTYN
    Edited by Joel Marcus & Marion L. Soards
25 THE UNDERSTANDING SCRIBE:
    MATTHEW AND THE APOCALYPTIC IDEAL
    David E. Orton
26 WATCHWORDS:
    MARK 13 IN MARKAN ESCHATOLOGY
    Timothy J. Geddert
27 THE DISCIPLES ACCORDING TO MARK:
    MARKAN REDACTION IN CURRENT DEBATE
    C. Clifton Black
28 THE NOBLE DEATH:
    GRAECO-ROMAN MARTYROLOGY
    AND PAUL'S CONCEPT OF SALVATION
    David Seeley
29 ABRAHAM IN GALATIANS:
    EPISTOLARY AND RHETORICAL CONTEXTS
    G. Walter Hansen
30 EARLY CHRISTIAN RHETORIC AND 2 THESSALONIANS
    Frank Witt Hughes
31 THE STRUCTURE OF MATTHEW'S GOSPEL:
    A STUDY IN LITERARY DESIGN
    David R. Bauer
32 PETER AND THE BELOVED DISCIPLE:
    FIGURES FOR A COMMUNITY IN CRISIS
    Kevin Quast
33 MARK'S AUDIENCE:
    THE LITERARY AND SOCIAL SETTING OF MARK 4.11-12
    Mary Ann Beavis

34 THE GOAL OF OUR INSTRUCTION:
   THE STRUCTURE OF THEOLOGY AND ETHICS
   IN THE PASTORAL EPISTLES
   Philip H. Towner
35 THE PROVERBS OF JESUS:
   ISSUES OF HISTORY AND RHETORIC
   Alan P. Winton
36 THE STORY OF CHRIST IN THE ETHICS OF PAUL:
   AN ANALYSIS OF THE FUNCTION OF THE HYMNIC MATERIAL
   IN THE PAULINE CORPUS
   Stephen E. Fowl
37 PAUL AND JESUS:
   COLLECTED ESSAYS
   Edited by A.J.M. Wedderburn
38 MATTHEW'S MISSIONARY DISCOURSE:
   A LITERARY CRITICAL ANALYSIS
   Dorothy Jean Weaver
39 FAITH AND OBEDIENCE IN ROMANS:
   A STUDY IN ROMANS 1–4
   Glenn N. Davies
40 IDENTIFYING PAUL'S OPPONENTS:
   THE QUESTION OF METHOD IN 2 CORINTHIANS
   Jerry L. Sumney
41 HUMAN AGENTS OF COSMIC POWER:
   IN HELLENISTIC JUDAISM AND THE SYNOPTIC TRADITION
   Mary E. Mills
42 MATTHEW'S INCLUSIVE STORY:
   A STUDY IN THE NARRATIVE RHETORIC OF THE FIRST GOSPEL
   David B. Howell
43 JESUS, PAUL AND TORAH:
   COLLECTED ESSAYS
   Heikki Räisänen
44 THE NEW COVENANT IN HEBREWS
   Susanne Lehne
45 THE RHETORIC OF ROMANS:
   ARGUMENTATIVE CONSTRAINT AND STRATEGY AND PAUL'S
   DIALOGUE WITH JUDAISM
   Neil Elliott
46 THE LAST SHALL BE FIRST:
   THE RHETORIC OF REVERSAL IN LUKE
   John O. York
47 JAMES AND THE Q SAYINGS OF JESUS
   Patrick J. Hartin

48 TEMPLUM AMICITIAE:
    ESSAYS ON THE SECOND TEMPLE PRESENTED TO ERNST BAMMEL
    Edited by William Horbury
49 PROLEPTIC PRIESTS
    PRIESTHOOD IN THE EPISTLE TO THE HEBREWS
    John M. Scholer
50 PERSUASIVE ARTISTRY:
    STUDIES IN NEW TESTAMENT RHETORIC
    IN HONOR OF GEORGE A. KENNEDY
    Edited by Duane F. Watson
51 THE AGENCY OF THE APOSTLE:
    A DRAMATISTIC ANALYSIS OF PAUL'S RESPONSES TO CONFLICT
    IN 2 CORINTHIANS
    Jeffrey A. Crafton
52 REFLECTIONS OF GLORY:
    PAUL'S POLEMICAL USE OF THE MOSES–DOXA TRADITION IN
    2 CORINTHIANS 3.12-18
    Linda L. Belleville
53 REVELATION AND REDEMPTION AT COLOSSAE
    Thomas J. Sappington
54 THE DEVELOPMENT OF EARLY CHRISTIAN PNEUMATOLOGY
    WITH SPECIAL REFERENCE TO LUKE–ACTS
    Robert P. Menzies
55 THE PURPOSE OF ROMANS:
    A COMPARATIVE LETTER STRUCTURE INVESTIGATION
    L. Ann Jervis
56 THE SON OF THE MAN IN THE GOSPEL OF JOHN
    Delbert Burkett
57 ESCHATOLOGY AND THE COVENANT:
    A COMPARISON OF 4 EZRA AND ROMANS 1–11
    Bruce W. Longenecker
58 NONE BUT THE SINNERS:
    RELIGIOUS CATEGORIES IN THE GOSPEL OF LUKE
    David A. Neale
59 CLOTHED WITH CHRIST:
    THE EXAMPLE AND TEACHING OF JESUS IN ROMANS 12.1–15.13
    Michael Thompson
60 THE LANGUAGE OF THE NEW TESTAMENT:
    CLASSIC ESSAYS
    Edited by Stanley E. Porter
61 FOOTWASHING IN JOHN 13 AND THE JOHANNINE COMMUNITY
    John Christopher Thomas
62 JOHN THE BAPTIZER AND PROPHET:
    A SOCIO-HISTORICAL STUDY
    Robert L. Webb

63 POWER AND POLITICS IN PALESTINE:
    THE JEWS AND THE GOVERNING OF THEIR LAND 100 BC–AD 70
    James S. McLaren
64 JESUS AND THE ORAL GOSPEL TRADITION
    Edited by Henry Wansbrough
65 THE RHETORIC OF RIGHTEOUSNESS IN ROMANS 3.21-26
    Douglas A. Campbell
66 PAUL, ANTIOCH AND JERUSALEM:
    A STUDY IN RELATIONSHIPS AND AUTHORITY IN EARLIEST CHRISTIANITY
    Nicholas Taylor
67 THE PORTRAIT OF PHILIP IN ACTS:
    A STUDY OF ROLES AND RELATIONS
    F. Scott Spencer
68 JEREMIAH IN MATTHEW'S GOSPEL:
    THE REJECTED-PROPHET MOTIF IN MATTHAEAN REDACTION
    Michael P. Knowles
69 RHETORIC AND REFERENCE IN THE FOURTH GOSPEL
    Margaret Davies
70 AFTER THE THOUSAND YEARS:
    RESURRECTION AND JUDGMENT IN REVELATION 20
    J. Webb Mealy
71 SOPHIA AND THE JOHANNINE JESUS
    Martin Scott
72 NARRATIVE ASIDES IN LUKE–ACTS
    Steven M. Sheeley
73 SACRED SPACE
    AN APPROACH TO THE THEOLOGY OF THE EPISTLE TO THE HEBREWS
    Marie E. Isaacs
74 TEACHING WITH AUTHORITY:
    MIRACLES AND CHRISTOLOGY IN THE GOSPEL OF MARK
    Edwin K. Broadhead
75 PATRONAGE AND POWER:
    A STUDY OF SOCIAL NETWORKS IN CORINTH
    John Kin-Man Chow
76 THE NEW TESTAMENT AS CANON:
    A READER IN CANONICAL CRITICISM
    Robert Wall and Eugene Lemcio
77 REDEMPTIVE ALMSGIVING IN EARLY CHRISTIANITY
    Roman Garrison
78 THE FUNCTION OF SUFFERING IN PHILIPPIANS
    L. Gregory Bloomquist
79 THE THEME OF RECOMPENSE IN MATTHEW'S GOSPEL
    Blaine Charette

80 BIBLICAL GREEK LANGUAGE AND LINGUISTICS: OPEN QUESTIONS IN
CURRENT RESEARCH
Stanley E. Porter and D.A. Carson
81 THE LAW IN GALATIANS
In-Gyu Hong
82 ORAL TRADITION AND THE GOSPELS: THE PROBLEM OF MARK 4
Barry W. Henaut
83 PAUL AND THE SCRIPTURES OF ISRAEL
Craig A. Evans and James A. Sanders
84 FROM JESUS TO JOHN: ESSAYS ON JESUS AND NEW TESTAMENT
CHRISTOLOGY IN HONOUR OF MARINUS DE JONGE
Edited by Martinus C. De Boer
85 RETURNING HOME: NEW COVENANT AND SECOND EXODUS AS THE
CONTEXT FOR 2 CORINTHIANS 6.14–7.1
William J. Webb
86 ORIGINS OF METHOD: TOWARDS A NEW UNDERSTANDING OF JUDAISM AND
CHRISTIANITY—ESSAYS IN HONOUR OF JOHN C. HURD
Bradley H. McLean
87 WORSHIP, THEOLOGY AND MINISTRY IN THE EARLY CHURCH: ESSAYS IN
HONOUR OF RALPH P. MARTIN
Edited by Michael Wilkins and Terence Paige
88 THE BIRTH OF THE LUKAN NARRATIVE
M. Coleridge
89 WORD AND GLORY: ON THE EXEGETICAL AND THEOLOGICAL
BACKGROUND OF JOHN'S PROLOGUE
Craig A. Evans
90 RHETORIC IN THE NEW TESTAMENT
ESSAYS FROM THE 1992 HEIDELBERG CONFERENCE
Edited by Stanley E. Porter and Thomas H. Olbricht
91 MATTHEW'S NARRATIVE WEB: OVER, AND OVER AND OVER AGAIN
J.C. Anderson
92 LUKE: INTERPRETER OF PAUL, CRITIC OF MATTHEW
E. Franklin
93 ISAIAH AND PROPHETIC TRADITION IN THE BOOK OF REVELATION
J. Fekkes III
94 JESUS' EXPOSITION OF THE OLD TESTAMENT IN LUKE'S GOSPEL
C.A. Kmball
95 THE SYMBOLIC NARRATIVES OF THE FOURTH GOSPEL
D.A. Lee
96 THE COLOSSIAN CONTROVERSY:
WISDOM IN DISPUTE AT COLOSSAE
Richard E. DeMaris

99 ST
135 ooc